"50 Years Is Enough"

The Case Against the World Bank and the International Monetary Fund

edited by Kevin Danaher

South End Press
Boston, MA

332.152
F469

Cover design by Steve Lyons
Text design and production by Kevin Danaher
Printed in the U.S.A. on acid-free, recycled paper.

Library of Congress Cataloging-in-Publication Data
50 years is enough: the case against the World Bank and the International
Monetary Fund/edited by Kevin Danaher
p.cm.
Includes bibliographical references and index.
ISBN 0-89608-496-5 (cloth): $30.00
ISBN 0-89608-495-7 (pbk.): $14.00
1. World Bank. 2. International Monetary Fund. 3. Economic assistance.
4. Structural adjustment (economic policy). 5. Developing countries –
Economic conditions.
I. Danaher, Kevin, 1950-. II. Title: Fifty years is enough.
HG3881.5.W57A15 1994
332.1'52–dc20   94-15460
                                                                           CIP

South End Press   116 Saint Botolph Street, Boston, MA 02115

99 98 97 96 95 94   9 8 7 6 5 4 3 2

TABLE OF CONTENTS

Section III: UNHEARD VOICES: ENVIRONMENTALISTS, WOMEN & TRIBAL PEOPLES

ACKNOWLEDGMENTS

Our sincerest thanks to the following publications and organizations for granting us permission to reprint articles from their publications: *BankCheck Quarterly* (Chapters 1, 4, 6, 12, 15, 16, 23, 24, 26); Cato Institute (Chapter 31); *Global Perspectives*, newsletter of the Center for Global Education (Chapter 2); The Development Group for Alternative Policies (Chapters 9, 11); Greenpeace International (Chapter 35); Inter-Church Coalition on Africa (Chapter 20); *Left Business Observer* (Chapter 7); Maryknoll Peace and Justice Center (Chapter 17); Mozambique Information Agency (Chapter 14); *Multinational Monitor* (Chapters 8, 10, 18, 22, 25); Survival International (Chapter 21); Third World Network (Chapter 27); Service Employees International Union (Chapter 32); Swiss Coalition of Development Organizations (Chapter 28); Washington Office on Africa (Chapter 34); *The Washington Post* (Chapter 36).

My deepest appreciation goes to Jason Ward, Monica Berini and Clinton Hodgson, who helped with the production of this book in so many ways: researching articles, scanning, editing, writing correspondence and helping solve the many problems that occur in the process of putting a book together. Thanks to my colleagues at Global Exchange, who are always a source of motivation – they make it fun to come to work every morning. A special thank you to Lynn Lu at South End Press for being so smart, efficient and pleasant to deal with. To the many staffers at the organizations involved in the 50 Years Is Enough coalition I owe thanks for assistance and for being an inspiring example of how diverse groups can work together on tough issues and still maintain a sense of humor. Ross Hammond and his colleagues at the Development GAP have been especially helpful on this project. And, of course, big hugs and kisses to the three females who make my life such a pleasure: Medea, Arlen and Maya.

Kevin Danaher
April 25, 1994

PREFACE:
Redefining Development
Muhammad Yunus

The World Bank was created to encourage "development." To the World Bank, development means growth. Single-mindedly, it pursues growth to the best of its ability. But, as others have noted, unrestrained growth is the ideology of the cancer cell.

The World Bank focuses on economic growth until it is distracted by other issues like hunger, women, health, the environment, etc. The World Bank tries to adapt itself to these considerations without giving up its basic goal. It adopts the rhetoric of all these issues quickly, but it cannot easily translate that rhetoric into action. Conservatism at the Bank's core makes doing this extremely difficult.

Two things may have contributed to this conservatism. Firstly, the theoretical framework within which the World Bank operates does not assign any urgency or primacy to poverty reduction. As a consequence, its pronouncements about poverty reduction get translated only through humanitarian add-ons, such as safety-net programs.

Secondly, people who work at the World Bank were not hired to eliminate poverty from the world. They were chosen for qualities that may not have immediate relevance for poverty reduction.

The World Bank Needs to be Changed

In order for the World Bank to take poverty reduction seriously, these two issues have to be resolved. This may require going back to the drawing board and redesigning the Bank from scratch. The theoretical framework of the World Bank must be re-designed to give poverty reduction a central place. Goals must be defined in terms of measurable reductions of poverty each year for each country, and a date must be set for freeing the world from poverty once and for all. Methodologies and work habits must be designed that are pro-poor. The World Bank must hire people who have the ability and commitment to do the job with all the seriousness it deserves.

Until the World Bank is restructured to achieve poverty reduction, it should immediately create a window (like the International Development Association) with an exclusive mandate and managed by people hired exclusively to achieve the goals set in the mandate. Poverty reduction should *not* be mixed up with usual World Bank projects. The new window should formulate its own business practices rather than follow the existing procedures, which are not conducive to poverty reduction efforts. The hallmark of this window will be that it will not claim to have all the answers. It will have the humility to learn, experiment and continually seek better answers.

It is very important that the World Bank be changed to create a poverty-free world. The World Bank is the flagship of all the development banks in the world. All regional development banks, specialized development banks, bilateral development banks and national development banks follow the lead of the World Bank. Even non-bank development institutions follow the World Bank without ever raising a question. The World Bank's influence is global and total. Unless the course of this flagship is changed, the ships charting behind it will also remain on the same course.

All these changes can come about only if poverty is made totally unacceptable and if we believe that poverty can be eliminated at an affordable cost. The basic technology to eliminate poverty exists (and can be improved on). An unshakable political will is needed to end poverty and hunger.

The Grameen Bank: A Bank for the Poor

Current conceptualizations of poverty provide no help in the alleviation of poverty. These conceptualizations are based on the assertion that the poor are responsible for their poverty. They are poor because they are lazy. They are poor because they lack skill, initiative or entrepreneurial ability. They suffer from cultural backwardness, they lack ambition or they have bad habits (drinking, drugs, etc.). Working with this conceptualization produces programs and projects intended to make the poor give up their "bad habits" and acquire "necessary skills and attitudes." Obviously, we don't make much headway through these efforts because of the false premise.

In Bangladesh, we run a bank for the poor. We think of the poor differently. We think they are as capable and as enterprising as anybody else in the world. Circumstances have just pushed them to the bottom of the heap. They work harder than anybody else. They have more skills than they get a chance to use. With a supportive environment, they can pull themselves out of the heap in no time.

Back in 1976, we offered tiny loans to the poorest people in one village. People showed how good they were at using the money to earn income and pay the loans back. They were honest and hardworking but that's not how conventional bankers choose to see the poor. To them, the poor belong to the class of untouchables.

Encouraged by our initial results, we expanded our work to two villages, ten villages, one district and then five districts. At no point did we have any problem getting our money back. But all along, conventional bankers told us: "What you are seeing is not the real thing. The real thing is that the poor have no will to work, they have no ability. They will never return your money."

For a while, we felt confused. What was real? What we heard about the poor, or what we experienced with the poor? We relied on our experience. We kept on expanding. Today, Grameen Bank, the poor people's bank in Bangladesh, operates in 34,000 villages, exactly half the number of all the villages in Bangladesh. Grameen Bank currently lends money to 1.7 million borrowers, 94 percent of whom are women. The borrowers own the bank. We lend out over $30 million each month in loans averaging less than $100. The repayment rate for our loans is over 98 percent. Besides income-generating loans, we also give housing loans. A typical housing loan is $300. We have given more than 220,000 housing loans so far with a perfect repayment record. Studies done on Grameen tell us that the borrowers have improved their income, widened their asset base and moved steadily toward crossing the poverty line and toward a life of dignity and honor. Studies also tell us that in Grameen families the nutrition level is better than in non-Grameen families, child mortality is lower and adoption of family-planning practices is higher. All studies confirm the visible empowerment of women.

Our success shows that if the multilateral banking system were changed, the poor would have a chance to change their lives. If the development banks were changed, it would reduce poverty much faster.

We Do Our Business Differently

In many ways, we operate differently than other banks, including the World Bank. For one thing, we don't blame our borrowers if things don't go right; instead, we blame ourselves. We train our staff to find fault with themselves, not with borrowers. We tell our staff that "Things will go wrong only if you don't do it right."

We take quite a bit of time preparing our borrowers to learn how to make decisions within their five-member groups. We raise questions concerning their reactions should one of them fail to pay their weekly installment. We repeat the following advice many times to them so that they will remember it when the occasion arises: "Please never get angry with the person who cannot pay the installment. Please don't put pressure on her to make her pay. Be a good friend, don't turn into an enemy. As a good friend, your first response should be, 'Oh my God, she is in trouble, we must go and help her out.'" We advise them,

"First, find out the story behind the non-repayment. From our experience we can tell you that most often there is a very sad story behind each case of non-repayment. When you get the full story you'll find out how stupid it would have been to twist her arm to get the money. She can't pay the installment because her husband ran away with the money. As a good friend your responsibility will be to go and find her husband and bring him back, hopefully, with the money.

"It may also happen that your friend could not pay the installments because the cow that she bought with the loan money died. As good friends, you should promptly stand by her side, give her consolation and courage at this disaster. She is totally shaken by the shock of the event. You should cheer her up and help her to pull herself together. Ask Grameen to give her another loan, and reschedule and convert the previous loan into a long-term loan."

Grameen reminds its staff that no borrower should, at any time, get a feeling that she has added to her misery by joining the Grameen group. We are in the business of reducing people's misery, not increasing it. If we are not capable of doing that, we should close down our shop and find something else to do for a living.

The Poor Suffer Because of Debt Burden

Stories that we hear at Grameen about the enormous debt burden accumulated by a large number of countries around the world and the miseries caused by the structural adjustment programs imposed on them by the World Bank make us feel that the two banks work quite differently.

When we hear about how countries are made to pay these debts through their noses, surrendering the bulk of their export earnings, leasing out valuable resources at throw-away prices to make extra income, sacrificing social and environmental considerations to earn enough to repay their huge debts, we find it difficult to accept this as banking. Causing misery to people and to nations cannot be banking.

At Grameen, we follow the principle that the borrower knows best. Of course, the World Bank follows a very different principle. We encourage our borrowers to make their own decisions. When a nervous borrower asks a Grameen staff: "Please tell me what would be a good business idea for me," the staff knows how to respond to the request. She is trained to respond in the following way: "I am sorry, I am not smart enough to give you a good business idea. Grameen has lots of money, but no business ideas. If Grameen had good business ideas also, do you think Grameen would have given the money to you? It would have used the money itself and made more money."

But it is quite different with the World Bank. They don't just give you money. They give you all the ideas, expertise and everything else. Your job is to follow the yellow lines, the green lines, the red lines, read the instructions at each stop and follow them. The World Bank is eager to assume all the responsibilities. They don't want to leave any responsibility for the borrower, except the responsibility for the failure of the project.

The World Bank approaches its borrowers through a string of powerful missions. The missions are so plentiful that at no point are you very far away from the next World Bank mission. Despite all the arrogance of expertise, supervision and money, the projects don't always work out. Yet the borrowers are blamed for these failures. Is this fair?

We Need the World Bank on the Side of the Poor

Banking can be done in a humane way, in a pro-poor way. We must make serious efforts to find the solution and put it into practice. The World Bank is the most powerful financial institution in the world. To eliminate poverty from the surface of the earth, we must learn to bring the full force of this institution behind this effort. This needs to be done with all urgency and seriousness.

"International solidarity is not an act of charity. It is an act of unity between allies fighting on different terrains toward the same objectives. The foremost of these objectives is to aid the development of humanity to the highest level possible."

Samora Machel (1933-1986),
First President of Mozambique

"The third world war has already started. It is a silent war. Not, for that reason, any less sinister. This war is tearing down Brazil, Latin America and practically all the Third World. Instead of soldiers dying, there are children. It is a war over the Third World debt, one which has as its main weapon interest, a weapon more deadly than the atom bomb, more shattering than a laser beam."

Luís Inacio Lula da Silva,
Head of Brazil's Workers' Party

INTRODUCTION
Kevin Danaher

As World War II raged across Europe and Asia, the leaders of England and the United States realized that, in order to ensure a liberal, capitalist world economy after the war, they would need multilateral institutions that could enforce rules favoring the free movement of capital internationally. In July 1944 the two governments convened a conference at Bretton Woods, New Hampshire. There they developed the plans for two institutions that would shape the world economy for the next 50 years.

The International Monetary Fund (IMF) was established to smooth world commerce by reducing foreign exchange restrictions. It also created a reserve of funds to be tapped by countries experiencing temporary balance of payments problems so they could continue trading without interruption. This pump-priming of the world market would benefit all trading countries, especially the biggest traders, the United States and Britain.

Also founded at Bretton Woods was the International Bank for Reconstruction and Development (World Bank). The World Bank was given the task of making post-war development loans for infrastructure projects (roads, utilities), which, because they were unprofitable, were not likely to be initiated by private capital. The Bank was also mandated to promote private foreign investment by means of guarantees or participation in loans and other investments made by private investors.

The founders of these institutions hoped that by establishing groundrules before the end of the war, they could gird themselves against the twin threats of state-managed economies under a socialist model and international anarchy brought on by cutthroat varieties of nationalistic capitalism. They saw that if the major powers did not ensure some access to big capital for the elites of less prosperous countries, those elites could adopt policies with the potential for unravelling the world capitalist economy.

The unwritten goal of the World Bank and the IMF -- one that has

1

been enforced with a vengeance -- has been to integrate countries into the capitalist world economy. Despite all the rhetoric about development and the alleviation of poverty, the central function of these multilateral lending institutions has been to draw the rulers and governments of weaker states more tightly into a world economy dominated by large, transnational corporations.

Over the past five decades, the World Bank and the IMF have steadily gained power and influence, becoming the key arbiters determining which countries will receive international loans. This status gives the Bretton Woods institutions the power to enforce economic policies written in Washington, where both the Bank and the Fund are based. For many in the Third World, this harkens back to colonial times.

The policies imposed by the World Bank and the IMF are designed to facilitate the repayment of debt: that is, the steady transfer of wealth out of Third World countries to the bankers of the industrial countries. This transfer of wealth has had devastating consequences for the poor majority. Money that could have been invested in health, education and housing has instead been transferred to wealthy bankers. Accordingly, Third World countries under IMF/World Bank tutelage have seen infant mortality rates increase, schools and housing deteriorate, unemployment skyrocket and the general health of the people decline.

This is why author Susan George uses the term "financial low-intensity conflict" to depict the war being waged between rich and poor. It is *not* simply a war between "North and South," as it is so often portrayed in the mainstream press and academic literature. Rather, it is a collaborative effort between southern elites and their northern counterparts. The Third World rulers get new infusions of cash and remain unaffected by the austerity policies imposed by the technocrats from the IMF and the World Bank. Northern elites get loan payments and can sleep well at night knowing that their allies in the South will keep a tight grip on the workers and keep the money flowing.

Notice that, despite all their pressure to cut back the size of Third World governments, the IMF and World Bank do not pressure Third World leaders to reduce military spending. Without a strong repressive apparatus, it would be impossible to enforce the harsh policies dictated from Washington.

The Record Speaks for Itself

There is a parable about a villager who goes to a local wise man and asks to borrow the wise man's donkey. The wise man lies, saying the donkey is not there. Just then, the donkey brays. The wise man pauses, then says: "Well, who are you going to believe, a donkey or a wise man?"

Despite the steady decline of Third World economies under the tutelage of economists from the World Bank and the International Monetary Fund (IMF), these institutions keep insisting that their wise men and their "free market" policies will eventually foster development. Third World leaders are told that, in order to get more loans to pay off the old loans, they must implement "structural adjustment" reforms. These include:

- selling state enterprises to the private sector in order to make governments more efficient
- raising producer prices for agricultural goods so farmers will have the incentive to grow and market more food
- devaluing local currencies (in line with their world market value) to make exports more competitive in foreign markets
- reducing government budget deficits by cutting consumer subsidies and charging user fees for social services such as health care and education
- encouraging free trade by dropping protectionist measures and by reducing regulation of the private sector
- creating incentives to attract foreign capital

Yet the central question that is consistently avoided by the enforcers of these policies is, do they work?

Look at the case of Africa. Thirty of the 47 governments in sub-Saharan Africa have been pressured into implementing structural adjustment reforms. The effects have been devastating to the poor. As early as 1988, the United Nations concluded: "The most vulnerable population groups, in particular women, youth, the disabled and the aged, have been severely and adversely affected."[1]

Though western economists claimed that these policies would reduce debt burdens, by 1992, Africa's external debt had reached $290 billion, about 2.5 times greater than it was in 1980. The record of the IMF/World Bank gurus is also dismal in Latin America and Asian debtor countries such as the Philippines.

Asian countries such as Japan, China and South Korea that have experienced high growth rates have done so *not* through a dogmatic "free market" strategy as espoused by the Bank and the Fund, but through highly state-directed economies.

Usually, we are exposed to analyses from people in the top 2 percent of the world's income pyramid. In contrast, the book you are holding includes strong representation of Third World voices explaining the many damaging effects of the neoliberal economic strategy imposed on them by "experts" from Washington. As Martin Khor, Director of the Third World Network in Malaysia, sums it up:

"Structural adjustment is a policy to continue colonial trade and economic patterns developed during the colonial period, but which the Northern powers want to continue in the post-colonial period. Economically speaking, we [countries in the South] are more dependent on the ex-colonial countries than we ever were. The World Bank and IMF are playing the role that our ex-colonial masters used to play."

Section I of this book places the World Bank and IMF in a global and historical context. The articles in this section explain how the Bank and the Fund have been used to keep most Third World debtor nations in a subordinate position in the global division of labor.

Section II draws evidence from 13 countries to show that the policies being pushed by the World Bank and the IMF are not working for the vast majority. While there are significant variations -- e.g., Latin America has been more influenced by the IMF, while Africa has been mainly under the tutelage of the World Bank -- the similarities in the impact of neoliberal economic policies are striking.

A central problem with the structural adjustment policies is that they are developed and imposed in an undemocratic manner. Unelected elites from the North and South get together and devise these policies without any input from the poor majority who will be on the receiving end. It is hardly surprising that the poor end up being hurt by policies they have no say in devising or implementing. Leonor Briones of the Freedom from Debt Coalition in the Philippines explains that:

"The very logic and framework of structural adjustment policies require the repression of democratic rights. This is because these policies demand drastic fiscal, monetary and economic measures that cannot help but raise very strong reactions from the public. And such reactions have to be repressed. It is not surprising that many structural adjustment programs are successfully implemented in countries like my own, under a dictatorship."

Section III focuses on vulnerable "subjects" of the World Bank and the IMF: women, the environment and tribal peoples. It is telling that population groups and other living things that are relatively powerless tend to get trampled by the policies of the Bank and the Fund.

Section IV examines the inner workings and ideology of the Bank and the Fund. It contains testimony from people who have worked inside the IMF and World Bank. They reveal the shocking level of wasteful spending and insensitivity to the poor that characterize these institutions. They also document the cozy relationship between Third World elites and the international bankers. As the former head of the World Bank's Health Department, Michael Irwin, reports:

> "The Bank staff, living and working comfortably in the Washington area and venturing forth in luxury, with first-class flights and hotels, are out of touch with both the realities and the causes of poverty in the Third World. World Bank staff, who deal almost exclusively with ministers and senior civil servants on their 'missions,' are simply bureaucrats talking confidentially with autocrats, getting only information that the borrower governments want the Bank to have."

Section V contains articles about alternative approaches to development that have sprung up in opposition to World Bank/IMF policies. This section suggests ways in which we could reorganize the global economy to meet the basic human needs of the majority.

The book concludes with suggestions for further reading and a guide to organizations struggling to rectify the globe-spanning problems analyzed herein. There are dozens of organizations producing educational materials, organizing protests, sponsoring conferences and pressuring legislators for reform. Whether or not these efforts will be successful depends, to a large extent, on whether you get involved!

Notes

1. UN General Assembly, Report of the Secretary General, "Critical Economic Situation in Africa: United Nations Programme of Action for African Economic Recovery and Development, 1986-1990," August 10, 1988, p. 29.

World Bank/IMF: 50 Years Is Enough
Bruce Rich

As the World Bank slouches toward its 50th anniversary, more and more voices are questioning its credibility and its legacy. On May 27, 1993, 11 African heads of state gathered in Libreville, Gabon, where they heard U.S. civil rights leader Jesse Jackson denounce the effects of Bank policies on the poor in the developing world. "They no longer use bullets and ropes. They use the World Bank and IMF," Jackson declared. In June, Republicans in the U.S. House of Representatives proposed an amendment to eliminate all U.S. funding of one of the Bank's two principal lending branches, the International Bank for Reconstruction and Development (IBRD). The motion was defeated by only two votes.

The past two years have been particularly difficult for the Bank. Its management defied the recommendations of the Morse Commission Report on India's Sardar Sarovar Dam and failed to develop meaningful measures to arrest the relentless decline of project quality documented in the Wapenhans report (the internal report found that more than one-third of Bank projects were essentially failing). A review of the Bank's past half-century shows that these problems are not new.

From Reconstruction to Development

The founders who gathered for the Bretton Woods Conference in July 1944 foresaw two primary functions for the Bank in the post-World War II era: first, reconstruction of Europe, and later, guaranteeing loans made by private banks for projects in poorer, developing countries. But as an agent of reconstruction, the Bank was stillborn. What war-torn Europe needed was not interest-bearing loans for specific projects that required lengthy preparation, but rapidly disbursing grants and concessional loans for balance of payments support and imports necessary to meet basic needs. In all, the Bank made only four loans for reconstruction, totalling US$497 million. It was the U.S.-initiated Marshall Plan, not the Bank, that was the engine of reconstruction, disbursing $41.3 billion by 1953.

Nor was there much demand for World Bank loan guarantees. When the World Bank took the next step and assumed its role as a direct lender for projects in developing countries, it ran into yet another problem. According to the Bank's third annual report for the years 1947-48, "the number of sound, productive investment opportunities thus far presented to the Bank is substantially smaller than was originally expected." Rather than question the need for the Bank's services, the report blamed the prospective borrowers for not borrowing, citing their lack of technical and planning skills and economic instability. The Bank's third president, Eugene Black, reiterated before the United Nations Economic and Social Council in 1950 that the reason the Bank had made so few loans was "not the lack of money but the lack of well-prepared and well-planned projects."

If there was insufficient demand for World Bank projects, the Bank decided, it would create sufficient demand. Warren Baum, who held positions in senior Bank management through the 1980s, admitted in 1970 that the Bank had to help design projects in a ceaseless struggle to keep the money flowing: "We do not get enough good projects to appraise unless we are involved intimately in their identification and preparation."

Distinguished economist Albert Hirschman reminisced about his experience in the early 1950s as an advisor to the newly created Colombian National Planning Council while he was working for the Bank, "which," he observed, "had taken an active part in having the Planning Council set up in the first place and then in recruiting me for it." Hirschman recollected that he . . .

> "wanted to learn as much as possible about the Colombian economy . . . in the hope of contributing marginally to the improvement of policy making. But word soon came from World Bank headquarters that I was principally expected to take, as soon as possible, the initiative in formulating some ambitious economic development plan that would spell out investment   . . . and foreign aid targets over the next few years . . . One aspect of this affair made me particularly uneasy. The task was supposedly crucial for Colombia's development, yet no Colombian was to be found who had any inkling of how to go about it. That knowledge was held only by a few foreign experts."

The Pressure to Lend

The Bank's sad record of supporting military regimes and governments that openly violated human rights began on August 7, 1947, with a $195 million reconstruction loan to the Netherlands. Seventeen days before the Bank approved the loan, the Netherlands had unleashed a war against anti-colonialist nationalists in its huge overseas empire in the East Indies, which had already declared its independence as the Republic of Indonesia. The Dutch sent 145,000 troops (from a nation with only ten million inhabitants at that time, economically struggling at 90 percent of 1939 production), and launched a total economic blockade of nationalist-held areas, causing considerable hunger and health problems among Indonesia's then 70 million inhabitants. In the United Nations, the World Bank was condemned for providing the Dutch government with the resources it needed to continue its economic recovery while waging full-scale war half-way around the world. Historians credit threats by the U.S. Congress to cut off all bilateral aid to the Netherlands as critical in prompting the Dutch to halt the war and grant Indonesia independence in 1949. The Bank's intransigence was a marked contrast and an ominous portent for the future.

In 1966, the Bank directly defied the United Nations, continuing to lend money to South Africa and Portugal despite resolutions of the General Assembly calling on all UN-affiliated agencies -- including the Bank -- to cease financial support for both countries. Portugal's colonial domination of Angola and Mozambique, and South Africa's apartheid were, the resolutions declared, flagrant violations of the UN charter. But the Bank argued that Article IV, Section 10 of its Charter, which prohibits interference in the political affairs of any member, legally obliged it to disregard the UN resolutions. As a result, the Bank approved loans of $10 million to Portugal and $20 million to South Africa after the UN resolution was passed. Even a personal plea from UN Secretary General U Thant to Bank president George Woods was of no avail.

The 1960s also saw an increase in the Bank's pressure to lend, as some of its borrowers began to pay back more annually to the Bank than it disbursed in new loans. In 1963, 1964 and 1969 India transferred more money to the World Bank than the Bank disbursed to it, despite large cash infusions from the newly created International Development Association (IDA). According to the 25-year history of the Bank written by Edward Mason and Robert Asher, the increase in lending in the 1960s began by the 1970s to "create unmanageable demands for reverse flows." Mason and Asher noted that "an institution limited to a zero net transfer of capital can hardly be characterized as a development institution." To solve the problem, the Bank had two choices: forgive or write down World Bank debt, or increase the volume of lending to the same countries, thereby piling on more debt. The latter scenario would work best if the Bank could obtain more funds to disburse as grants or concessional, low-interest loans.

On a Mission from McNamara

World Bank president Robert McNamara temporarily solved the dilemma by increasing lending (IBRD and IDA combined) at a phenomenal rate, from $953 million in 1968 to $12.4 billion in 1981. If ever there was an example of unsustainable growth, McNamara's World Bank was it. His views on management help to clarify his legacy. In the 1960s, he proclaimed that "running any large organization is the same, whether it's the Ford Motor Corporation, the Catholic Church, or the Department of Defense. Once you get to a certain scale they're all the same." But McNamara's master stroke wasn't in how he managed the Bank; it was in how he redefined its mission. It was McNamara who introduced the idea of the Bank as benevolent patron of the poor, and it was McNamara who gave the Bank its first environmental mandate.

McNamara's mission for the Bank to help the poor was couched in idealistic, moralistic terms. ("All of the great religions teach the value of each human life . . . The extremes of poverty and deprivation are simply no longer acceptable. It is development's task to deal with them," he exhorted in 1973 at the Bank/Fund annual meeting in Nairobi.) But the means were infused with a disquieting lack of accountability and with a structure of top-down control. As pressure to lend intensified, the immediate solution was to employ the same approaches and technologies everywhere, with predictable results: they were inefficient at best and often so environmentally and socially inappropriate that they were destined to fail.

At the 1972 Stockholm Conference on the Human Environment, McNamara claimed that the Bank's environmental office -- which he had established in 1970 -- reviewed "each project processed by the Bank" and conducted "careful in-house studies" of the ecological components, using comprehensive environmental criteria embodied in checklists that "encompass the entire spectrum of development." In two years, he claimed, the Bank had established a formidable environmental record, which, he implied, was worthy of emulation: "While in principle the Bank could refuse a loan on environmental grounds . . . the fact is no such case has yet arisen. Since initiating our environmental review, we have found that in every instance the recommended safeguards can and have been successfully implemented."

But the statements had no basis in reality. In 1972, the environmental office consisted of one senior advisor and a recently hired assistant. The environmental review of every project and "successful implementation" of "safeguards" were, in any meaningful sense of the words, non-existent.

Some of the most egregious Bank environmental follies of the 1980s began in the 1970s as a major component of the "poverty" strategy: huge agricultural colonization and land-clearing schemes on poor soils in tropical forests in Latin America and Asia. The performance of Bank agricultural projects approved during the McNamara period was abysmal in the Bank's own terms of meeting appraised economic rates of return, avoiding huge cost and time overruns, and reaching the poor. The 1989 review of evaluation results produced by the Bank's Operations Evaluation Department examined 82 Bank agricultural projects, most approved between 1975 and 1982, the prime years for McNamara-style "poverty" lending. Nearly 45 percent were judged to be unsatisfactory.

Beyond the wasted money and the environmental devastation, there was an even more sinister side to the Bank during the McNamara years: the World Bank's predilection for increasing support to military regimes that tortured and murdered their subjects, sometimes immediately after the violent overthrow of more democratic governments. In 1979, Senator James Abourezk, a liberal Democrat from South Dakota, denounced the Bank on the Senate floor, noting that the Bank was increasing "loans to four newly repressive governments [Chile, Uruguay, Argentina and the Philippines] twice as fast as all others." He noted that 15 of the world's most repressive governments would receive a third of all World Bank loan commitments in 1979, and that Congress and the Carter administration had cut off bilateral aid to four of the 15 -- Argentina, Chile, Uruguay and Ethiopia -- for flagrant human rights violations. He blasted the Bank's "excessive secretiveness" and reminded his colleagues that "we vote the money, yet we do not know where it goes."

The Bank abandoned even the most cynical pretensions to intellectual integrity and rigor when, shortly after cutting off lending to the democratically elected Allende government in Chile in the early 1970s, it geared up to lend to Ceaucescu's Romania, one of the most centrally planned and repressive regimes on earth. Between 1974 and 1982, the period of Bank lending, Romania became even more centrally planned and repressive. Some Bank staff had trouble seeing the economic logic of lending to Ceaucescu. According to former Bank staff member

Art Van de Laar, at one meeting, McNamara responded to questions about Romania with a statement that he had "great faith in the financial morality of socialist countries in repaying debts." At that point, a Bank vice-president ironically observed that "Allende's Chile had perhaps not yet become socialist enough."

A 1979 World Bank country economic study on Romania cites Ceaucescu's pronouncements and, under a section entitled, "Importance of Centralized Economic Control," concludes that "it remains probable that Romania will continue to enjoy one of the highest growth rates among developing countries over the next decade and that it will largely succeed in implementing its development targets."

In many ways, Romania was the ideal Bank borrower: policy dialogue and loan negotiations were streamlined and efficiently focused in the Executive Branch of the government, and the Bank's comparative advantage in lending huge amounts for gigantic infrastructure schemes was identical with the government's priorities for massive power projects, heavy industry, irrigation and large-scale agro-industrial schemes. By 1980, Romania was the IBRD's eighth-biggest borrower out of a total of 19; in 1982, it ranked eleventh in loan commitments out of a total of 43 borrowers that year.

New Ideologues and Policy-Based Lending

It is ironic that at the same time it was pushing money for centralized planning in Romania, new ideologues in the Bank were making their presence known, fervently pushing free-market solutions to all the world's ills. Partly because of the political unsustainability of the austerity measures imposed by the International Monetary Fund (IMF), the Bank entered into "policy dialogue" with Southern governments about appropriate "market oriented" policies, making its first structural adjustment loan in 1980. Although the Bank subsequently acknowledged that it had failed to assess the possible negative social impact of these loans, they nevertheless grew to a quarter of its portfolio by mid-decade and have remained near that level ever since. The policies associated with adjustment programs -- export promotion, trade liberalization, privatization, deregulation, wage restraint and budget and credit cuts -- led not only to a deepening and spreading of poverty around the globe, but also to intensified environmental damage.

During the 1980s, however, the Bank's environmental rhetoric remained very much the same. In 1981, Bank President A.W. Clausen claimed in one of his first speeches that "for a decade now, the Bank has required . . . that every project it finances be reviewed by a special environmental unit -- nearly two thirds of the projects reviewed have raised no serious health or environmental questions, and I'm pleased to say that it has been possible to incorporate protective measures in all the projects we have financed over the past decade."

It was only after dozens of Congressional hearings and mounting NGO campaigns around the world that Clausen's successor, Barber Conable, admitted in 1987 that "the World Bank has been part of the problem in the past" as far as the environment was concerned. But a recent loan decision serves as a good example of how Conable's attempted reforms have failed to influence Bank practice.

On June 29th, the second to last day of the Bank's 1993 fiscal year, the Bank's Board approved a $400 million loan to India for coal-fired power generation over objections by Germany, the United States and Belgium on environmental, social and economic grounds. The representatives of these nations refused (in vain) to approve the loan because, among other things, the loan agreement fails to adequately rehabilitate 140,000 poor people displaced by previous Bank projects for coal-mining and coal-fired electricity production in India. It also fails to evaluate alternatives that could provide as much electricity at less economic and ecological cost (and less indebtedness) for India.

The Bank plans to pour money into coal-fired power production with half-billion-dollar loans to India every 18 to 24 months. If the whole program is realized it would add 16,000 megawatts of coal-burning power plants over the next decade in India alone, which would account for an estimated 2.5 percent of the world's increase in global warming and would increase CO_2 emissions over the same period.

Mission Accomplished?

Has the Bank succeeded in helping the poor or even the governments of the poor? Consider the figures in its 1992 Annual Report. In that year, the Bank (both the International Bank for Reconstruction and Development and the International Development Association) paid out $16.441 billion in gross disbursements to its borrowers. However, net disbursements (disbursements less the amount of money repaid to the Bank on outstanding loans and credits) totaled $6.258 billion. In the same year, the Bank's borrowers paid companies in rich Organization for Economic Cooperation and Development (OECD) nations $6.547 billion for procurement of goods and services on outstanding World Bank loans. In other words, when all is said and done, the nations that borrowed money from the World Bank paid $198 million more to OECD economies for Bank-associated procurement than the borrowing countries actually received from the Bank in 1992.

Meanwhile, the number of unemployed people has grown rapidly around the world (projected by the International Labor Organization to reach one billion in 1994), and wage levels have plummeted, often to levels half as low as at the beginning of the 1980s. Small producers have been displaced by larger-scale export schemes, and education and health-care systems have deteriorated. The result has been a rapid expansion of poverty and a concentration of national incomes: Brazil, Jamaica and Ghana are cases in point.

On this, the 50th anniversary of the birth of the World Bank, it is good to remember that, for most of its life, it has been a creature of the Cold War; geopolitically, the most consistent rationale for development assistance over the decades has been checking the advance of communism, or even that of non-communist regimes and systems friendly to the Soviet Union. For decades, the United States and other leading industrialized countries gave World Bank management a relatively free hand. They were not overly concerned whether the Bank was propping up particularly nasty regimes or traducing its purported poverty and environmental goals, since it was above all an invaluable institution for helping to win the Cold War -- and on this last point they were right. But the Cold War is over.

The World Bank is an institution out of time and place. Fifty years of the Bank as we know it is enough. If, indeed, the role of multilateral institutions is an important one in the new world order, the World Bank must literally remake itself, open its files, end its secret ways and document and learn from its mistakes -- not merely on projects, but in the foundations of its economic policy prescriptions. It needs to trade in the policies developed by old cold warriors and grasp the essential meaning of its favorite new phrase: sustainable development. The world (which, after all, provided the Bank with a name) has had enough lies and enough secrecy.

2

Global Economic Counterrevolution: How Northern Economic Warfare Devastates the South

Walden Bello

B
arbarians at the gates: The image is evoked frequently these days to describe the defensive condition of the West, and not just by right-wing extremists like Pat Buchanan.

Listen to Jacques Attali, the well-known French Socialist party stalwart who until recently headed the European Bank for Reconstruction and Development. In his latest book [*Millennium: Winners and Losers in the Coming World Order*], he writes off the billions of people of the southern hemisphere as "millenial losers." Africa is a "lost continent," according to Attali, while Latin America is sliding into "terminal poverty." With no future of their own, says Attali, the peoples of the South can only look forward to "migrating from place to place looking for a few drops of what we have in Los Angeles, Berlin, or Paris, which for them will be oases of hope, emerald cities of plenty and high-tech magic."

What worries Attali, though, is that the poor of the South "will redefine hope in fundamentalist terms altogether outside modernity. This dynamic threatens true world war of a new type, of terrorism that can suddenly rip the vulnerable fabric of complex systems." In other words, the gates must remain well-guarded against the insurgent tide.

Attali is hardly a reactionary. Indeed, the ease with which he and liberals like him have been seduced by the image of "the beleaguered North" testifies to how many in the West now perceive that the interests of the rich, white North and the poor, colored South are irreconcilable. We may dismiss the popularity of David Duke as an anomaly and attribute violence against foreigners in Germany to a handful of neo-Nazis, but intellectuals are a weathervane, and thinking like Attali's points to a dangerous closing in Westerners' thinking.

It is not popular these days for opinion leaders in Europe and the

United States to suggest that the North may have had a hand in creating the massive movement of people from the South. Surely, however, the migration cannot be separated from the draconian policies of debt collection that produced a staggering net transfer of financial resources -- $155 billion -- from the South to the North between 1984 and 1990.

Moreover, this massive decapitalization, which triggered the virtual collapse of economies throughout the South, was not simply the unfortunate consequence of repaying debt, as Northern media have portrayed it. It was, in fact, the intentional outcome of a global economic counterrevolution set in motion in the 1980s by Northern states and economic institutions under the leadership of the Reagan administration.

"Development": Defeat Solidarity

To understand this counterrevolution, we must place it against the background of the 1960s and 1970s, which the United Nations labeled the "first two development decades." These years were marked by the growth of a more assertive, more confident South. Though a mixed bag politically, the newly emerging independent countries of Asia and Africa, as well as the older states of Latin America, were determined to achieve development through economic programs that included vigorous state leadership, domestic market protection and strong controls on Western investment.

While the East-West conflict split the South on some issues, it did not prevent its coming together in the Non-Aligned Movement, the United Nations Commission on Trade and Development (UNCTAD) and the Group of 77 [comprising the bulk of African, Asian and Latin American countries] to press for a fundamental redistribution of wealth on a global level.

The rhetoric of solidarity seemed on the verge of becoming reality in the early 1970s, when OPEC countries managed to seize control of the price of oil. OPEC's success triggered further attempts by Third World countries to create cartels in bauxite, tin and other raw materials, as well as in agricultural commodities. Southern governments expected the OPEC producers to stand united with them to demand a comprehensive deal on a wide range of commodities. This would mark the beginning of the "New International Economic Order."

OPEC did not deliver, but even the near emergence of a unified Southern economic bloc controlling strategic commodities gave the Northern countries a bad scare. Anti-South sentiment became a mass phenomenon in the United States, where it contributed to Ronald

Reagan's election in 1980. Preceding the resurgence of chauvinism and racism in Europe by a decade, this earlier reaction in the U.S. probably stemmed from the coincidence of the Third World economic challenge with such direct political threats to U.S. hegemony as the defeat in Vietnam and the Iran hostage crisis.

In any event, the Reagan administration came to power with an agenda to discipline the Third World. While U.S. military adventures against radical Third World movements and governments dominated the news, even more lethal was the economic warfare the U.S. unleashed against the South on a global level.

The Reagan project was certainly helped by the fall in raw-material prices to their lowest point since the 1930s. But the rollback of the South was not primarily a result of market forces; it was engineered. The U.S.-dominated World Bank spearheaded the effort. The main mechanism employed was the aid program, which was transformed from an instrument of limited wealth redistribution and pacification under Cold War liberals like World Bank head Robert McNamara to a device that completely reshaped Third World economies under Reaganites at the Treasury Department and the World Bank.

Structural Adjustment Loans: The Weapon of Choice

Right-wing economists had identified strong state leadership, protection of domestic markets and controls on foreign investment as strategic building blocks of a subversive "New International Economic Order." Dismantling them became a priority, and for this task the World Bank deployed the formidably named "structural adjustment loan" (SAL).

SALs were not tied to one specific project, but access to these multi-million-dollar loans was made contingent on a Third World government's agreement to carry out a drastic program of liberalization. This included reducing the state's role in the economy, lowering barriers to imports, removing restrictions on foreign investment, eliminating subsidies for local industries, reducing spending for social welfare, cutting wages, devaluing the currency and emphasizing production for export rather than for local consumption.

While World Bank economists tried to sell these measures as necessary to promote "efficiency," Third World leaders accurately perceived them as striking at the heart of the Southern project of gaining more economic independence at the national level and seeking income redistribution at the global level. Not surprisingly, initially there were few takers.

The opportunity for the Treasury Department and the World Bank to have their way came in the early 1980s: as more and more Third World countries ran into greater difficulties servicing the huge loans made to them by Northern banks in the 1970s, the banks made the adoption of the World Bank structural adjustment program essential to debt rescheduling. They argued that the structural reforms ensured debtors' abilities to continue paying their debts beyond the short term. Unable to gain access to further private bank financing without the World Bank seal of approval, governments surrendered. By the end of 1985, 12 of the 15 debtors designated as top-priority debtors -- including Argentina, Mexico and the Philippines -- had submitted to structural adjustment programs.

Over the next seven years, SALs proliferated as the economies of more and more Third World countries came under the surveillance and control of the Bank. About 187 SALs had been administered by the end of the decade, many of them coordinated with equally stringent standby programs administered by the International Monetary Fund (IMF). Whereas in the previous division of labor between the two institutions, the World Bank was supposed to promote growth and the IMF was supposed to monitor financial restraint, their roles now became indistinguishable. Both became the enforcers of the North's economic rollback strategy.

The cooperation between the Bank and the Fund was brought to a higher level with the establishment in 1988 of the Structural Adjustment Facility (SAF) to closely coordinate both institutions' surveillance and enforcement activities, especially in sub-Saharan Africa. Out of a total of 47 countries in that region, 30 are currently implementing adjustment programs administered by the Bank or the Fund. Since most of these countries have very weak political structures, an IMF-World Bank condominium has been imposed over much of sub-Saharan Africa under the guise of providing aid.

Structural adjustment programs functioned extremely effectively as a mechanism to collect Third World debt and cause a massive redistribution of financial resources from the South to the North. But more importantly, they achieved the strategic objective: imposing "reforms" that have since transformed scores of Third World economies. From Argentina to Ghana, state intervention in the economy has been drastically curtailed, protectionist barriers to Northern imports have been eliminated wholesale, restrictions on foreign investment have been lifted and, through export-first policies, internal economies have been more tightly integrated into the capitalist world market dominated by the North.

The crowning achievement of this strategy came in 1991: India, a leader of the Non-Aligned Movement and long the champion of state-led nationalist development, promised a thoroughgoing restructuring of its economy in exchange for a structural adjustment loan to enable it to service its debts to Western banks. Conservative publications like *The Economist* gave the event almost as much significance as the dismantling of socialism in the Soviet Union.

"Bitter Medicine," No Cure

Like all counterrevolutions, the costs of dominating the South have been ghastly. The average Gross National Product for nations in sub-Saharan Africa fell by 2.2 percent per year in the 1980s; by 1990, per capita income on the continent was back down to its level at the time of independence in the 1960s. A United Nations advisory group reported that throughout the continent, "health systems are collapsing for lack of medicines, schools have no books, and universities suffer from a debilitating lack of library and laboratory facilities." Structural adjustment programs have also promoted massive environmental damage, as many African countries were forced to cut down forests rapidly and exploit other natural resources more intensively to gain the foreign exchange they needed to make mounting interest payments.

Latin Americans regard the reverse financial flow from their continent as the "worst plunder since Cortez" and refer to the 1980s as the "lost decade." Per capita income in 1990 was at virtually the same level as ten years earlier. Severe malnutrition stalks the countryside, paving the way for the return of cholera, which people thought had been eradicated.

Technocrats at the World Bank and the IMF view this social devastation as the "bitter medicine" Southern countries must swallow to regain economic health. But after more than a decade of structural adjustment programs, the technocrats still haven't come up with an unqualified success story. They sometimes point to Chile as a model, but change the topic when conversation turns to the hunger and malnutrition pervasive in that land, where wages have declined by over 40 percent in real terms since the early 1970s. At other times, World Bank types wax eloquent over Mexico's resumption of growth, but become evasive when they have to explain why more than 50 percent of the population is now unemployed or underemployed, and why the real purchasing power of the minimum wage is about two thirds of what it was in 1970.

Perhaps it is the migrants who most clearly perceive the truth about structural adjustment: it was intended not as a transition to prosperity but as a permanent condition of economic suffering to ensure that the South would never rise again to challenge the North. If that is the case, flight is a rational solution. Migrants are not obsessed nomads seeking the emerald cities, as Attali would have it; they are refugees fleeing the wasteland that has been created by the economic equivalent of a scorched-earth strategy.

Attali paints one possible outcome to the North-South "tragedy": "a war unlike any seen in modern times, [one that] will resemble the barbarian raids of the seventh and eighth centuries." The image of permanent war is shared by the U.S. Presidential Commission on Integrated Long-Term Strategy. Conflict with the Third World, the Commission tells us, "is a form of warfare in which 'the enemy' is more or less omnipresent and unlikely ever to surrender." The Commission goes on to say that whereas "in the past we have sometimes seen these attacks as a succession of transient and isolated crises, we now have to think of them as a permanent addition to the menu of defense planning problems."

But another outcome is possible. It can come about if people emerge who are brave enough to accept the North's responsibility for the economic devastation of the South and lead the effort to forge the only lasting solution to the global crisis: the creation of a North-South alliance that would shatter the shackles of structural adjustment and unleash the long-repressed promise of Southern sovereignty.

3

IMF/World Bank Wreak Havoc on Third World
Davison Budhoo

avison Budhoo, a prominent economist from Grenada, cre-
ated a worldwide sensation when he resigned from the IMF in
1988 in disgust over what he called the Fund's "increasingly
genocidal policies." He is author of **Enough Is Enough**, *and* **Global**
Justice: The Struggle to Reform the International Monetary Fund*.*
Budhoo is Executive Director of the Bretton Woods Reform Movement
(BWRM), which is spearheading a campaign against IMF/World Bank
structural adjustment programs.

1994 marks the 50th anniversary of the founding of the World Bank
and the International Monetary Fund at Bretton Woods, New Hampshire.

But as the North congratulates itself and celebrates, the South and
its three billion poor will tear out their hair in rage. For the operations
of these agencies there have been catastrophic. Instead of development and favorable adjustment, the Third World today is in an accelerated spiral of economic and social decline. That decline is linked directly to the World Bank and the International Monetary Fund.

IMF-World Bank structural adjustment programs (SAPs) are designed to reduce consumption in developing countries and to redirect
resources to manufacturing exports for the repayment of debt. This
has caused overproduction of primary products and a precipitous fall
in their prices. It has also led to the devastation of traditional agriculture and to the emergence of hordes of landless farmers in virtually
every country in which the World Bank and IMF operate. Food security has declined dramatically in all Third World regions, but in Africa
in particular. Growing dependence on food imports, which is the lot of
sub-Saharan Africa, places these countries in an extremely vulnerable
position. They simply do not have the foreign exchange to import
enough food, given the fall in export prices and the need to repay debt.

Basic conditionalities of the IMF-World Bank include drastic cuts in social expenditures, especially in health and education. According to the UN Economic Commission for Africa, expenditures on health in IMF-World Bank programmed countries declined by 50 percent during the 1980s, and spending on education declined by 25 percent. Similar trends are evident in all other Southern regions.

IMF-World Bank programs come with other requirements. Governments are generally forced to remove subsidies to the poor on basic foodstuffs and services such as rice and maize, water and electricity. Tax systems are made more repressive, and real wage rates are allowed to fall sharply -- in Mexico during the 1980s, the real wage rate declined by over 75 percent. Today, in that country, a family of four on the minimum wage (and over 60 percent of the employed labor force is on the minimum wage) can buy only 25 percent of its basic needs.

With IMF-World Bank-inspired devaluation come inflation and increases in the prices of all imported foodstuffs. Removal of price controls domestically leads to sudden increases in the prices of commodities used by the poor. Big increases in interest rates cause bankruptcies in domestically owned small businesses and further unemployment. Removal almost overnight of trade restrictions throws domestic industries into disarray and liquidation and compounds unemployment. Dismantling foreign exchange restrictions allows the elite classes to export funds overseas, carte blanche, as capital flight, thus worsening the balance of payments. Privatization of all government-owned productive enterprises as an ideological prerogative of the IMF-World Bank is an incalculable loss.

Even on the basis of objectives established by the IMF-World Bank themselves, SAPs have not been successful. An internal study within the IMF completed in 1988 reveals that the 40-odd programs implemented between 1983 and 1987 failed in their objectives of enhancing economic growth, reducing fiscal and balance of payments deficits, lowering inflation and stabilizing or decreasing external debt. Subsequent programs, as the United Nations Development Program (UNDP) and UN Economic Commission for Africa have shown, have failed even more dismally in relation to IMF-World Bank self-imposed objectives.

Anti-People

But the greatest failure of these programs is to be seen in their impact on the people. Using figures provided by the United Nations Childrens Fund (UNICEF) and the UN Economic Commission for Africa, it has been estimated that at least six million children under five years of age have died each year since 1982 in Africa, Asia and Latin America because of the anti-people, even genocidal, focus of IMF-World Bank SAPs.

And that is just the tip of the iceberg. Even more pervasively, these programs have created economic, social and cultural devastation whenever and wherever they are introduced. The prestigious and highly Northern-oriented UNDP has determined that some 1.2 billion people in the Third World now live in absolute poverty (almost twice the number ten years ago), over half of sub-Saharan children are starving or malnourished, 1.6 billion people in the Third World are without potable water and well over two billion are unemployed or underemployed. In some countries of Africa, infant mortality rates are double what they were ten years ago, before SAPs were widespread.

Recently, UNDP reported (in its 1992 *Human Development Report*) that, mainly because of inherent inequities built into SAPs, the income gap between rich and poor in the Third World doubled in the course of the 1980s. Today, the richest fifth of the world (including most of Europe and North America) receives 150 times more in income than the poorest fifth (located almost exclusively in the South). "This [disparity] was a big shock to me," said the Chief Adviser to UNDP at a press conference. "I had never expected a ratio of 150 to 1; perhaps 40 to 1." In scathingly cynical terms, the Report concluded that "the World Bank and the IMF should be the buffer to protect developing countries, but their recent record shows that they have become institutions for recycling debt, not recycling resources."

On the environmental side, millions of indigenous people have been driven out of their ancestral homelands by large commercial ranchers and timber loggers. Several millions more have been displaced by massive dams that benefit primarily elite classes and transnational corporations. Both types of activities were approved and financed by the IMF-World Bank. It is now generally recognized that the environmental impact of the IMF-World Bank on the South has been as devastating as the economic and social impact on peoples and societies.

These policies, which are really the outpouring of a new and savage push for instant and highly unjust expropriation of the resources and economic sustenance of the South, must be brought to a halt. How can this be done? Three possible lines of approach can be suggested.

The first is to abolish these institutions. This is the view taken by independent researchers (such as Susan George and Walden Bello) and by human rights organizations (such as PROBE International and the Peoples' Tribunal on IMF-World Bank Crimes against Humanity,

Berlin 1988). Senior officials of the Swedish official aid agency, SIDA, have also suggested this. While abolition is fully justified, it is unrealistic to think that it will happen. The governments of the North will never agree to abolition, simply because these institutions are too important to them as instruments to achieve their economic and political objectives. This has been proven over and over again by the Group of Seven [France, Germany, Italy, Canada, Japan, England and the U.S.] who, at every meeting, enhance rather than diminish the powers of these bodies.

A second possible way out is to let the World Bank and the IMF continue to operate, but to control them through the creation of a special UN agency. This is the solution put forward by the UNDP in its 1992 Report. The difficulty with this solution is that the UN today, like the IMF-World Bank themselves, is under the total control of a small clique of Northern countries. The form may change, but the substance of the policies of major industrialized countries in relation to the South, as expressed in the operations of the IMF-World Bank, will remain the same.

The third possible solution is for peoples and countries to force change on the institutions, by confronting them with irrefutable evidence of their gross injustices, inequities and contradictions.

In this respect, several things can be done immediately. There are, for instance, various Articles of Agreement in the constitutions of the World Bank and IMF that have not been implemented at all, simply because implementation would have improved the position of developing countries vis-a-vis the staff of the IMF and World Bank. In this regard, there is provision for a conflict resolution body to intervene in cases of conflict of a technical nature between management of the institutions and member governments. These Articles should be made operational immediately. Also, the IMF Council, as defined in the Articles of Agreement to mean a Peoples' Parliament within the management structure of the institution, should be established forthwith. This would not only serve to help democratize the institution, but would create a meaningful checks-and-balances mechanism against abuse. There should also be created a Third World Watchdog Committee, comprising highly qualified technical people, to help developing countries in their negotiations with the institutions.

Leaders of the industrialized world have much to ponder and do about the IMF-World Bank, apart from preparing 50th Anniversary celebrations and handing out more accolades and power to their staff. But the most likely outcome is that, as always, they will do nothing.

4

The Free Trade Connection
John Gershman

Free trade is the latest prescription for economic ills. Though at the very heart of the neoliberal approach to economic growth, which supports the withdrawal of the state from the economy and the enhancement of the role of the market in economic relations, free trade is only one component of a larger system. Structural adjustment programs are laying the political and economic groundwork for the policies that free trade agreements will institutionalize.

If the 1980s were the decade of the debt crisis and structural adjustment, the 1990s promise to be the decade of free trade. With global free trade under the auspices of the General Agreement on Tariffs and Trade (GATT) stalled by debates between the U.S. and the European Community over agricultural subsidies, the most comprehensive free trade agenda is in the Americas.

Since the announcement by President Bush in June 1990 of the Enterprise for the Americas Initiative (EAI) and the opening of free trade talks with Mexico (since expanded to include Canada), there has been a rush to free trade in the hemisphere. The North American Free Trade Agreement (NAFTA) was recently signed into law by President Clinton. Mexico has signed free trade agreements with Chile and the Central American countries, among others. And the U.S. has signed over 20 framework agreements with countries and groups of countries under the auspices of the EAI.

The current rush toward free trade follows on the heels of ten years of structural adjustment, a logical "next step" in the overhaul of the global economy. How do the agendas of free trade and structural adjustment reinforce each other?

Structural adjustment goes beyond a simple imposition of a set of macroeconomic policies like currency devaluation, privatization, trade liberalization and cuts in government spending. It represents a political project, a conscious strategy of social transformation at two levels: global and domestic.

Structural Adjustment: The Global Agenda

At the global level, structural adjustment rolled back attempts to build Southern unity. The 1970s saw increased Southern assertiveness, including demands for new international economic and information orders and a strengthening of UN agencies. Despite the fact that this unity was often more rhetorical than real and was ultimately largely ineffective beyond providing Southern elites with some nationalist legitimation to use at home, it did frighten some Northern elites. The U.S. defeat in Vietnam; the success of popular nationalist revolutions in Angola, Mozambique and Nicaragua; the perceived hostility of the United Nations to U.S. interests and a heating up of the Cold War in the late 1970s and early 1980s set a global stage that seemed increasingly inhospitable to U.S. interests.

The debt crisis changed all that, opening doors of opportunity to reassert U.S. hegemony and to confront an assertive South. The U.S., determined to open up long-insulated nationalist economies, found allies among Northern governments, commercial banks, international institutions like the World Bank and Southern technocrats.

The change was easy to observe in the Reagan administration, which originally viewed the World Bank as a liberal cash cow subsidizing Third World states opposed to U.S. economic policies. After 1982, however, the Bank and the International Monetary Fund (IMF) became the major instruments of an active attempt to restructure North-South relations, as well as to guarantee the interests of commercial banks.

The prescription was one of structural adjustment, and the program, for those prescribing it, was a great success. In 1985, 12 of the top 15 indebted countries had submitted to structural adjustment programs. By 1990, more than 187 adjustment loans had been provided to countries in Latin America, Asia, Africa and Eastern Europe. Of the 47 countries in sub-Saharan Africa, 30 are currently undergoing World Bank or IMF adjustment programs. As a debt collection mechanism, structural adjustment programs would make any credit agency's mouth water: between 1984 and 1990 the net transfer of resources from South to North totaled $155 billion.

Structural Adjustment: The Domestic Agenda

Domestically, structural adjustment involves an economic assault on the living standards of the poor and a political assault on the organized bases of popular resistance to austerity and adjustment. These two components represent the substance of the now-infamous package of neo-liberal economic policies of which policy elites from Warsaw to Santiago are enamored.

The economic costs have been no less than catastrophic. Real wages in Chile are 40 percent lower than in the early 1970s, while those in Mexico fell 50 percent in the last decade. Living standards in much of Latin America have fallen back to the level they were at 30 years ago. At the same time, income has been redistributed from the poor to the rich. In Mexico, for example, the workers' share of national income fell from 49 percent to 29 percent between 1981 and 1990. In Chile, the richest ten percent capture 47 percent of national income, compared with 36 percent in 1970. Mexico and Chile are considered by the Bank and the IMF as success stories.

The political assaults involved both brutal repression and the conscious engineering of new legal and political institutions that would disadvantage workers and the poor. Chile represents perhaps the clearest example. Under Pinochet, labor laws were changed to shift collective bargaining from an industry-wide level to the plant level, weakening labor's power. Community organizers and trade unionists were among the chief targets of Pinochet's brutal regime, under which thousands disappeared, were murdered or were imprisoned. In Mexico, labor unions dominated by the Partido Revolucionario Institucional (Institutional Revolutionary Party, PRI) serve to shelter the government from direct worker opposition. They also serve as the base for repressing autonomous trade union organizers, including Cleto Nigmo, an organizer at Ford's Cuautitlan plant who was murdered in January 1991.

The Rush to Free Trade

So why the sudden rush to free trade? Focusing again on the Americas, we see the coincidence of interests among Southern elites, transnational corporations (TNCs) and U.S. elites.

Southern elites are in a pickle. Their economies risk getting left high and dry without guaranteed access to Northern markets. After a decade of suppressed wages and reduced social spending, their domestic markets are too small to have any significant purchasing power. This reinforces the export-oriented strategies for growth that have been promoted through structural adjustment.

But the integration of Europe, the return to the world capitalist economy of both Eastern Europe and the Commonwealth of Independent States, continued obstacles to gaining access to Japanese markets and rising protectionist sentiment in the U.S. make those markets more uncertain, an unsettling prospect for Southern elites. For them, guaranteed access to the U.S. market is essential to attract foreign investment and to maintain debt payments. Free trade agreements provide that access.

For TNCs, free trade agreements institutionalize flows of capital, goods and services that already exist. Corporations are also able to leverage changes in foreign investment codes and intellectual property regulations, opening up more areas of the economies to foreign capital while protecting their monopolies on advanced technologies and products.

In the U.S., the NAFTA and the EAI attempt to confront the competitiveness challenge posed by Europe and Japan. The free traders claim that they will create a "ladder" of comparative advantage, with the U.S. at the top, specializing in high-wage, high-tech goods. Mexico, Chile and Brazil would be a notch below, specializing in labor-intensive and some capital-intensive goods, while the rest of the region would be at the bottom, producing raw materials and doing basic assembly operations. As the U.S. moves into more and more high-tech and information-intensive industries, other countries would take over those industries left behind, moving up the ladder, so to speak.

This rhetoric disguises some unpleasant realities. What the "ladder" actually provides is the institutional infrastructure for TNCs to develop integrated production facilities using the entire western hemisphere as their area of operations. TNCs have already located some high-tech operations in Mexico, for example, where they can get world-class quality and productivity at one tenth of U.S. wages. The ladder quickly becomes a slippery slope for workers, small farmers and small businesses. Free trade agreements represent a "corporate bill of rights," in Canadian activist Maude Barlow's appropriate and tragic turn of phrase. They enable corporations that move or threaten to move production to the South to exploit increasingly cheap labor and deregulated economies, to whipsaw trade unions into taking wage cutbacks and to bully states into lowering environmental and other regulations. Hard-won standards in the U.S. are thus undermined, while at the same time, U.S. firms are expected to compete against cheaper imported goods. The circle completed, free trade becomes the "boomerang" of the debt crisis, in author Susan George's phrase.

Where to go from here? Calls for broad Southern unity under the Non-Aligned Movement or the Group of 77 are not likely to have significant impact. While they will remain important fora, they currently lack the cohesion to challenge Northern political and transnational corporate power. More critical are the calls for regional economic integration that would provide Southern states with some bargaining power. The Mercosur bloc of Brazil, Argentina, Paraguay and Uruguay could play such a role, although not in its present form. A variation on Malaysian Prime Minister Mohammed Mahatir's proposal for an East Asia Economic Group that would exclude, rather than include, Japan, could be another.

But if these strategies are to have a broader, more meaningful impact, they must promote higher common labor and environmental standards, as well as redistributive policies such as agrarian reform to enhance the rights of workers and raise living standards of the poor. A multilevel strategy that links local, national, regional and global struggles is the challenge and the opportunity presented by the free trade agenda.

> *"Structural adjustment is a mechanism to shift the burden of economic mismanagement and financial mismanagement from the North to the South, and from the Southern elites to the Southern communities and people. Structural adjustment is also a policy to continue colonial trade and economic patterns developed during the colonial period, but which the Northern powers want to continue in the post-colonial period. Economically speaking, we [countries in the South] are more dependent on the ex-colonial countries than we ever were. The World Bank and IMF are playing the role that our ex-colonial masters used to play."*
>
> Martin Khor, Director,
> Third World Network,
> Malaysia

5

The Debt Boomerang
Susan George

If the goals of managers in the official institutions that rule over Third World debt were to squeeze the debtors dry, to transfer enormous resources from South to North and to wage undeclared war on the poor continents and their people, then their policies have been an unqualified success.

If, however, their strategies were intended -- as the official institutions always claim -- to promote development beneficial to all members of society, to preserve the planet's unique environment and gradually to reduce the debt burden itself, then their failure is colossal.

The most obvious aspect of this failure -- or success, depending on your point of view -- is financial. Every single month, from the outset of the debt crisis in 1982 until the end of 1990, debtor countries in the South remitted to their creditors in the North an average $6.5 billion in interest payments alone. If payments of the principle are included, then debtor countries have paid creditors at a rate of almost $12.5 billion per month -- as much as the entire Third World spends each month on health and education.

Moreover, the debt crisis has given creditor countries the chance to intervene in the management of dozens of debtors' economies -- using the International Monetary Fund (IMF) and the World Bank. Their job is simple: to make sure the debt is serviced. Since the average citizen of a low-income debtor country earns less than one fiftieth of what the average citizen of a high-income creditor country earns, this process is like trying to extract blood from a stone.

To accumulate hard currency and service its debts, a country must increase its exports and reduce government spending. Most debtor governments have accepted this and forced their people to cooperate with the draconian policies of the IMF and World Bank to ensure that debts are serviced. Much good has it done them. A decade has passed since the Third World debt crisis first erupted, yet in spite of harsh measures faithfully applied, this crisis is today more intractable than ever.

Bureaucratic Immunity

Debtor countries have deprived their people of basic necessities in order to provide the private banks and the public agencies of the rich countries with the equivalent of six Marshall Plans (the program of assistance offered by the U.S. to Europe after the Second World War).

Have these extraordinary outflows served to reduce the absolute size of the debt burden? Not a bit: in spite of paying out more than $1.3 trillion between 1982 and 1990, the debtor countries as a group began the 1990s with a full 61 percent more in debt than in 1982. Sub-Saharan Africa's debt increased by 113 percent during this period.

The economic policies imposed on debtors by the major multilateral agencies and packaged as "structural adjustment" have cured nothing at all. They have, rather, caused untold human suffering and widespread environmental destruction, emptying debtor countries of their resources and rendering them less able each year to service their debts, let alone invest in economic and human recovery.

The World Bank and the IMF structural adjusters have by now had plenty of time to make their measures work. But they have failed. Had they been corporate executives they would doubtless have been sacked long ago for incompetence. But no such accountability applies to these international bureaucrats acting on behalf of the creditor governments. They need never submit to the judgment of their victims. They answer only to their own equally unaccountable superiors and, at the top of the bureaucratic tree, to a Board of Governors reflecting the majority voting strength of the richest creditor countries. These lavishly compensated international civil servants are consequently still to be found in Washington and throughout the Third World living exceedingly well.

There are other beneficiaries. For business corporations operating in debtor countries, structural adjustment has enhanced profitability by reducing both wages and the power of unions. For many international banks, debt service payments at unusually high interest rates in the early 1980s helped to fuel several years of record earnings. From the corporate or banking perspective, the World Bank and the IMF pass the test with flying colors.

Third World elites don't have much cause for complaint, either. They have weathered the "lost decade of the 1980s" with relative ease and have sometimes profited handsomely from it. They, too, benefit from plummeting wages. Their money is often in safe havens outside their own countries. Each time the IMF requires a devaluation of the national currency to encourage exports, those whose holdings are in foreign currencies automatically become richer at home. And although public services may deteriorate or close down, rich people can afford private ones. So it is not surprising that Third World governments have failed to unite and demand debt reductions.

The debtors' lack of unity ensures the draining of their economies and a continuing South-to-North resource flow on a scale far outstripping any the colonial period could devise. The debtor governments have from time to time called for debt relief, but have never collectively confronted the creditors. As a reward for docility, creditors have allowed most debtor-country elites to maintain their links to the world financial system, providing them with at least a trickle of fresh money and offering them frequent opportunities to purchase local assets at bargain prices through so-called debt-for-equity swaps of privatization programs.

Third World debt should not, therefore, be seen as a straightforwardly "national" problem. Different social classes in debtor countries have vastly divergent interests and are unequally affected. Although debt has visited unprecedented pain on the vast majority of Third World people, the crisis is not necessarily a crisis for everyone.

While the topmost layers of Third World societies remain largely insulated from debt distress, ordinary people in the South sacrifice to pay back loans they never asked for, or that they even fought against, and from which they derive no gain. Knowledge of their plight is by now fairly widespread in the developed, creditor countries, thanks to the efforts of thousands of concerned people patiently explaining the human and ecological consequences of the debt crisis in the Third World.

Fallout in the North

Yet the pressures exerted by dozens of non-governmental organizations in both the North and South have so far failed to alter basic debt-management policies. Although the Fund and the Bank now claim they seek to "mitigate the social costs of adjustment," official response to the crisis advances at a calculated snail's pace, inching from one feeble and ineffective plan to the next while leaving the status quo essentially untouched.

Until now, those in the North who have tried to change the debt management strategies have rightly based their arguments on ethical and humanitarian grounds.

The impact of Third World debt fallout in the North is much less well known -- doubtless because the consequences of debt are far more serious and life-threatening in the South than in the North. But although people in the South are more grievously affected than those in the North, in both cases, a tiny minority benefits while the overwhelmng majority pays.

Northern taxpayers have carried commercial banks through the Third World debt crisis from the start, and virtually all of them are blissfully unaware of the fact. We have paid Northern banks between $44 and $50 billion in tax relief on bad debts -- enough to meet the entire Third World's health spending for one year.

There is another less measurable cost: the strong correlation between debt and worldwide military conflict. Loans have frequently been employed by Third World governments to buy arms from Northern manufacturers for use against both internal and external opponents. Debt promoted the Gulf War. Saddam Hussein saw the invasion of Kuwait as one way of wiping out the colossal debts he owed both to that country and to the allies -- much of it used to finance his arms build-up. George Bush granted massive debt forgiveness to an allied Arab nation like Egypt as a reward for staying on his side.

Third World debt is not the only cause of, say, increased illegal drug exports to the U.S. and Europe, or of accelerated deforestation hastening the greenhouse effect. But it is, at the very least, an aggravating factor. Debt-burdened Latin American governments become hooked on dollars from their coca-producing regions. This severely dampens their incentive to encourage legal crops. Increasing drug exports, in turn, escalate the costs of law enforcement and contribute to social breakdown in the North.

A Stake in Change

Such harmful effects did not suddenly spring fully armed from the head or the belly of the World Bank. They result from a set of policies aimed at promoting a capital-intensive, energy-intensive, unsustainable Western model of development, which was favorable only to Third World elites, Northern banks and transnational corporations.

Not surprisingly, massive overborrowing coupled with high interest rates led to the debt crisis. This crisis in turn provided official debt managers in the 1980s and 1990s with a perfect lever to entrench the very development model that had caused the original problem. Relying on unbridled free-market forces and export-led growth, they have devastated the unprotected: the poorest, most vulnerable groups and the environment.

They are still doing it and, quite simply, they have to be stopped.

Any standard of human decency or ethical imperative demands a change in debt management, but so does enlightened self-interest. Everyone outside the narrowest of elite circles has a stake in positive change. If enough people in the North realize that the Third World debt crisis is their crisis, they may well insist on radically different policies, speak out and seek to join with similar forces in the South.

For this to happen we must first think for ourselves, recognize the modern mythology that prevent us from acting and then act. There are some obvious directions we can take to help the "natural majority" to become effective. Workers, farmers, trade unionists, activists, parents, immigrants, taxpayers -- we all have to make a common cause against the common danger.

We do not want to prescribe a program but to state some principles:

First, those who borrowed were rarely elected by their peoples. They squandered money on arms or used it to further entrench their own power and privilege, counting on their poorer compatriots to make sacrifices to pay back the loans when due. Democratically elected governments should not be expected to assume the debt burdens of dictatorial predecessors.

Those who made the loans were either irresponsible or intentionally attempting to make the debtors subservient to their interests. The creditors have been richly rewarded and are in no danger if the debt is cancelled or converted to provide genuine development. They should play by normal rules and not expect the public to pay for their costly mistakes.

The debt has already been largely or entirely repaid. The North is, in fact, substantially in debt to the South, and it has received, since 1982, the cheapest raw materials on record.

But cancellation and other debt reduction measures must not be used as an excuse or a pretext to further cut the debtor countries out of the benefits of the world economy. The guiding precepts should be popular participation in decision-making at every level, social equity and ecological prudence.

So long as the policies of the rich North represent a mixture of crude carrot-and-stick maneuvers, coupled with basic contempt for the South, its problems and its peoples, we can expect more lethal North-South tensions, more powerful boomerangs hurtling back at us, a further forced retreat of the rich countries to Fortress America or Fortress Europe.

Alternatively, we could decide that it is time -- high time -- we began to live together on this improbable planet as *homo sapiens* with a good deal more *sapiens*.

The Six Boomerangs

Environment: Debt-induced poverty causes Third World people to exploit natural resources in the most profitable and least sustainable way, which causes an increase in global warming and a depletion of genetic bio-diversity. This ultimately harms the North, too.

Drugs: The illegal drug trade is the major earner for heavily indebted countries like Peru, Bolivia and Colombia. The social and economic costs of the drug-consuming boom in the North is phenomenal -- $60 billion a year in the U.S. alone.

Taxes: Governments in the North have used their taxpayers' money to give banks tax concessions so they can write off so-called "bad debts" from Third World countries. But in most cases, this has not reduced the actual debts of poor countries. By 1991, British banks had gained from tax credits more than half their exposure. The eventual total relief will amount to $8.5 billion.

Unemployment: Exports from rich countries to the Third World would be much higher if those countries were not strapped by debt, and this would stimulate manufacturing and employment in the North. The loss of jobs due to "lost exports" is estimated to account for one fifth of total U.S. unemployment.

Immigration: The International Labor Organization estimates that there are about 100 million legal or illegal immigrants and refugees in the world today. Many go to the richer countries of the North to flee poverty and the effects of IMF-imposed economic policies.

Conflict: Debt creates social unrest and war. Iraq invaded Kuwait in 1990 largely in retaliation for Kuwait's insistence that Saddam Hussein's regime repay a $12 billion loan.

6

The Doctrine of Odious Debts
Patricia Adams, Interviewed by Juliette Majot

n her book *Odious Debts*, economist Patricia Adams traces the path of international loans, investigating the reasons why they are made and their impacts on the environment and Third World populations. In this interview, Adams explains the Doctrine of Odious Debts and offers a way to both resolve the debt crisis justly and further democracy and accountability in the Third World.

Juliette Majot: **Your book covers a wide range of topics as you follow the trail of international loans: environmental destruction, crony capitalism, loose international lending and government corruption. You decided to devote an entire chapter to what you call odious debts and titled your book after it. Why?**

Patricia Adams: When I tracked money that went out of public and private lending institutions during the heyday of investment in Third World development in the 1970s, I became fascinated with establishing whether or not the resulting debts were legitimately incurred. Where did the money go? How much disappeared? Were the investments sound? Who decided the loans were a good risk in the first place?

According to research by activists around the world, these loans were going to investments that were environmentally disastrous and economically unsound. I wondered how lenders and borrowers could afford so many economic mistakes, and how they could deviate so far from the values of their peoples.

It's clear that both lending and borrowing has been going on in the name of the people, but with no accountability to them.

So this question of legitimacy became very important to me. The term "odious debts" is not mine. It is an established international principle, and there are historical precedents of debts being repudiated on the grounds that they were odious.

JM: **What are the actual conditions under which a debt could be considered odious?**

PA: Any debt that has been incurred by a government without the informed consent of its people, and one that is not used in the legitimate interest of the State is theoretically an odious debt. For example, the principles in the Doctrine of Odious Debts were first used by the U.S. to repudiate Cuba's debts after Spain "lost" Cuba in the Spanish-American War. The repudiation was based on the grounds that Spain had borrowed the money without the consent of the Cuban people and had used the money to suppress the Cubans' legitimate rebellion against Spain's colonial rule. The legal scholar who coined the phrase "the doctrine of odious debts," Alexander Sack, also said that debts incurred to subjugate a people or to colonize them should also be considered odious to the indigenous people.

By those rules, many of the debts currently on the Third World's ledgers could be considered odious. There are advantages to putting current debts through odious debt proceedings: the principle puts appropriate responsibility onto the lenders to lend money to duly empowered and legitimate governments, and, because lenders could go after the real signatories of debts declared odious (the Ferdinand Marcoses and Mobutu Sese Sekos of the world) corruption becomes less attractive to some borrowers.

JM: **Is the principle applicable to loans from both private- and public-sector lending institutions?**

PA: Absolutely. It has to be. The Third World owes the Bank about $182 billion -- more money than any other single bank in the world. Some of that debt, according to legal precedent, is almost certainly odious.

JM: **But shifting the responsibility of debt onto the lender, at least where the World Bank is concerned, would require significant changes in the way the Bank does business. Are those kinds of changes possible?**

PA: Not at the World Bank. But I don't think the World Bank is worth reforming. I think it should be closed down in an orderly manner. For one thing, the World Bank is in the business of deficit financing, a practice which I believe is economically unsound. For another, the World Bank is, by its constitution, accountable neither to the people who finance it directly, nor to those who borrow from it. And finally, we've got to get over this notion that the Third World needs the North, or the West, or whatever you want to call it. This deeply imbedded belief that the Third World is quite helpless without the North and is incapable of handling its own economies and minding its environment is degrading. It merely serves the World Bank's style of running roughshod over traditional social structures and economies.

JM: **Does this mean you are advocating closed economies?**

PA: No. I'm advocating that people have control over their own resources. Trade between parties on mutually agreed upon terms can work to the benefit of both. But trade hurts when trading partners victimize a third party, for instance, the Penan people of Sarawak, whose forests are being traded away for the benefit of others. This third party victimization is characteristic of trade today -- in both foreign and domestic trade.

In fact, this third-party victimization is what characterizes much economic activity today, and the World Bank has a lot to do with that. When you consider the types of economies that were actually functioning before the advent of modern international deficit financing, you can see the tragedy of what has happened over the past 45 years.

The World Bank seemed a reasonable institution for emergency lending -- for putting back together the bricks and mortar of Europe after World War II. But there is a distinction between emergency lending and long-term development lending. Many developing countries had functioning economies before the World Bank started investing money in them. Those economies were diverse, reflecting the ecological niches on which they were based. And they were usually governed by political structures that maintained a degree of honesty and accountability between community members that protected the ecological base on which they depended.

Perhaps they were not the kind of economies that the West wanted to see, not ones that were big importers of western goods. But today, after 45 years of international lending, many of these economies aren't functioning well at all. The people, particularly the poor, and the environment have suffered greatly as a result.

JM: **One of your conclusions is that the debt crisis actually spared the environment from further devastation in some cases.**

PA: Ironically, yes. Debt led to a slowdown in new loans, and in turn, some big projects that would have been extremely damaging to the environment haven't been built. Destroying the environment often costs a lot of money. Look at the Balbina Dam. Brazil's electricity utilities poured buckets of money into a bad project that was being made uneconomic by its environmental problems.

JM: **Are you suggesting that a reduction in Third World debt would necessarily lead to an increase in environmental destruction?**

PA: If debt reduction leads to a resurrection of the types of irresponsible lending practices seen during the past two decades, the environment will suffer further. I see no reason why debt reduction would reduce environmental destruction. The asset sale, as I call it, has been going on for many decades. It started before the debt crisis. What we need to aim for is reducing debt and environmental degradation at the same time.

JM: **And how do we do that?**

PA: The first step is a moratorium on those debts considered to be odious. Lenders whose loans have been declared odious can go after the individuals who signed the contracts and made off with the money. The next step is to decentralize control of physical resources by recognizing the property rights of indigenous peoples and other communities. Democratic mechanisms, which in many cases existed for generations before being undermined by the modern state, need to be re-established. If the people who share a commons -- be it a river, a forest, or a national treasury -- are not forced to account to each other either on the river bank, in the town hall or through an open and accountable government, then an unmanageable commons is created. In that case, everyone has an incentive to exploit, and no one has the power to control. In both environmental and financial matters, governments and people should try to eliminate unmanageable commons. They must set up systems where the people who pay, whether with their environment or their finances, have control over the decisions that affect them.

7

Whatever Happened to Third World Debt?
Doug Henwood

In the October 1993 issue of its *World Economic Outlook*, the International Monetary Fund muses on the question, "Is the debt crisis over?" The answer is a qualified yes.

It's become commonplace in the business press that the Third World debt crisis, which began in 1982 when Mexico announced that it could no longer service its debts, came to an end sometime in the late 1980s. Of course, by this the business press means that Third World debt is no longer capable of bringing down the global financial system, as seemed possible in the mid-1980s.

You have to hand it to the global money elite -- they handled the matter masterfully. They managed to use the crisis to get everything they wanted from Third World governments -- a free-market transformation of the southern hemisphere in the Reagan-Thatcher mode, including the dismantling of nationalist-protectionist development strategies, cuts in social spending and public investment, privatization of state enterprises and financial deregulation. The result was to widen the income gap between North and South and to transform previously recalcitrant countries into pliant servants of big capital. While using the debt as a political lever, the IMF, the World Bank and the First World treasury ministers and central bankers bought their private commercial banks enough time to rebuild their financial strength -- in part by shifting risk to public institutions like the World Bank and away from private banks. In 1985, commercial banks held 49 percent of Third World debt, and official agencies, 36 percent; in 1993, the banks held 35 percent, and officialdom, 45 percent. Latin America's creditors changed more dramatically, with official agency debts more than doubling (+137 percent) while bank debt shrank by 11 percent before inflation. This relief from 1970s debacles left banks free to move on to the debacles of the late 1980s, like loans to takeover artists and real estate developers.

While debt reduction has been the mantra of the new policy, debt has still grown. Since 1989, when the Brady debt reduction initiative (named after Bush's dim Treasury Secretary, Nicholas Brady) was announced, the amount the world's poor countries owe to the rich has grown by 23 percent, to just under $1.5 trillion. Under Brady, bank debts were extinguished and new tradable bonds issued in their place, fresh loans were offered by the World Bank and loan guarantees by the U.S. government; it was a complex way of writing off part of the debt and shifting risk to public creditors. Official creditors accounted for 57 percent of the 1989-93 debt increase, but even bank debt grew over the period. The IMF helpfully provides the tables that permit these calculations, though the Fund doesn't bother to point out the oddity of proclaimed debt reduction coexisting with actual debt growth. Instead, they proclaim the success of market reforms in Latin America, and then ask, "In the light of these successes" -- one wonders what failure would be -- "is the debt crisis over?" The answer is, the Fund proclaims, "that the international financial system is no longer at risk, but much remains to be done. Many low-income and lower-middle-income countries continue to experience serious debt-related problems." Livelier Latin American debtors have restructured and gotten over the worst, while the poorest countries, mainly in Africa, remain under a crushing load. Meanwhile, a new problem debtor, actually a constellation of a dozen debtors, has emerged -- the former Soviet Union.

Despite the debt reduction schemes, the best thing that ever happened to the debtor countries has been the more-or-less steady decline in interest rates since their 1981 peak. That's not surprising, since the proximate cause of the debt crisis in the first place -- proximate, that is, as opposed to longer-term causes like colonialism and neocolonialism -- was the 1979-81 spike in U.S. interest rates engineered by Federal Reserve chair Paul Volcker. Interest rates on much Third World debt are tied to the six-month London Interbank Offered Rate (LIBOR), the interest rate banks offer each other in the unregulated London dollar market. The effective interest rate -- annual interest payments as a percent of outstanding debt -- has fallen, but nowhere near as sharply as LIBOR. Had the effective rate fallen as hard as LIBOR since 1989, interest payments would have been $41 billion rather than $85 billion in 1994. Still, the effective interest rate drop has enabled debtor countries to keep annual interest payments constant while total indebtedness grew.

In the 1970s, poor countries found it easy to borrow money from Northern banks. They could do so with few questions asked -- meaning that kleptocrats could steal the money and stick their public with the bill, and less thievish countries could spend the money as they saw fit. That changed with the onset of the debt crisis. Countries had to swallow the very bitter medicine of austerity to earn a few dollops from the IMF and the rest of the gang. Even so, the flow of new lending wasn't enough to cover the cost of servicing old debts. As the 1980s drew to a close, the only outside money available to poor countries (most of them need outside money because their economies are too weak to generate enough of a surplus to fund growth, especially with foreign creditors and investors skimming the cream) was in the form of portfolio and direct investment. (Portfolio investment is the flow of outside capital into paper assets, like stocks and bonds, while direct investment is the flow of outside capital into real assets, like plantations, mines and Coca-Cola plants.) On paper, however, these flows look pretty impressive. Portfolio flows quadrupled between 1989 and 1992. But, as the IMF is compelled to admit, these flows have been concentrated in a handful of countries -- Argentina, Brazil, Mexico, Korea and Turkey alone account for over three quarters of the flow.

Mexico is an interesting case, since it is a heavy debtor and the darling of the market reformers. The value of existing U.S. direct investment, before inflation adjustment, fell between 1982 and 1987. But it took off in the late l980s, rising 133 percent between 1988 and 1992. Yearly direct investment flows into Mexico from all countries followed a more dramatic pattern, falling 86 percent between 1981 and 1984, then rising 1,305 percent since. During the days of heavy debt service and capital flight, financial resources drained out of the country -- a net drain of $28 billion from 1983 to 1988. However, the capital-friendly policies of the Salinas regime have since lured a remarkable influx of money -- $73 billion in financial inflows plus $21 billion in direct investment between 1989 and 1993. The euphoria over Mexico and other "merging markets" has a very bubble-like feel to it, with expectations levitating far above present realities.

That bubble may be bursting. Early Wall Street reaction to the Chiapas rebellion was extremely complacent; the uprising was dismissed as a local affair that could be quickly, if not bloodlessly, repressed. Now that that seems not to be the case, hot money is leaving quickly. The exodus can be traced in part to the general mini-panic that took over world financial markets in February, but it's been amplified by the recognition that the Mexican miracle isn't quite as miraculous as it seemed when NAFTA was passed.

But direct investment can't leave quickly; it sticks around to make things. So far, it has yet to deliver an export miracle. Exports have grown since the late 1980s, but imports have grown three times as fast. The import surge is doubtless caused in part by foreign investment -- U.S. automakers, for example, use capital equipment from the U.S. when outfitting Mexican plants, which counts as a Mexican import from the U.S.; presumably, the balance on this kind of trade will soon reverse, as new plants export finished goods to the U.S. Financial balances have improved since the worst days of the debt crisis in the early 1980s, but Mexico still remains heavily in the red, thanks to interest payments and the withdrawal of profits by foreign investors. Evidently, foreign investors are doing very well in Mexico; while U.S. multinationals lost money on their Mexican subsidiaries in the early 1980s, their profit rate (profits divided by value of investments) now averages around 19 percent.

If Mexico is to be the new South Korea, it needs to make some radical changes. Fixed investment (plants, machinery, housing) is about 19 percent of GDP, a bit more than half South Korea's rate of 36 percent. Mexico put in a much better investment performance in the 1960s and 1970s, averaging about four fifths of Korean investment levels, but the debt crisis led to an investment collapse in the 1980s, while Korean investment accelerated. Over the last 30 years, Korea has never had periods of retrenchment and austerity like Mexico had over the last decade; instead, it's seen consistently ripping growth rates, not only in GDP, but in real wages as well. Growth, not stringency, leads to new growth. Mexican real wages shrank in the 1980s and have risen only slowly since. GDP growth was barely positive in 1993, the worst performance in years.

Mexico and the U.S. NAFTAns tout foreign investment as the engine of Mexican growth, but South Korea offers a contrary precedent. Foreign investment -- adding together direct and financial investments -- played a relatively small role in Korean industrialization, averaging under 2 percent of total fixed investment between 1963 and 1990; it's since risen to 5-7 percent. For the last 30 years, Mexico has been consistently more open than Korea, with foreign investment averaging almost 5 percent of total fixed investment between 1963 and 1989, and rising since to 25 percent or more (figures are spotty and should be taken as approximations, not revealed truth). This makes sense -- with foreign investment, profits are shipped abroad rather than being available for reinvestment. Also, reliance on foreign investors lessens national control over development strategy, since managers at distant headquarters make crucial decisions, leaving little say for local governments.

The Chiapas rebellion has exposed the popular failures of Mexican economic strategy, but the comparison with South Korea shows that the strategy fails on conventional measures as well. And Mexico is the star of the post-debt crisis era. For other countries, the situation has undeniably gotten less critical, but prosperity is nowhere near being around the corner. As even the World Bank admits, the nations it calls severely indebted low-income countries (SILICs) -- mainly in Africa -- are still in trouble and would require "deeper reductions" in indebtedness than creditors have been willing to provide "to restore external viability." External viability means credit-worthiness in the eyes of banks and a profitable stability in the eyes of foreign investors. Internal viability -- the basics of civilized life, like food, housing, education and health services -- is apparently a concern beneath mention.

> *"Since the 'lost decade' of the 1980s, it has become painfully clear that the World Bank and the IMF are intended to benefit the wealthy and the powerful, yet they continue to pretend that they are serving the community of nations. Of particular concern is the way in which their structural adjustment programs run counter to their sectoral policies; thus, their programs on reproductive health and education are constantly undermined by their macroeconomic policies, which destroy investments in public health and education. Sustainable development will never be achieved until these contradictions are confronted."*
> Peggy Antrobus, Founder,
> Women and Development Institute,
> Barbados

8

Brazil: Drowning in Debt
Marcos Arruda, Interviewed by
Multinational Monitor

Marcos Arruda is coordinator of the Institute of Alternative Policies for the Southern Cone of Latin America (PACS-PRIES), based in Brazil, Chile, Uruguay and Argentina. He is a professor of philosophy of education at the Institute of Advanced Studies in Education/Getulio Vargas Foundation in Rio and a member of the Amsterdam based Transnational Institute. Arruda is also a member of the international economy division of the Workers Party shadow government. This interview was conducted by the staff of **Multinational Monitor**.

Multinational Monitor: **What is the origin of Brazil's debt crisis?**

Marcos Arruda: During the 1970s, there was an enormous flow of petrodollars seeking easy investments throughout the world. The Northern countries sent ambassadors offering very cheap loans to finance investments in Southern countries. The 1970s was the decade of the two oil crises of 1974 and 1979, and it was also the decade of military regimes all over the world, many of them sponsored by the CIA. During the 1970s, 18 out of 21 Latin American nations were under military dictatorships. So the bankers actually dealt with our dictators on the big loans that created our countries' overwhelming indebtedness.

The military dictatorship in Brazil used the loans to invest in huge infrastructure projects -- particularly energy projects -- that were useful to the private sector. After the government investments cleared the path, private capital was drawn in with subsidies, fiscal investment incentives, even co-investments with state companies, and private investors reaped the profits.

The state projects were intended to serve as radiators of development. The idea behind creating an enormous hydroelectric dam and plant in the middle of the Amazon, for example, was to produce aluminum for export to the North. The project involved the use of subsidized energy from the hydroelectric facility, minerals from Para (a state in northern Brazil) and a plant set up by transnational companies, including Alcan and Alcoa, in connection with a Brazilian state company. The government took out huge loans and invested billions of dollars in building the Tucuri dam in the late 1970s, destroying native forests and removing masses of native peoples and poor rural people who had lived there for generations.

The government would have razed the forests, but deadlines were so short that they used Agent Orange to defoliate the region and then submerged the leafless tree trunks under water. Now the trees are rotting, and we are having to pay millions of dollars to clean up the excessive amount of organic matter that is decomposing under water.

The hydroelectric plant's energy is sold at $13 to $20 per megawatt when the actual price of production is $48. So the public sector of Brazil -- meaning taxpayers -- is providing subsidies of $28 to $35 per megawatt. We are financing cheap energy for transnational corporations to sell our aluminum in the international market, often to themselves; Alcoa in the United States or Alcan in Canada buy what Alcoa sells from Brazil, a product with very little value added.

We think these sorts of projects are destructive to the environment and financially irrational for the Brazilian government. The government is now responding to this irrationality with the magic word "privatize."

MM: **What has been the overall effect of the debt on the Brazilian economy?**

MA: Let's take the decade of 1980-89, which is now being called a lost decade -- as I am sure the 1990s will be. From 1980 to 1989, Brazil paid a total of $148 billion as service on its debt -- $90 billion in interest and the rest in principal. In 1980, the debt was $64 billion. Ten years later, having paid $148 billion on that debt, Brazil now owes $121 billion. This illustrates the vicious cycle of the debt, which has a simple logic: the more we pay, the more we owe. We argue that unless we break this cycle, there is no way out.

The way to break the cycle is to cancel the debt. But even cancellation will not solve the whole problem. Why? Because it is the very model of development that we have adopted in Brazil that is at the root of the process of indebtedness. And this holds true for all of the South. Our government and the rich of our countries have talked us into the idea that the more we imitate the North, the more we will develop. The International Monetary Fund (IMF) and the World Bank have come up with the same recipe for the development of the entire South, saying, "If you follow this prescription, you will clean up your economy, you will reshape your financial flows and you will be on good terms with the international financial community." But we've done it for 13 years now, and the results are devastating.

The main component of the adjustment process prescribed by the World Bank and the IMF for Brazil and the South as a whole involves restructuring our economy so as to drive all savings to investments in exports. The logic was: exports are the main source of foreign currency; sell your products abroad and you will have currency to pay the debt. So everywhere in the South there has been a massive effort to produce enough goods for export at the expense of the internal economy.

Let us think of our national economy as divided between the domestic economy and the external economy that produces for other countries. How can you drive investments in the internal economy to the external sector of the economy? By reducing the effective demand of the internal economy, reducing the real purchasing power of wage earners and using the surplus investment to produce for exports. This has meant ten years of impoverishment and decapitalization of the domestic economy, which the national figures do not reflect.

The GDP figures show that we have had fair results because our exports did very well. Brazil alone averaged exports of between $25 and $30 billion every year.

However, what counts in paying the debt is not how much you export. What matters is the trade surplus, the difference between what is exported and what is imported. So the other mechanism to gain international currency to pay the debt was to compress imports. Since most of our industries still have to buy equipment and technology from abroad, the primary method for import compression involved deindustrialization, the cutting-down of internal production. For the most part, our industry could not replace its equipment over the last ten years, so it is worse off now than it was ten years ago.

Through the various adjustment measures, we actually were able to produce a trade surplus of approximately $69 billion in the 1980s. But we paid $148 billion to service the debt. How did we cover that deficit? First, we depleted our international reserves, which a nation maintains to cover imports that it cannot cover with its export earnings. Second, we took out new loans to pay old loans. That is the crucial element of the vicious cycle of indebtedness: you stop borrowing to invest in production, and you borrow to pay the former debt. The money does not even come in; it goes from one banker's book to another, in the process becoming a liability of the Brazilian government.

MM: **What is your argument in favor of cancellation of the debt?**

MA: Many loans were illegal according to our countries' existing constitutions. They were often secured under unconstitutional terms, requiring, for example, that a country give up its sovereignty and accept a biased court to decide contractual disputes. They were also often secured without any knowledge of Congress, which is itself a violation of the law. We believe that there should be an audit of our debt, and we should decide how much of it is legal and how much is illegal and therefore should be recognized as nonexistent.

There are other important reasons the debt should not be paid in full. First, the creditors knew who they were lending to. The banks should be responsible for their irresponsible loans. They were lending money to unaccountable governments. The bankers knew that sooner or later the governments would be taken down and those loans would be called into question. They entered into those transactions anyway. So the creditors have to pay part of the price.

Second, our debt increased sharply as a result of the unilateral U.S. decision at the end of the 1970s to increase interest rates. Those interest rate increases multiplied the amount of Third World debt -- at least that which was negotiated under flexible term interest rates -- three or four times. This is another factor that was external to the actual borrowing process and should be taken into account when we decide how much we should pay.

Third, there is a secondary market for debt, in which the free market establishes how much any given Third World country's debt is worth. Why don't we use the free market rule to evaluate how much we should be paying as interest on the debt? In the case of Brazil, if you take the debt as $120 billion and you take into consideration that the market value of our debt titles is 30 cents per dollar, the country should have to pay interest on only $36 billion out of the $120 billion. And yet, this year alone, Brazil is probably going to pay between $10 and $12 billion in principal and interest.

But the Brazilian government is not interested in confronting the creditors because it continues to cling to the myth that we cannot grow without foreign capital. This may be true for small countries like Puerto Rico or Uruguay, but it is not true for large countries like India or Brazil, especially given our immense natural resource base. If we decide that the existing model of development is not desirable, then we can go another way. Each part of the world can go a people's way: a Latin American way, an African way, a Hindu way, instead of the white Western way of conceiving development.

MM: **What elements have made up the imposed Northern method of development?**

MA: After 1985 and the build-up of the Third World debt, the World Bank declared that it would make loans to Third World countries to begin to pay back or buy back their debts, but only if the countries agreed to abide by conditions. These included opening up their economies, bringing down tariff and non-tariff barriers, facilitating international investment in their countries, reducing the size of their governments, privatizing state companies and accepting debt-for-equity and debt-for-nature swaps. Latin America's oil producing countries, Mexico and Venezuela, have accepted or are in the process of accepting these conditions. Just imagine the pressures on the other countries that do not produce oil. Argentina sold out and is now giving in to the conditions of the World Bank and the IMF.

Southern governments have reshaped the economy of their countries to the priorities of the North. The deal offered by the North was that it would help Third World countries diminish the size of their debt if they continued to pay. We argue that we cannot continue to pay. We have to use the surplus we are producing to invest in the internal economy. We have to redistribute wealth so that people's demand for products increases, the economy grows again and only then can the surplus be used to pay the debt.

MM: **What has been the effect of privatization in Brazil?**

MA: Brazil has sold some of the most productive state companies to the private sector at very low prices. If the government prices the companies too low, it ends up giving out public assets that were the result of investments over decades.

Who buys these discounted companies? Usually companies of the same industry that already have oligopolistic power. Take the steel sector, which is run by a small number of companies. State investment in that sector was very important in regulating the market as well as not allowing it to be totally controlled by a cartel. Now we are selling the state steel companies and we're increasing the oligopolistic power of the cartel in that sector.

By criticizing the privatization policy, we are not saying that we reject all privatization. I belong to the Workers Party, which argues that we need a deep restructuring of the state of Brazil. But that restructuring does not involve transferring the best and most productive assets of the state to the private sector. Rather, we advocate democratizing the state.

MM: **What do you mean when you talk about a Latin American**

model of development or about democratizing the state?

MA: First of all, we want to move away from the logic of the free market, which is not truly free. The United States and Japan protected their economies when they were in the process of industrialization. Now we should have the same right to protect our economies.

The second element is to submit capital to the rule of human needs, putting human beings and their labor at the center of our projects. We have to give people the power to manage, control and participate in decision-making about the direction in which their companies, factories or farms are going to move. There must be more collective ownership and co-management of production. Collective decisions should be made about trade and about which technologies to adopt.

We argue against an economy centered on capital and based on the logic that the main purpose of economic activity is to produce more and more. That means depleting nature, destroying natural resources and using up non-renewable sources of energy.

We have to use the economy of enough as the criterion to plan the economies of the South and the North. There has to be a redistribution of wealth and resources from North to South. The North is using most of the world's energy resources. The North is the cause of most of the world's pollution, natural destruction and waste precisely because of its compulsive drive to always produce more. The North has to give up some of its excessive consumption. The world is one, and its resources are limited. One of the conditions necessary for structural transformation of the South is structural transformation of the North.

At this time, the world is moving in the opposite direction. In 1960 and 1970, the richest 20 percent of the world controlled 70 percent of the world's income. By 1980, the figure rose to 76 percent, and, by 1989, to 82.5 percent. So there is an acceleration of income concentration on a world scale, which means fewer people have greater wealth and more people are in need, everywhere on the globe. Something has to change for the earth to be viable over the next millennium.

MM: **How will the impeachment of Brazil's President Fernando Collor de Mello affect Brazil's basic economic development strategy?**

MA: After Collor stepped down, his successor, President Itamar Franco announced a new secretariat. The two men now responsible for economic decisions are Paulo Haddad, a professor and consultant, and Gustavo Krause, an economist who was mayor of a medium-sized city of the Northeast. Both tend to be conservative, the latter being a member of the parties that kept the reins of power during military rule. So far, in terms of economic development, they have defined only what the Itamar administration will *not* do or change.

They do not seem to recognize that the ten years of recession with inflation, which ruined our economy and caused severe suffering for the people, prove that the IMF's and the technocrats' concepts that have dominated economic planning for decades have failed with respect to the aims they proclaim. They do not intend to redefine "modernization" to give it a comprehensive meaning that includes social and human, scientific, technological, political and cultural development, rather than simply extensive and non-selective privatization.

They also seem to have decided that the politics of indebtedness -- and Brazil's relationship with international creditors -- will continue as under Collor. If these hypotheses are borne out, I foresee a new inflationary surge, deeper recession and growing masses of unemployed people. Without a deep change in the rhythm of debt repayment, and in our relations with creditors and transnational capital, we will never overcome the crisis, nor escape the position of being subordinate to priorities that are not our own.

"We cannot believe that the salvation of our country lies in an uncritical and undemocratic subjection of our country to IMF and World Bank policies."

Rev. Frank Chikane, Director,
South African Council of Churches

9

World Bank and IMF Adjustment Lending in Chile
The International NGO Forum

C hile, with a growing export-oriented economy, is often cited as "South America's tiger," a comparison with Korea and Taiwan. Since the mid-1980s, the economic indicators of Chile's "success" have included a steady growth rate, a rapid rise in exports, a positive trade balance, increased foreign investment and a relatively low inflation rate. These have often been paraded as proof that policies associated with structural adjustment programs (SAPs) can, indeed, bring about a healthy, sound economy.

But a closer look at the numbers leads to a strikingly different conclusion. The alleged "successes" of Chile have been enjoyed primarily by the economic elite and have led to an increasing concentration of income. In addition, despite its growth and improved trade balance, the country has fallen deeper into the debt trap; total external debt, including IMF credits and other short-term loans, rose from US$4.8 billion in 1976 to $19 billion in 1990. At the same time, investment in environmental protection has been minimal. In sum, Chile's growth is a product of an export model that is economically unsustainable, socially destructive and environmentally unsound.

Two Decades of Economic Adjustment and Shock Treatments

Chile's experiment with a more self-reliant development program under President Salvador Allende was abruptly put to an end by a bloody coup led by General Augusto Pinochet in 1973. The military regime enthusiastically embraced free-market policies and privatization and committed itself to eliminating "suffocating statism" by promoting the creation of a new economic elite. Most state enterprises were sold at rock-bottom prices or returned to their former owners. Exports and foreign investment were actively encouraged. Capital markets were liberalized and the currency devalued.

Shock treatments were applied in 1975 and 1982, causing the economy to contract by 12.9 and 14 percent, respectively. Despite its adherence to market-oriented policies, fiscal austerity and export promotion, Chile struggled for more than ten years to gain some semblance of economic stability. Even Milton Friedman and his fellow monetarists were eventually forced to temper their claims that Chile was an "economic miracle." Chile was in no better position than its Latin neighbors when the debt crisis hit in 1982 and, like many others, turned to the IMF for financial assistance. The conditionality that accompanied these funds assured further belt-tightening for the poor.

The Financial Dam Breaks

Chile had begun accumulating massive amounts of debt during the late 1970s. New private financial and industrial conglomerates blossomed under a shower of foreign credit, which was considerably cheaper than local capital. With easy access to external financing, not only was this new elite -- the *grupos* -- able to concentrate wealth in a few hands, it also contributed to an enormous increase in foreign debt. Private-sector external debt grew from $1.6 billion in 1978 to $8.1 billion in 1981. In 1982, the bubble burst. A financial crisis was provoked by the overextended *grupos,* a drop in copper prices and poor foreign-exchange-rate management. The government unilaterally decided to assume responsibility for the private debt, which represented 65 percent of total debt in 1981, even though it had never guaranteed those loans. Chile logically turned to the IMF during this credit crunch.

The IMF rapidly approved a $523 million standby loan to Chile and a $307 million compensatory financing facility loan, as Chile had already eagerly implemented the measures normally required for IMF financing. The 1983 program was a short-term emergency operation. The Chilean authorities devalued the *peso* and instituted strict demand-management policies, including the elimination of wage indexation and the lowering of the wage floor. Through the rest of the decade, IMF and World Bank assistance to Chile totaled $3.7 billion.

Benefits for the Elite Paid for by the Poor

Although Chile's economy showed a more consistent growth pattern by the mid-1980s, only a very few have benefited from the upturn. Most Chileans have had to bear a high cost for the prescribed shock therapies, while the economic benefits have not trickled down. Instead, the IMF programs have resulted in a larger concentration of income, further widening the gap between the rich and the poor.

In 1978, the richest ten percent of the population enjoyed 37 percent of Chile's national income, while the poorest 50 percent of the population had 20 percent of that income. By 1988 the top ten percent had 47 percent of the income, and the poorest, only 17 percent. Consumption patterns followed the same trend. In 1969, the poorest 20 percent consumed 7.6 percent of the country's output; this share dropped to 4.4 percent in 1988. Meanwhile, the rich saw their share increase from 44.5 percent in 1969 to 54.6 percent in 1988.

Although GDP per capita has been rising slowly (from $1,207 in 1979 to $1,318 in 1988), this figure disguises the price the poor have paid to make that growth possible. Over 40 percent of Chile's 14 million citizens live in poverty, and some two million, in extreme poverty. The restructuring of the Chilean economy throughout the 1970s and early-'80s led to high unemployment and contributed to a severe decline in real wages. Labor was unable to protect itself, since trade unions were systematically repressed under the Pinochet regime.

Unemployment officially peaked at around 20 percent in 1982; it would have reached 30 percent if it had not been for an emergency employment program financed by a military government increasingly concerned about the political implications of severe unemployment. The projects funded, however, only provided temporary work at sub-minimum wages, sometimes as little as one quarter of the official minimum wage. Wages declined dramatically during this period, not only because of high unemployment, but also because export growth was predicated on it. The IMF, in fact, included "wage restraint" as one of the conditions of its 1985 structural adjustment loan, which also included shifting expenditures from social services to export-oriented infrastructure.

Under adjustment, the quality of life for the poor further deteriorated with the increasing privatization of education and health care. Public funds are now being used more and more to subsidize private health care and education. Currently, an employee may apply the mandatory seven percent deduction from wages for health care toward a public or private program. The rich invest this money in private programs, while the poor must rely on an increasingly pauperized public-health sector. Even Finance Minister Alejandro Foxley, at a 1991 IMF meeting, openly acknowledged the deteriorating situation, noting the poor conditions that existed for public-health and education workers.

Promotion of "Cheap" Exports Plunders Natural Resources

Chile's structural adjustment programs have concentrated upon the elimination of trade barriers, the promotion of private domestic and international investment and the diversification of export production.

The country has seen an increase in its export earnings, which grew from $3.8 billion in 1985 to $8.3 billion in 1990. Although it has also been able to reduce its dependence on mining from 86 percent of export earnings in 1970 to 54 percent in 1990, most of its exports are still primary products or minimally processed ones. And, in promoting exports, the government has eagerly invested in infrastructure, such as roads and ports, to facilitate this exploitation. These investments and the rapid extraction of resources have often had deleterious effects on the natural environment.

The avid promotion of private control over "non-traditional exports," for instance, has resulted in enormous environmental damage. The development of cellulose and wood products has led to massive deforestation, not only destructive to the environment and indigenous peoples, but also damaging to the future productive capacity of the forestry sector. The government received a one-shot source of income by selling off huge tracts of forests to a small number of local and foreign investors. Since then, up to 40,000 hectares of native forest have been felled and replanted with non-native pine and eucalyptus plantations, causing serious ecological damage through soil erosion and the increased use of pesticides and agrochemicals. The Penhuenche Indians not only lost an important source of income with the felling of the araucaria trees, but they also lost access to native lands.

Similarly, the export of fishmeal has been developed by a modern fishing industry that has overharvested Chilean coastal waters, which, when combined with the dumping of toxic wastes, is squeezing out small-scale, sustainable fishing. The fruit industry, the major agricultural export earner, is also creating enormous unaccounted environmental costs, since it relies heavily on chemical fertilizers and pesticides. It is also one of the industries most susceptible to the whims of the international market: a whole year's crop was lost in 1991 as U.S. consumers joined in a boycott of Chilean fruit caused by rumors of poisoned grapes.

How Healthy Is an Economy Based on Exports?

Chile, like all developing countries, is vulnerable to price fluctuations in the world market for its primary exports. Ironically, a state-owned company, CODELCO, is responsible for most of the country's copper production and remains a key source of foreign-exchange revenue for the government. In recent years, Chile has compensated for declining world prices by rapidly expanding copper production. Its economy has evolved from one in which 33 percent of its total production was oriented toward exports in 1960 to one that earmarks 57 percent of production for exports in 1990.

Furthermore, Chile is relying increasingly on foreign capital to expand its export sector, with more than half of all foreign investment going to mining projects. Foreign capital has been attracted by extremely liberal laws regulating investment and the repatriation of profits. And once the profits have been extracted, particularly in the case of non-renewable raw materials, investors typically move on to greener pastures.

Buried Under a Continuing Burden of Debt

Chile's debt peaked in 1987 at over $21 billion. Financing from the IMF and World Bank gave it sufficient breathing room to develop strategies to reduce its overall debt by about $3 billion by 1989. The government employed aggressive export-promotion policies and, between 1985 and 1991, eliminated a significant amount of debt through debt-equity swaps through which foreign companies gained important access to land and mining interests. With the stamp of approval from the IMF, the country was also able to ease short-term pressures by rescheduling $12 billion of its commercial debt in 1987 and another $1.8 billion in 1990. In addition, commercial banks have granted new credits, since U.S. banking authorities have upgraded Chile's credit rating.

In June 1991, Chile became the first country to obtain a reduction of its official debt to the United States -- $16 million was written off of its outstanding $40 million food aid debt, as it was seen as the only country that was involved in "economic revitalization under the auspices of the IMF, the World Bank and the IDB" and was improving relations with commercial banks while opening up to foreign investment.

None of these measures, however, has fundamentally resolved Chile's debt problem. The debt-swap program has essentially run its course, the rescheduling of commercial debt has only postponed repayment and the debt-reduction plans have involved only token amounts of debt. Furthermore, debt has been climbing again and is likely to pass its 1986 high point. After two decades of economic stabilization and adjustment under the watchful eyes of the IMF and the World Bank, the Chilean people and their environment continue to pay a price for a policy that has served a very different set of interests.

10

Structural Adjustment and Costa Rican Agriculture
Alicia Korten

Castulo Cabrera's seven-hectare lone field of corn runs along Costa Rica's northern border, surrounded by 7,000 hectares of freshly planted orange trees. Ticofruit, an agro-export company that sells canned orange juice to the United States and Europe, owns the 7,000 hectares and the orange trees. The company is rapidly buying land that was only recently distributed to small farmers as part of Costa Rica's agrarian reform program. While his neighbors sold their land and their labor to Ticofruit, Cabrera stood firm, explaining, "I don't want to sell. This piece of land has given me a home, helped me feed my children, been part of my culture. Where would I go if I sold?"

Cabrera is one of the few to maintain such independence in a community that is dying as a result of economic policies outlined in the World Bank's structural adjustment program (SAP) and implemented largely by the U.S. Agency for International Development (AID). Costa Rica accepted its first structural adjustment loan in April 1985 and is now touted by the World Bank as a structural adjustment success story.

From Food to Flowers

Costa Rica's structural adjustment policy calls for earning more hard currency to pay off foreign debt; forcing farmers who have traditionally grown beans, rice and corn for domestic consumption to plant non-traditional agricultural exports (NTAEs) such as ornamental plants, flowers, melons, strawberries and red peppers. Over the past eight years, AID has pumped $5 million into NTAE promotion in Costa Rica.

Structural adjustment programs encourage this transition by shifting state supports from domestic to foreign market producers. For example, industries that export their products are now eligible for tariff and tax exemptions not available to domestic producers. One such incentive, a tax rebate called CATs (Certificados de Abono Tributario), eats up five percent of Costa Rica's annual budget, according to the

World Bank.

While structural adjustment agreements have approved subsidies for exports, they have simultaneously removed support for domestic production. Structural adjustment agreements prohibit the Costa Rican government from buying grains from producers at inflated prices and selling to consumers at subsidized prices. The agreements also require Costa Rica to remove quotas that have traditionally protected basic grains farmers from low international prices. Yet, while the North pressures Southern nations to eliminate subsidies and "barriers to trade," Northern governments pump billions of dollars into their own agricultural sectors, making it impossible for basic grains growers in the South to compete with the North's highly subsidized agricultural industry.

Structural adjustment policies are not creating a level "free market" playing field, as supporters suggest. Rather, they systematically favor export over domestic production. The agreements shift public spending subsidies from basic staples, consumed mainly by the Costa Rican poor and middle classes, to luxury export crops produced for affluent foreigners.

The Risks of NTAEs

SAP supporters say that technical assistance and training programs will ensure that small farmers successfully convert to producing NTAEs. However, these crops inherently favor foreign investors over small farmers, who rarely have the contacts within international markets and access to international transport systems necessary to sell crops for export. Such crops also require higher capital investments and more complicated production processes than basic grains.

Small-scale basic grains farmers find it difficult to join the cut-throat NTAE market. "When we talk about nontraditionals we are not talking about small farmers. The capital is too high. The risk is too high. If we encourage them to plant non-traditionals, we place them in a very risky situation," explains Jilma Ramirez, a program manager at the Costa Rican Coalition of Development Initiatives, founded and financed by AID.

Costa Rica's agricultural landscape is littered with tales of failed NTAE promotion projects. Norberto Fernandes, a small farmer in northern Costa Rica, received a loan in 1990 to switch from growing corn for the domestic market to red peppers for export. He says an NTAE promoter passed through his village "promising riches, a new car, a better house, education for my children" if he jumped on the bandwagon. When his new crop of red peppers came in, Norberto was told they did not meet export quality control standards. He had to sell his 30 cows to repay the loans.

Technicians say villagers such as Fernandes fail because they do not properly follow the technical advice given to them. The farmers, however, feel promoters deceived them about the difficulty of growing the new crop.

Small farmers say these policies are forcing them off the land and that the small farmer is disappearing as a productive social class. Carlos Hernandez, a leader of the national farmer's union Consejo Campesino para Justicia y Desarrollo (Peasant Council for Justice and Development), explains that national policies forced Cabrera's neighbors to sell their land to Ticofruit. "By decreasing support for basic grains, the government has little by little forced the small farmer to sell. When the farmer sees his farm is no longer an economic alternative, he sells his land and converts to wage labor."

The number of Costa Rican farmers selling produce to the National Production Council, a state apparatus that is technically supposed to buy all the country's basic grains, dropped from 70,000 in 1984 to 27,700 in 1989. Even the World Bank admitted in its 1988 *Costa Rica: Country Economic Memorandum* that "smallholders unable to move into the new (non-traditional crop) activities might have to sell their land and become landless workers."

AID official Arturo Villalobos agrees that the land concentration caused by small farmer sales "has been a terrible blow to Costa Rican democracy, social harmony and the environment."

Opening the Negotiations

Central American small farmers have created a regional alliance to respond to the structural adjustment and free trade policies that are threatening their existence. La Asociacion de Organizaciones Campesinas Centroamericanas para la Cooperacion y el Desarrollo (ASOCODE, Association of Central American Peasant Organizations for Cooperation and Development) was founded one year ago and represents more than 80 percent of Central America's organized farmers, over four million heads of households. "Structural adjustment and free trade agreements have given us a common concern," says Wilson Campos, ASOCODE's coordinator. "We are all struggling to find our place within an increasingly global economy."

The group "represents the moment of greatest consolidation within Central American small farmers," according to the president of the Central American Food Security Program (CADESCA), Salvador

Arias.

ASOCODE hopes to open the structural adjustment dialogue to popular sectors. Members are concerned about the secretive nature of structural adjustment and free trade negotiations, arguing that grass-roots groups cannot influence policy if they gain access to documents only after agreements are signed.

The group has sent a letter to the Central American Presidents demanding a permanent seat at the regional bargaining table, with representatives attending every negotiation meeting. They also want governments to help peasant groups buy public sector agricultural processing and storage facilities if they are privatized as SAPs require.

"We want these institutions to stop tying loans to the restructuring of economic policies we have fought for decades to establish," states Campos. "And we want our countries to maintain the right to subsidize domestic market production and protect domestic producers through tariffs."

Campos believes dialogue with governments and lending agencies may be possible. Civil society is benefiting from an increasingly tolerant political environment as civil strife decreases in many Central American countries. Furthermore, the group was encouraged by the invitation -- the first in the history of the region -- of a delegation of farmer leaders to the regional presidential economic summit in December 1992.

However, if demands are not met, Campos says, the group is prepared to "organize protests, block highways and take over lands ... Through the negotiations process, we are also strengthening our ability to respond through actions."

Repression on the Rise

As more people are marginalized, the Costa Rican government relies increasingly on the civil guard to maintain stability. The police force grew from 6,000 in 1980 to 7,800 in 1989. In 1992, the state approved funds for an additional 2,500 police officers.

The state offers foreign companies the use of these squads. A contract signed with Stone Container, a U.S. forest company with a 10,000 hectare plantation in southwest Costa Rica, "approves the expedient use of the Civil Guard, at Stone's request, to evict people that invade lands that are rented or bought by Stone."

Elias Villalobos describes what happened to him and his family when the civil guard evicted him and 21 other squatter families from an abandoned farm Stone had rented. "Fifty-five rural guards bulldozed our farms, our crops, our trees -- they erased all that we had worked for. They came into our houses and dragged us outside -- men, women, even the little children. They pushed my two-year-old child and knocked his hand into a pot of boiling water. We were afraid for our lives. They shot their guns but they didn't kill anyone . . . Then they burned everything that remained. They burned 19 houses and didn't even give us time to take out our belongings."

Twenty-five farmers were wounded and one killed by gunfire during land evictions in 1991 and 1992. For Costa Rica, a country that abolished its army in 1948 and prides itself on a nonviolent tradition, such accounts offer evidence of the country's eroding social base.

Ever-Deepening Debt

The results of Costa Rica's structural adjustment program have been mixed at best. The program has brought inflation under control and increased non-traditional export production, as advocates promised. However, the program has not succeeded in one of its' principal goals: debt reduction.

In addition, structural adjustment policies have left Costa Rica increasingly dependent on a stable foreign demand for agricultural exports to earn the foreign exchange necessary to maintain its new import-dependent industries and to feed its own citizens. Since the International Monetary Fund gave Costa Rica its first stabilization loan in 1980, foreign debt has soared from $2.1 billion to what would have been a $5 billion debt in 1991 if Costa Rica had not received a $1 billion debt forgiveness package in 1990.

One reason Costa Rica has been unable to put a dent in its debt obligations is that demand for imports is increasing faster than rising export profits. In 1980 imports exceeded exports by $527 million; by 1992 the gap had expanded to $711 million. Agricultural export farms are highly dependent on imported intermediary goods, such as pesticides and machinery. Reduced tariffs are increasing the flow of imported luxury goods into the country. Also, the country must import grains to meet its food needs as domestic grains growers disappear.

Durable imports made between January and April 1993 have jumped by 191 percent compared to 1991 imports made during the same months, largely due to foreign cars now flooding the country. Agricultural raw material imports have increased 39 percent, agricultural intermediary goods by 122 percent and non-durable imports, such as food, by 122 percent during this same period.

Another reason the foreign debt is not declining is because Costa

Rica gains only a small percentage of the total foreign exchange profits earned from agricultural export operations. For every $100 consumers spend on tropical fruit products, agro-export countries receive roughly $15. "The $85 balance goes mainly to the transnational corporations like Monsanto and John Deere that sell agricultural inputs, ones like Sea-Land and Coordinated Caribbean Transport (Transway) that control shipping, companies like Cargill and Volkart that handle most world commodity trade, corporations like General Foods and RJ Reynolds that process and distribute the commodities, and finally those like Safeway that market the goods," according to Tom Barry, director of the Inter-Hemispheric Resource Center.

Who Benefits?

Many, even some AID officials, believe the structural adjustment program is undermining Costa Rica's democratic tradition by converting land owners into landless agricultural laborers and forcing the state to use repressive measures to maintain stability within its borders. AID economist Miguel Sagot outlines the regressive impacts of Costa Rica's structural adjustment program. "There are an increasing number of unanswered questions regarding structural adjustment. For example, who benefits -- the already powerful or the poor? There is suspicion that structural adjustment has increased the income gap within Costa Rica." Sagot further notes, "Social services . . . have also deteriorated in the last years. Many people believe this is because the government has switched its budget priorities from social services toward export promotion. And, as Costa Rica's debt sky-rockets, one has to wonder to what degree the success of the program is due to heavy borrowing. It is questionable whether Costa Rica will ever be able to repay the debt it is accumulating."

Yet Sagot notes that if Costa Rica does not continue with structural adjustment, it will be locked out of North American free trade agreements and lose its access to loans. And Costa Rica's leaders seem willing to sacrifice social equity, environmental sustainability and long-term economic stability for a place in the global economy.

11

World Bank and IMF Adjustment Lending in the Philippines
The International NGO Forum

The Philippines is often referred to as "the sick man of Asia." The country labors under the weight of a US$29 billion foreign-debt burden and a $9 billion domestic debt. Payments on the foreign debt have amounted to $18 billion since 1986, yet total debt has increased over the same period by more than $3 billion.

A seemingly permanent regimen of International Monetary Fund (IMF) stabilization and World Bank adjustment programs has been imposed, designed primarily to ensure continued payment to the country's external creditors, including the international financial institutions. The IMF's insistence that debt payments take priority is mirrored in a Ferdinand Marcos-era decree, still in force, which provides for automatic appropriations for debt servicing. This means that every year, roughly 40 percent of the national budget and 31 percent of export earnings are devoted to debt payments. Unless debt servicing can be trimmed to a sustainable level, resources simply will not be available for economic growth.

No-Growth Policies: The Consequences of Odious Debts
The people of the Philippines have suffered from both the effects of a debt-dependent development strategy and macroeconomic policies that have favored the wealthy, particularly those close to government. Heavy borrowing during the Marcos administration mostly financed inefficient industrial investments or disappeared through capital flight and corruption. IMF and World Bank stabilization and structural adjustment policies, designed to raise the revenues needed to pay these debts, have favored industry and agribusiness -- neither of which are labor intensive -- over food-crop agriculture. Every year, 900,000 young people enter the job market. With unemployment and underemployment standing at roughly 48 percent, there is little hope that these people can be absorbed into the work force.

Economic growth has also been a victim of these policies. While inflation has decelerated to about 12 percent, the current-account deficit has been reduced and international reserves of the Central Bank have recovered substantially, the tight fiscal and monetary policies that led to these successes have also resulted in severe recession.

IMF Success Means Suffering for the Poor

Stabilization programs to treat balance of payments crises have been regular features of Philippine economic planning since the early 1960s, and the World Bank implemented at least two major structural adjustment programs (SAPs) in the 1980s. Yet the economy continues to be characterized by periodic balance-of-payments problems and excessive dependence on imports.

Stabilization polices in the Philippines have focused on restricting domestic demand so as to ensure adequate resources for foreign-debt servicing. They have included such measures as slashing government expenditures, increasing taxes and tax collection and reducing subsidies to dissuade people from consuming artificially cheap goods.

Although the IMF stabilization programs instituted since 1984 have been successful in meeting their objectives of increasing international reserves and decreasing inflation and the budget deficit, they have had a devastating impact on the majority of Filipinos. While IMF stabilization policies were not solely responsible for the economic crisis of the mid-1980s, the constriction of demand that these policies fostered and the lack of measures to cushion the impact on the poor caused severe hardship for millions.

According to a recent World Resources Institute (WRI) study, "Real wages in both agricultural and nonagricultural activities declined every year from 1980 until economic recovery started to take hold in 1987, falling by about 25 percent between 1981 and 1987 . . . Rising unemployment and falling real wages raised the percentage of population living in poverty since the poor had nothing to offer except their labor."

Underemployment and unemployment have been particularly severe in rural areas. The landless poor have tried to survive by migrating to marginal uplands and coastal areas that the government insists on controlling, but has failed to protect. The result has been serious deforestation, destruction of fisheries, soil erosion and the consequent smothering of coral reefs and the siltation of dams and irrigation systems. More recent stabilization programs have likewise stifled economic growth, which was less than one percent in 1991.

Liberalization and Recession

The first structural adjustment program in the Philippines, implemented between 1980-83, was designed to promote exports, liberalize the tariff structure, simplify import procedures and restructure selected industries. A loan of $200 million from the World Bank helped pay for industrial inputs, including raw materials and capital goods. The second SAP, launched in 1984, included reforms in industrial incentives and the extension of on-going trade-policy reforms.

Structural adjustment policies, though never fully implemented, exacerbated the economic crisis of the mid-1980s by supporting the disinvestment in agriculture and wrenching the unprepared Philippine manufacturing sector open to global trade. Domestic producers were not provided with incentives to encourage them to improve production methods and reduce the social costs of domestic industrial adjustment. Trade liberalization, it turned out, was no substitute for direct industrial reform, the real need in the Philippines.

According to a study led by author Walden Bello, the first World Bank structural adjustment loan led to

> "the concentration of capital through new banking laws, the channeling of capital to the export sector leading to financial loss, plant closings and bankruptcy for many local businessmen . . . By the Bank's own estimates, roughly 100,000 workers in 'inefficient' garment and textile firms would lose their jobs. This amounted to about 46 percent of the work force in the garment and textile sectors and about five percent of total employment in manufacturing."

The failure of stabilization and adjustment policies in the Philippines is due in part to their failure to address the country's deeper structural problems of inequity and dependency, or to consider social or environmental costs. This is particularly true in the agrarian sector, where land ownership is highly concentrated and small farmers lack access to the credit, as well as the technological and market expertise needed to benefit from a liberalized market. The World Resources Institute study found that "stabilization policies that sharply increased poverty and unemployment accelerated the degradation and deforestation of upper watersheds and the over-exploitation of coastal fisheries and mangroves."

The removal of price controls and subsidies under successive adjustment programs has had a harsh effect on small farmers and consumers. The lifting of price controls on the sale of processed rice resulted in a near doubling of price between 1985 and 1986. Because small rice farmers sell an average of 90 percent of their crop, they are as vulnerable as non-farming consumers to shifts in market prices for this most basic of commodities. When subsidies for production were removed, farmers were forced to reduce the amount of land under cultivation and/or limit the use of material inputs. Both responses resulted in decreased production. In the case of rice production, there is now a shortfall of about 15 percent in annual consumption needs.

Tight monetary policies have led to high interest rates, which have severely curtailed domestic borrowing. The majority of poor farmers compete for scarce money with industrialists and larger farmers, who pose less of a credit risk. With little collateral, small farmers are forced to borrow from usurers at interest rates of 50 to 400 percent. Rice traders generally provide loans for production inputs and then extract payment at harvest time. The lack of affordable credit has forced many small farmers to lose their mortgaged land. With an increasing number of landless laborers in the countryside, real rural wages and income have declined, and the incidence of starvation has doubled since 1985. The latest figures indicate that approximately 75 percent of rural households live in abject poverty.

The removal of the government subsidy on imported oil, demanded by the IMF, has been beneficial for the environment, but has had a harsh impact on the poor. This measure, along with a one-percent tax on oil imports and a temporary nine-percent import levy on all goods (including oil), has been an easy way for the government to reduce the budget deficit and has curtailed environmentally harmful activities in the forestry, fishing and mining sectors. But, in the absence of policies to cushion the impact on the poor, small farmers and fishermen have suffered disproportionately. The imposition of "Green Revolution" techniques in rice farming has locked farmers into buying fertilizer (an oil-based product) and gasoline for irrigation pumps. Depletion of coastal fishing stocks has forced fishermen to travel farther to find fish, increasing their fuel costs. Increases in transportation costs also raises the cost of most consumer goods and travel for the poor majority.

A People's Alternative

Structural adjustment programs in the Philippines have promoted agricultural exports at the expense of food security. The WRI study concludes, however, that adjustment should instead promote labor-intensive food crop production in lowland rainfed areas and tree-cropping in the more fragile and erosion-prone upland areas. Resource rent taxes and environmental charges are policy reforms that can help alleviate or reverse the adverse environmental effects of adjustment programs. Changes in land tenure and property rights are institutional reforms that can, by giving households a more secure stake in resource management, mitigate rural environmental degradation associated with structural adjustment and promote productivity, equity and resource conservation. In the economic model used by the WRI researchers:

> "Both output and employment . . . increase under the assumption of land reform, as do agricultural and fisheries production. Manufacturing sector output also expands in response to the increase in consumer demand. Income distribution improves markedly: incomes of the poor rise by 14 percent while those of the rich fall by 5 percent. Land prices rise relative to other factor costs. Land shifts into lowland crop production, not into erosion-prone crops or timber production. Energy use rises marginally."

In addition to advocating different development policies, groups in the Philippines have been pushing for an alternative debt-management strategy. The Freedom from Debt Coalition (FDC), a network of over 200 citizen-action groups, advocates limiting debt-servicing to ten percent of export earnings. Based on calculations of 1989 exports, this would have freed up an estimated $1.74 billion, which could have been used to stimulate domestic economic development. According to the FDC, the money should not be used for military expenditures, other unproductive budget items such as discretionary (pork barrel) funds, or non-fiscal transactions, like the oil price stabilization fund subsidy, debt buy-back operations and interest payments on maturing government securities.

The FDC promotes specific policy changes, including alternative stabilization and adjustment measures, structural reforms and new social policies. They include: 1) reform of the existing regressive tax system; 2) creation of a leaner and more efficient bureaucracy; 3) expansion of basic social services that improve human capital and promote production activities; 4) greater public investment in the rural areas; 5) new monetary policies and related institutional changes, such as lower interest rates, abolition of the existing banking cartel and expansion of credit to the rural sector, possibly through strengthening the network of cooperatives; 6) abolition of all but "natural monopolies" (which should also be properly regulated); 7) industrial-output promotion; 8) appropriate trade policies to complement new industrial policies; 9) currency devaluation to promote exports, but accompanied by measures to soften the inevitable impact on an import-dependent economy; 10) an agrarian-reform program and 11) protection of the rights of workers to join unions, to strike and to enjoy humane working conditions.

Support for the FDC's proposals would provide funds for the kinds of structural transformations that the Philippines so desperately needs. Increased funding for education, health and nutrition, and science and technology is also needed to promote greater productivity and to increase equity. As Leonor Briones, the President of the FDC has stated, the country's adjustment policies need to be transformed so that people are no longer "adjusted out of jobs, homes, schools and in extreme cases, out of existence."

"The very logic and framework of structural adjustment policies require the repression of democratic rights. This is because these policies demand drastic fiscal, monetary, and economic measures which cannot help but raise very strong reactions from the public. And such reactions have to be repressed. It is not surprising that many structural adjustment programs are successfully implemented in countries like my own, under a dictatorship. We shouldn't let our own governments off the hook when they have blindly and slavishly implemented these programs at the expense of the interests of their own people. When we complain to the World Bank and the IMF, they tell us, 'So sorry, we don't talk to people. We only talk to governments. We only talk to your president. We only talk to your central bank governor. We only talk to your minister of finance.' This is a joint production of the international finance community with the cooperation of local elites and leaders in our own country. The majority of the people are shut out of the negotiations."

Leonor Briones, President,
Freedom from Debt Coalition,
Philippines

12

Jamaica: The Showpiece that Didn't Stand Up
Kathy McAfee

Newly appointed U.S. ambassador to Jamaica William Holden announced his mission at his swearing-in ceremony in November 1989. It was, once and for all, "to silence the trumpets of socialism" in Jamaica and the Caribbean. In the 1970s, such a declaration by the chief emissary of the U.S. or any foreign country would have been met with strong protest, if not expulsion. Jamaica's government in the 1970s was run by the social democratic Peoples National Party (PNP) and its charismatic leader, Michael Manley. But the government of the "new Michael Manley," elected in February of 1989 after eight years out of power, had little reason to object. The trumpets had long been laid aside.

Manley and the PNP returned to power over a state with its independence greatly curtailed by foreign control and a society choking in the stranglehold of debt. To regain sovereignty over Jamaica's economic and political affairs, the government would have had to confront the world's most powerful economic institutions, the IMF and the World Bank. It would have had to risk a showdown with the economic power, and very possibly the military might, of the United States.

As the decade opened, no trumpets blew louder than those of the White House and State Department prophets of privatization. No drum was banged with more clamor than that of "free market democracy." But the very policies that the U.S. government dictates in the name of freedom are a grave threat to genuine democracy. Even as it slashed its own aid to Jamaica, the U.S. was tying its limited support more tightly to the austerity requirements of the multilateral institutions. By pushing impoverished people over the brink into hunger, these policies are bound to result in social chaos and political upheaval, which can ultimately be contained only by authoritarianism and repression.

During a decade of structural adjustment, the people of Jamaica were forced to make great sacrifices to keep their nation in the debt-refinancing game, watching resources and capital flow out of their country into the coffers of Northern creditors. Unless the rules of the game are changed, or until Jamaica, along with other governments, refuses to play, their suffering will be in vain. But in the face of enormous odds, the PNP appeared to lack not only the means but also the political will to attempt to break out of debt bondage.

Jamaica: "Open for Business"

Toward the end of his first tenure as prime minister, Manley had first tried to apply, and then had resisted, an IMF stabilization program. Manley's PNP lost the violently contested 1980 election to the Jamaica Labor Party, led by Edward Seaga. Seaga, a Boston-born, Harvard-trained businessman with close ties to U.S. presidential candidate Ronald Reagan, came into office with the full support of Washington. During the election campaign, Seaga boasted of promises of substantial new loans and aid from the IMF and the U.S. government.

The Reagan administration pulled out all the stops to assist Seaga and keep its new Caribbean free enterprise showboat afloat. U.S. economic aid jumped from $38 million in 1978-79 to $208 million in 1981-82, making Jamaica the third largest per capita recipient of U.S. aid in the world.[1] The U.S. Agency for International Development (AID) warned in 1983 that: "The failure of the [AID] program in Jamaica would confirm the view of those in the Caribbean and elsewhere in the Third World that cooperation with the IMF and stimulation of the private sector is a hopeless endeavor."[2]

By 1985, AID was spending $48 for every person in Jamaica for Jamaica projects. This was 27 times more per capita than AID provided to sub-Saharan Africa that same year, the peak year of AID funding for Africa.[3] USAID spent more on its Jamaica program -- an average of almost $120 million yearly from 1981 to 1989 -- than on any other Caribbean country.

The spigots of international lending also opened. Seaga borrowed more during his first two years in office than Jamaica had borrowed in the entire preceding decade. A new IMF deal, which originally promised $698 million over three years, was accompanied by more than $400 million in new funds from other members of the World Bank-led consortium of donor governments and aid agencies, the Caribbean Group for Cooperation in Economic Development (CGCED).[4] World Bank aid to Jamaica in 1981-82 constituted more than 67 percent of the Bank's total lending in the Caribbean. In contrast to their policies toward the Manley government, the multilaterals were lenient with Seaga at first. Despite Jamaica's failure to meet IMF economic targets, the Fund agreed to a series of additional loans. The World Bank advanced five more adjustment loans between 1983 and 1987. A major factor in these decisions was the United States, which controls the largest share of voting power in both the IMF and the World Bank.

U.S. banker David Rockefeller assembled a high-profile Business Committee on Jamaica to attract investors to the country. The U.S. government dropped its warning against tourism to Jamaica. Reagan urged the world to "watch Jamaica," declaring that "Free-enterprise Jamaica, and not Marxist Cuba, should be the model for Central America in the struggle to overcome poverty and move toward democracy." Buoyed by this flood of support, Seaga proclaimed Jamaica "open for business."

Free Enterprise Debacle

The linchpin of Seaga's economic strategy was to seek new foreign investment in order to increase Jamaica's exports. To make that investment more convenient and profitable, he reduced government protection of Jamaican producers and opened the country to more imports from abroad. He promoted expansion of the country's free trade zone (FTZ), state-of-the-art sweatshops where Jamaican women, with no union representation, earn as little as 50 cents an hour for assembling garments for export. Seaga played down the loss of jobs resulting from the closure of Jamaican-owned factories unable to compete with the foreign manufacturers for credit and foreign exchange. To reduce demand for legal foreign exchange, channel dollars to favored interests and supporters and resist pressure for further devaluation of the Jamaican dollar, Seaga allegedly condoned import and resale of dollars from the profits of the *ganja* (marijuana) trade, estimated to be the country's second highest source of foreign exchange earnings.

Unfettered free enterprise, however, did not stanch the hemorrhage of wealth from Jamaica. Instead, the outflow increased. Between late 1980 and the end of 1982, Jamaica's trade deficit tripled. New IMF loans to plug the gap were made contingent on stronger austerity measures. The Jamaican dollar was devalued by 43 percent, greatly reducing the buying power of the poor. Nevertheless, after a brief period of increase in Jamaica's GDP in 1983, economic growth again ground to a halt. The rate of inflation accelerated to 30.1 per cent in 1984-85.[5] Unemployment climbed to 30 percent overall and to 78.6 percent and 58.6 percent among females aged 14-19 and 20-24.[6] In 1985, in the context of low world market prices for bauxite and alumina, Kaiser/Reynolds and Alcoa shut down their operations in Jamaica. (Jamaica again experienced limited GDP growth in the second half of Seaga's term, mainly from increased tourism, laundered *ganja* dollars, lower fuel import costs and the partial recovery of world market prices of bauxite and alumina.)

Jamaica was paying back more to its foreign creditors -- mainly in interest -- than it was getting in new support: a net outflow of $881 million from 1986 through 1988, including $349 million to the IMF alone. By the end of Seaga's term, the country's debt had doubled, reaching $4.4 billion. This meant that Jamaica owed more than $1,800 for every Jamaican citizen, at a time when the country was losing about $230 per Jamaican every year from its international trade.[7]

The IMF loans and the accompanying conditions failed in their primary objective. Rather than increasing, Jamaican earnings from exports to the United States, Canada and Europe fell by 2.6 per cent from 1980 to 1986. Moreover, the conditions attached to the stabilization and structural adjustment loans were so harsh that even Seaga himself protested: "Jamaica," he said in 1985, "is not a country that has the large-scale capital resources that can indulge in a totally free economy."

The social side effects of structural adjustment medicine were severe. From 1981 to 1985, total government per capita spending on health fell by 33 percent. As a consequence, according to a study by the ACE: "Health capital stock and equipment have deteriorated badly; hospital services have been closed; real incomes of doctors, nurses and other health personnel have fallen; charges have been introduced in public hospitals; patient care has deteriorated and patients are often asked to take their own linen and food to the hospitals."[8]

The study notes that: "Over the period January 1981 to June 1985, the consumer price index for housing increased by 95 percent in the capital city and by 115 percent in the rural areas. The minimum wage, if earned by the two adult members of the household, covered less than 40 percent of the cost of the basket [of minimum essential foods] over this period . . . A fifth of the public workforce was let go in just one year, from October 1984 to October 1985."[9]

All this was more than many poor Jamaicans were willing to withstand. For three days in January 1984, after the Seaga government announced yet another austerity measure, a gasoline price increase, the capital city of Kingston and much of the rest of the country were paralyzed by road blockages and demonstrations which left at least ten people dead or wounded.

Manley's Return: "You Can't Go Back Easily"

By early 1988, Seaga was so unpopular that World Bank officials apparently concluded that it was preferable to encourage Manley's return to office. Interviewed in June 1988, the Bank's Roger Robinson said: "Five years ago, people were still thinking about 'meeting local needs,' but not any more. Now the lawyers and others with access to resources are interested in external export investment. Once you have that ingrained in a population, you can't go back easily, even if the PNP and Michael Manley come in again."[10]

"Michael Manley," Robinson added with undisguised satisfaction, "is making all the right noises" to reassure the Bank and potential foreign investors and to spurn what Robinson called the "irrational" self-reliance strategies of the 1970s. "The PNP even gave support to Jamaican potato farmers, when it's well-known that potatoes coming in from Miami make better French fries!" he exclaimed.

Almost immediately after Manley's re-election in February 1989, Jamaican government officials were again shuttling back and forth between Kingston and Washington, the site of World Bank headquarters and of many of the IMF negotiations. There, they met with a corps of callous, denationalized technocrats, accountable to no country, whose primary allegiance is to their own lucrative careers in the institutions they serve.

For three months, the government was locked in intense negotiations with the IMF for a new stand-by agreement to replace the $106 million deal accepted by Seaga in September 1988. That agreement called for a limit on wage increases to ten percent (despite an anticipated inflation rate of 15 percent that year), interest rate hikes, credit constriction and further government spending cuts. A new standby agreement for $65 million in IMF Special Drawing Rights was reached in May 1989, but Jamaica was only allowed to withdraw a quarter of that loan.

On 31 October 1989, the government announced the suspension of a new round of negotiations. Meanwhile, Bank of Jamaica officials searched for further sacrifices to placate the IMF and persuade its representatives to continue the current agreements and prepare the ground for new loans in the spring. Without an IMF agreement, further World Bank loans and other sources of credit would be hard to obtain. On 8 November, the government announced a further devaluation of the Jamaica. In addition, the government lowered food price subsidies designed to protect the poor. New price ceilings raised the legal maximum prices for bread, cooking oil, milk, flour, cornmeal, rice and other staples by amounts averaging 13 percent. The government's importing agency announced that it would stop buying and reselling salted codfish, an important protein source and essential ingredient in Jamaica's most famous national dish.

The devaluation and price hikes provoked outcries of anger and despair from the public and even from the right-leaning press. The conservative *Gleaner* newspaper calculated that a worker earning the standard minimum weekly wage of J$100 a week, after buying a minimal basket of food for a family of four, barely enough to last a few days, would be left with only J$32.50 to cover school costs, transportation, rent, utility bills and all other expenses. (Food prices in Jamaica are only slightly lower than those in the United States, where the minimum wage is 11.5 times as high.)

The U.S. showed little inclination to help the Manley government cope with the $4.4 billion debt burden it inherited. In fiscal 1988-89, Jamaica paid a net amount of $213 million to the IMF and $75 million to the World Bank; its net outflow to all multilateral creditors was $263 million, and the debt was reduced to $3.95 billion. Manley reminded a U.S. Congressional delegation to Jamaica in November 1989 that the country would have to pay half of its export earnings and 40 percent of all government revenues to cover debt service costs in the coming year. "That means we're running a 50-cent dollar country," he said.

The prime minister begged the Congressmen to persuade multilateral lenders to bend their rules against debt rescheduling, not just for Jamaica but for other debtor nations. He reminded them that the U.S.-sponsored Brady Plan, even if it were to offer substantial relief of debts owed by poor countries to commercial banks, would be of little help to Jamaica, whose external commercial debt is only 14 percent of its total foreign debt. Manley reassured the U.S. representatives that, drastic as the crisis might be, he had no intention of approaching it "in a confrontationist way. We had enough of that in the 1970s," he said.

Jamaica on the Auction Block

Faced with the debt crisis, credit cuts and intensified U.S., IMF and World Bank pressure, the PNP tried to ride out the storm by postponing more drastic currency devaluation, while grasping every possible source of foreign exchange. An infamous example was the sale of $80 million worth of bauxite and alumina in advance to the Alcan corporation and to U.S. speculator Mark Rich. Jamaica got quick cash from the deal, but the futures buyers will reap the profits of expected increases in alumina prices well into the future. The country's 20 percent block of shares in the only national telephone company was sold to the British Cable and Wireless Ltd. company.

Other public land, rights and property are also on the auction block. The apparent conversion of Manley to a pro-capitalist privatizer allowed the *Enterprise*, voice of the Private Sector of Jamaica association, to gloat in an editorial:

> "Schools can't find teachers. The entire system seems to be on the verge of collapse. Nurses are fleeing . . . Everyone knows about the pressure on the dollar and the foreign exchange shortage. But underneath the bad news there is some movement like a tide beneath the waves that should give U.S. some hope. The government has quietly dropped the nonsensical rhetoric of the recent past and is divesting state enterprises at an even faster rate than its predecessor . . . The old gospel that government should be operated in the interests of the poor is being modified, even if not expressly rejected, by the dawning realization that the only way to help the poor is to operate the government in the interest of the productive!"

There is scant evidence that the private sector is either efficient or inclined to invest substantially in productive activity in Jamaica. But as long as it seeks accommodation with the IMF, the government has little choice but to shift resources in its direction and away from social needs. The Fund's rules are so stringent that they require even profitable public enterprises to be sold and efficient services to be cut back.

The government was forced to swallow other onerous conditions to obtain new foreign loans from other sources. In November 1989, the government concluded a $62 million agreement for a World Bank-designed Agricultural Sector Adjustment loan package. Its release was contingent upon obtaining an agreement between Jamaica and the IMF. Among other conditionalities of the agriculture loan were the near-elimination of tariffs and quantitative restrictions on livestock imports. One government official said this would be likely to destroy local industries: U.S. producers were already in the country proffering U.S. beef to hotel managers before the ink on the agreement was dry. Another condition of the World Bank loan is the reduction of government participation in commodity marketing boards. A Jamaican economist observed:

> "The Bank believes the government should have no say at all in what is bought and sold to whom and for how much. But the alternative of total privatization means one

or a few big producers will monopolize every sector and manipulate it for their own benefit; this has already happened to our coffee [most of which now goes to Japan]."[11]

The Bank also urged disbanding the Jamaica Commodity Trading Corporation, a step not even Seaga was willing to take because of the corporation's importance in enabling the state to stabilize food prices and capture revenue from the sale of foreign-donated surplus food. In addition, the Bank wanted the Jamaica Agricultural Credit Bank to raise its interest rates to, or close to, market rate levels, even though the source of the Credit Bank's funds is not the World Bank. Said a government official concerned with agriculture: "We told the World Bank team that farmers can hardly afford credit now, and that higher rates would put them out of business. The Bank told us in response that this means 'The market is telling you that agriculture is not the way to go for Jamaica.' They're saying in effect that we should give up farming altogether."

A bizarre aspect of the agriculture loan agreement, the official reported, is that not one penny would go to aid Jamaica's farmers! Instead, he said, the funds would be converted into Bank of Jamaica certificates of deposit, to shore up the government's credit reserves in preparation for the next IMF test:

> "The Bank is fully aware that we will have to use the money for other foreign exchange needs and not to add anything to our agriculture budget. But down the road, when more farmers go out of business, they'll tell U.S. it's because we didn't use their loan money wisely."

During negotiations for a World Bank housing project loan, the Bank insisted on further increases in mortgage interest rates, even though the rates were already so far out of the reach of most Jamaicans that the National Housing Trust (NHT), paid for mainly by a tax on all Jamaican wage-earners and responsible for 80 percent of the country's housing financing, was banking its money instead of building homes. Even higher interest rates, the Bank reportedly acknowledged, might mean even less construction of housing. More important, in the Bank's view, was the fact that the NHT's operations "would become more profitable," a party to the negotiations reported. Similar criteria were expected to be applied by the Bank to a "Trade and Finance Sector Adjustment." Said a Jamaican official:

> "The Bank's logic is that the less that goes into government, the more there will be for the private sector, and that the private sector, not government, should determine

how resources are used. They tell us we should let the market determine the exchange rate, even if it means the Jamaica dollar crashes.[12] If that happens, they say, wages will drop further, and we'll be flooded with free zone-type manufacturing. We'll reach the limit of our ability to import, so that way our foreign exchange problem will be solved! The World Bank and the IMF don't have to worry about the farmers and local companies going out of business, or starvation wages or the social upheaval that will result. They simply assume that it is our job to keep our national security forces strong enough to suppress any uprising."

He might have added that the creditors also know they can count on the U.S. government to lend a hand.

The Resistance Continues

Jamaicans have fought in the past against overwhelming odds; they struggle today with remarkable resilience and creativity to survive increasing impoverishment. But the popular organizations that were encouraged, up to a point, by the PNP in the 1970s have been badly damaged by the economic pressures and political assaults of the 1980s. Workers in the country's cane fields, factories and export-processing sweatshops continue to organize, demonstrate and protest, but with little support from the party they put in power.

Independent progressive organizations work valiantly to keep up with the demands from farmers, workers, unemployed youth and the urban poor for organizing assistance and logistical support, and important victories have been won. But more visible, at least in the mass media, is the frustration, despair and social dislocation that spews forth in the form of ghetto gunfights, politically manipulated violence, soaring cocaine use, drug wars and a sense of near-panic among many in the middle classes. Progressive Jamaican non-governmental organizations, such as the Social Action Centre and other member groups of the Association of Development Agencies, have made effective use of video, comics, theater and other popular education techniques in creative grassroots campaigns to link foreign debt issues to the problems of daily life in urban and rural communities.

The level of popular consciousness in Jamaica, upon which the potential for an alternative development approach depends, remains relatively high. It is evident in popular theater and music, which, at its best, combines righteous anger against poverty, pollution, sexual and other forms of violence and foreign control with calls for African liberation, Caribbean unity, racial harmony and peace. But the Rastafarian-inspired, feminist and other artists who convey these messages face tough competition for the hearts and minds of Jamaicans from satellite TV's "Dallas" and "Dynasty," evangelical fanaticism and the CNN (Cable News Network) news.

Achieving true sovereignty for Jamaica will necessitate an appeal to Jamaica's poor majority for continued struggle and sacrifice, guided by a clear vision of an alternative to the failed development-through-indebtedness strategy. It will also require greater economic leverage based on alliances with other Caribbean nations and the strengthening of ties with the region's Central American and South American neighbors, as well as with Cuba. Above all, winning Jamaica's freedom will require a mobilization of the Jamaican people, not by the blaring of any trumpets, but by the careful heeding of their own voices and by support of battles against exploitation in which they are already engaged. The path to Caribbean liberation is perilous indeed. But its dangers could hardly be greater than the immense human suffering, social disintegration, environmental destruction and political instability that Jamaica and most of her neighbors are now facing, or will soon inevitably encounter, if they are forced to continue on their present course.

Notes

1 . Barry, Preusch and Wood, *The Other Side of Paradise* (New York: Grove Press, 1984).

2. Cited by Medea Benjamin and Kevin Danaher in "Jamaica, Free Market Fiasco," *Food First News*, 1986.

3. Calculated from USAID, *Overseas Loans and Grants*, September 1986, and USAID, *Congressional Presentation*.

4. Fitzroy Ambursley, "Jamaica from Michael Manley to Edward Seaga," in Ambursley and Cohen (eds), *Crisis in the Caribbean* (New York: Monthly Review Press, 1983).

5. Government of Jamaica, "Economic Performance," submission to the CGCED, Spring, 1988.

6. Interamerican Development Bank, *Annual Report*, 1984; Government of Jamaica, Labor Force Survey.

7. *Hooked on Debt* (Kingston, Jamaica: Social Action Centre, 1990).

8. Norman Girvan, Ennio Rodriguez, Mario Arana Sevilla and Migueal Ceara Hatton, *The Debt Problem of Small Peripheral Economies: Case Studies from the Carribean and Central America*, 1990.

9. Increased poverty in Jamaica is documented by Joan French in *Hope and Disillusion: The CBI and Jamaica* (Kingston, Jamaica: ADA, 1990).

10. Author interview, November 1989.

11. Author interview, November 1989.

12. Until the mid-1970s, the Jamaican dollar was worth more than the U.S. dollar; by 1990 it was J$7 to US$1, and by 1992 it took more than J$25 to buy one U.S. dollar's worth of goods.

13

Ghana: The World Bank's Sham Showcase

Ross Hammond and Lisa McGowan

Ghana's Structural Adjustment Program, one of the longest-running IMF/World Bank-initiated economic reform programs in Africa, is regularly cited by Fund and Bank economists as the prime example of how structural adjustment cures failing economies and places them on a path to sustainable growth. Although there is overwhelming evidence of the program's failure, it continues to be used to legitimize adjustment programs elsewhere on the continent.

In 1983, the Ghanaian economy had reached a state of virtual collapse, the victim of falling cocoa prices, decreased government revenue, spiraling inflation and political instability. At the same time, $1.5 billion in loan repayments fell due as debts rescheduled in 1974 matured. Faced with possible bankruptcy, the Ghanaian government, led by Flight Lieutenant Jerry Rawlings, undertook a series of structural adjustment programs, designed and financed by the World Bank and the IMF. The programs became known collectively as Ghana's Economic Recovery Program (ERP), which was divided into three phases: Stabilization, Rehabilitation, and Liberalization and Growth.

As part of the ERP, the government has slashed public spending, devalued the currency (the *cedi*), invested in natural resource exporting industries and carried out a number of other IMF/World Bank-prescribed reforms designed to orient the economy to export production and open it to foreign investors.

As reward for its relentless pursuit of World Bank and IMF-inspired reforms, Ghana has been showered with foreign aid. In its decade-long quest for economic recovery, the government has drawn upon virtually every funding mechanism available at the Bank and Fund, contracting more than $1.75 billion in Bank loans and credits by the end of 1990. In fact, by 1988, Ghana was the third largest recipient in the world of credit from the International Development Association (IDA), the Bank's soft-loan window. Only India and China, each with populations over 850 million, received more than Ghana, whose population is only 15 million. IMF funding under the ERP has totaled over $1.35 billion, and total financial resources from bilateral and multilateral sources amounted to $8 billion over the first seven years of the program, making Ghana one of the most favored aid recipients in the developing world.

Macroeconomic Failures of the ERP

Despite massive amounts of foreign financing, Ghana can claim little real progress under its structural adjustment programs. The most regularly cited indicator of success -- real gross domestic product (GDP) growth averaging 3.88 percent annually between 1983 and 1990 -- is indisputably an improvement over the negative growth rates experienced in the immediate pre-adjustment period. However, this figure looks less impressive when one takes into account population growth (3.1 percent a year), huge inflows of foreign exchange from donors, relatively good weather conditions over the adjustment period and the initial goodwill of the Ghanaian people towards the ERP. Furthermore, an examination of the sectoral distribution of GDP growth shows that:

• growth has taken place principally in those areas receiving direct financial/investment support;

• while the minerals and forestry sectors have grown, manufacturing has declined;

• the performance of the domestic food and livestock sub-sectors, critical to the well-being of most Ghanaian consumers, has on balance been negative;

• the service sector (especially the transport, wholesale and retail subsectors) has grown from a 37-percent share of GDP to 42.5 percent, indicating that the economy is increasingly becoming a "buying and selling" one;

• by 1990, real annual growth of GDP had fallen to 2.7 percent, down from over 6 percent in the mid-1980s;

• inflation, which dropped from 123 percent in 1983 to 25.2 percent in 1989, jumped to 37.7 percent in 1990;

• the ratio of investment to GDP is lower than it was in the 1960s and 1970s and

• the tightening of credit (designed to control inflation) has decreased domestic investment and increased reliance on foreign borrowing -- by 1992 the interest rate had risen to 37 percent.

The evidence strongly suggests that growth in Ghana is aid-driven and, as such, is fragile and skewed toward those areas in which the donors are interested -- such as natural-resource extraction -- rather than toward domestic capacity building.

The goals of the latest phase of the ERP are to reduce inflation, generate a substantial balance-of-payments surplus, promote private investment and stimulate growth in the agricultural export sector. These goals have remained elusive, however, with the country's economy slipping notably during the past few years.

Cocoa Crowds out Food

The World Bank and IMF point to the growth of Ghana's agricultural export sector as chief among the ERP's successes. As a result of government incentives that included higher producer prices and increased investment, the volume of cocoa exports rose by more than 70 percent between 1983 and 1988. Cocoa is now responsible for more than 70 percent of Ghana's export earnings. Unfortunately, the world market price of cocoa has been dropping steadily since the mid-1980s. According to a U.S. Congressional study, world consumption of cocoa has increased by only 2 percent annually while supply has grown by 6 to 7 percent.

This emphasis on cocoa production has exacerbated local and regional income disparities. While approximately 46 percent of government expenditure in the agricultural sector has been invested in the cocoa industry, cocoa farmers comprise only 18 percent of Ghana's farming population and are concentrated primarily in the South, which has traditionally been favored by both government and donors over the disadvantaged Northern savannah region. Since the 1970s, land, power and wealth within cocoa-producing communities have become increasingly concentrated as well. Currently, the top 7 percent of Ghana's cocoa producers own almost half of the land cultivated for cocoa, while 70 percent own farms of less than six acres.

The government has not made economic incentives similar to those extended to agro-export producers available to those who produce food for domestic consumption. It has failed to promote food security through measures to raise productivity, yield and storage. As a result, Ghana's food self-sufficiency declined steadily during the 1980s, and the per capita income of non-cocoa farmers stagnated. Producers of rice, vegetable oils and other cash crops were hit hard by a flood of cheap imports, the product of trade liberalization measures and exchange-rate adjustments.

Unequal Burdens

It is the Ghanaian poor who have had to bear the greatest burden of adjustment. In the critical fishing industry, for example, as a result of a series of currency devaluations, inputs have become more expensive, particularly for small-scale operators who fish to meet local needs. Increased production costs are then passed on to the nation's consumers, most of whose real wages have been falling. Since Ghanaians obtain 60 percent of their protein from fish and fish by-products, the decrease in fish consumption resulting from higher prices has contributed to increased rates of malnutrition in the country.

Malnutrition and illness among the poor have also increased as a result of cuts in wages and public expenditures, currency devaluation and the introduction of user fees for health and educational services. In addition, illiteracy and drop-out rates have risen. When the minimum daily wage of 218 *cedis* was announced in 1990, the Trade Union Congress calculated that an average family needed 2,000 *cedis* a day for food alone.

The effects of eliminating thousands of government jobs under the adjustment program are spreading throughout the economy and to more and more people. Aside from the direct impact these cutbacks have had on urban unemployment rates, second-tier effects are being felt by the dependents of the newly unemployed, many of whom have been forced to take to the streets in search of income for their families. It is estimated that in Ghana an average of 15 people are at least partially dependent on each principal urban wage earner.

In contrast, rich Ghanaians have fared quite well under adjustment. Data generated by the 1987 Living Standards Measurement Survey indicate an increase in income inequality in the 1980s, compared to the 1970s. Landholdings and agricultural export earnings have become more concentrated, especially in the cocoa sector. Import-liberalization measures have led to increased food imports; the rich, with more money to spend, have more access to a wider range of higher priced food products, while more of the poor are going hungry.

Cutting Down the Forest for the Trees

The economic reform program has also promoted the export of timber, Ghana's third most important export commodity after cocoa and minerals, with a devastating effect on the nation's forests. The IDA and other aid agencies have tunneled aid and credit packages to timber companies to enable them to purchase new materials and equipment. As a result, timber exports, in terms of volume and value, have increased rapidly since the start of the ERP, rising from $16 million in 1983 to $99 million by 1988.

This quick-fix solution to Ghana's need for foreign-exchange earnings has contributed to the loss of Ghana's already depleted forest resources. Between 1981 and 1985, the annual rate of deforestation was 1.3 percent, and current estimates now place the rate as high as 2 percent a year. Today, Ghana's tropical forest area is just 25 percent of its original size. In its desperate drive for export earnings, the government has allowed timber companies and fly-by-night contractors to cut down the Ghanaian forests indiscriminately.

Such widespread deforestation is exacting a high toll on the country, leading to regional climatic change, soil erosion and large-scale desertification. Deforestation also threatens household and national food security now and in the future. Seventy-five percent of Ghanaians depend on wild game to supplement their diet, but with the forest stripped, wild game is increasingly scarce. For women, the food, fuel and medicines harvested from the forest provide critical resources, especially in the face of decreased food production, lower wages and other economic shocks that threaten household food security. These resources are lost when trees are cut for export.

They Call This Success?

After nine years of economic recovery programs and huge inputs of foreign aid, Ghana's total external debt has risen from $1.4 billion to almost $4.2 billion. Current investment and savings are too low to sustain the GDP growth rate in the absence of foreign funding, and capital flight has become a serious problem. Since 1987, Ghana has paid more to the IMF than it has received. Environmental degradation is fast-paced and is exacerbated by the policies of the ERP. All of these indicators suggest that the long-term prospects for Ghana's recovery are bleak and that Ghana's budget-cutting, free-trade program, so enthusiastically applauded by Western creditors and commentators, is hardly a model for the rest of Africa.

14

Mozambique: In the Coils of Structural Adjustment
Mozambique Information Agency

Wages serve the basic function of allowing workers to survive and to produce future workers -- their children. When wages are too low to guarantee this, then they are dysfunctional, and the economy is in very serious trouble.

From the World Bank offices in Mozambique's capital, Maputo, there issues a regular stream of triumphalist statements about how the structural adjustment measures forced on Mozambique have reversed the decline of the economy.

But for those on the minimum wage it doesn't look like that at all. Under structural adjustment, the real value of wages has fallen drastically, while subsidies on basic foods have been abolished or severely cut.

In January 1991, the minimum industrial wage of 32,175 meticais a month was worth US$31 at official exchange rates. Inflation and devaluation ate rapidly into this. When the minimum wage was raised to 40,000 meticais a month in December 1991, it was worth just $23. There has been no wage increase since then, but devaluation has gathered pace so that, as of late August 1992, the minimum wage is worth less than $14 a month.

It is theoretically possible for one person, buying the cheapest available foods, to keep himself alive in Maputo on this sum. But the Ministry of Health's nutrition department has shown that no family can survive on the minimum wage.

The results of the low-wage economy are readily visible on the streets of Maputo, where children eke out the family income by engaging in all manner of petty trade (such as buying packets of cigarettes at one price, and then selling them one by one at a slightly higher price).

Low wages generate theft and corruption, too. Scandals repeatedly occur in Mozambican schools, where low-paid teachers demand bribes to allow children to attend classes or, worse still, to pass exams. Theft in factories, in the ports, in the railways, is also linked to the failure to pay a living wage.

Not that the Mozambican government actually wants to pay starvation wages. The government discussed the problem of the minimum wage earlier this year, but it is no longer a free agent. Breathing down its neck are the ideologues of the World Bank and the IMF, who closely scrutinize the country's budget and make it very plain that the injections of foreign funding on which Mozambique depends are conditional on following the financial orthodoxy determined in the IMF'S Washington headquarters.

The problem for the govemment is that at the start of the structural adjustment program, back in 1987, it claimed paternity of the measures and said nothing about the negotiations with the World Bank and IMF. Apparently, in those early negotiations, the government fought tenaciously against some of the more disastrous IMF proposals and chalked up some significant victories. But with the passage of time, the unrelenting pressure from these U.S.-controlled financial institutions has gradually eroded any initial gains and has severely limited Mozambique's sovereignty.

Structural adjustment operates like those giant snakes that throttle their victims to death. Every time the the victim tries to breathe, expelling stale air from his lungs, the coils of the snake crush him still tighter.

The only solution is an honest and open public debate on economic policy. Unfortunately, negotiations with the IMF and World Bank are always shrouded in secrecy. These are among the least transparent, least accountable institutions in the world, determined to prevent the victims of their programs from discovering how they were decided.

The Mozambican authorities would be well-advised to make public the full content of all agreements and negotiations with the multilateral financial bodies. Only then can a fully informed discussion on the state of the economy take place.

15

Food for Thought: Senegal's Struggle with Structural Adjustment

Abdoulaye Ndiaye

Under heavy pressure from the U.S., France, the World Bank and the International Monetary Fund (IMF), Senegal instituted a Structural Adjustment Program (SAP) in the 1980s. Intended to remedy an economic crisis that started in the late 1970s, the move was fast and absolute. The results reflect what has become a common condemnation of SAPs throughout Africa, where the vast majority of the population was excluded from both the design and appraisal processes, while the participation of foreign experts in their design was significant. Abdoulaye Ndiaye, a Senegalese engineer, explains how structural adjustment has resulted in hardship for farmers.

Since the end of the 1970s, the government of Senegal has implemented major policy reforms intended to establish an equilibrium of public finance, a recovery in the balance of payments, sustained economic growth and improved employment.

A decade later, there is substantial evidence that these reforms have had a negative impact on the country's people. The introduction of SAP has raised fundamental questions about the development process in Senegal, including the limitations of the private sector to drive the process, the sources of financing for increased agricultural production and the support systems required to achieve greater self-sufficiency in food production.

At the center of the structural adjustment program is the "New Agricultural Policy" (NAP), introduced in 1984. Meant to reduce reliance on food imports, increase production of local cereals and develop rain-fed farming practices, NAP has been one of the SAP components that has most negatively affected the Senegalese population. There are good reasons why.

Among NAP's stated objectives was the promotion of exports (mainly peanuts), the privatization of agricultural input/output marketing and cutbacks and restructuring of the state's Rural Development Agencies (RDAs) -- all policies seemingly at odds with the program's other stated objectives of increased food security and improved rain-fed farming practices.

These conflicting objectives raise serious questions about the program's design. When NAP was abruptly implemented in 1985 without warning or a transition period, Senegalese farmers were unprepared to do without the agricultural inputs (such as seeds and fertilizers) that had been provided by the state. With the government out of the seed-distribution business, farmers were left on their own for obtaining key inputs. Given their low income levels, the challenge has been difficult, if not impossible, to meet.

For the entire agricultural sector, the use of fertilizer, which averaged 100,000 tons per year before the policy-reform program started, declined to less than 25,000 tons in 1989. Fertilizer subsidies were eliminated, leading to a five-fold price increase, while the expected private sector takeover of distribution has been minimal, causing major supply problems.

Private sector distribution of harvested crops has also fallen short of expectations. Though privatization formed the heart of NAP's marketing policy reforms, the private sector has not played a particularly strong role. Of the 1,700 collection points established for peanut commercialization identified in 1984, only 750 remained by 1988-89.

Major constraints inherent to the market conditions in most of Africa, such as small market size, poor infrastructure for transport and storage of goods, a small and weak private sector and limited access to information, will continue to be major factors playing havoc with the promoted "free market" system in Senegal.

The overall impact of NAP on the rural population of Senegal has been negative. There is little evidence of improvement of rural income in real terms, despite claims that a transfer of income from urban to rural areas is occurring due to more coherent pricing policies. Figures do not demonstrate improved access to credit in rural areas, and farmers are faced with the dilemma of how to finance production in the face of decreasing liquidity, stagnant rural incomes, difficult access to credit and rising consumer prices.

Given the nature of the NAP package, it is highly unlikely that the government of Senegal will achieve its stated goal of 80 percent national food self-sufficiency by the year 2000. Any intensification effort is seriously constrained by the reduced availability of fertilizer, quality seeds, agricultural equipment, extension services and relevant research.

The liberalization of both input and output marketing, and the elimination of subsidies have resulted in increased production costs and increased consumer prices at a time of stagnant national incomes. Also, the NAP has allocated scarce resources to export production, while failing to promote the consumption of local cereals in urban areas.

The macro-economic condition of the country is not much more encouraging. Despite implementing policy reforms designed to reduce the country's debt service, its foreign debt has sharply increased from 44 percent of GNP in 1980 to close to 80 percent in 1989. The policies are not without their social costs. Cuts in health services and education, rising unemployment in the public sector and a decrease in purchasing power have all contributed to the growing political instability of the country.

Ironically, the increased severity of hardship for the rural population has led to an increase in the number of development initiatives from grassroots organizations. These initiatives, which have been implemented with the support of national and international NGOs, include the promotion of reforestation, fallow practice, the use of natural fertilizers such as compost, alternatives to pesticides use and other environmentally sound practices, as well as local-level credit and savings programs.

The growing reliance on local level organizations to fill the void left by the withdrawal of the state has, however, created a difficult burden for NGOs, who have been very critical of the adjustment program currently in place. But, in the end, self-reliance is the principal hope for the poor of Senegal. The past decade's most positive development has been the emergence of the myriad community initiatives to empower and improve the living conditions of the people while maintaining the health of their environment, with or without assistance from the outside.

16

From Apartheid to Neoliberalism in South Africa
Patrick Bond

South Africa ran up high commercial bank debts in the early 1980s. The reliance on commercial credit provided an opportunity for one of the most successful components of the liberation struggle: a "financial sanctions" campaign that put intense pressure on South Africa's rulers. The current struggle over how much influence to allow the IMF and World Bank demonstrates how hard it is for a Third World country -- even one loaded with natural resources -- to resist the power of the multilateral lenders.

At the closing session of 1992's World Bank/IMF meetings, World Bank President Lewis Preston was asked by the press whether anything seemed different given the demise of the command economies. "There are still some socialists here," Preston replied, deadpan. "There are still even some communists around. But they are talking in very low voices, and they are mostly South Africans." The account in Johannesburg's *Business Day* newspaper raised a few eyebrows. Attending the meetings were the South African government's big business finance minister and the chief economist of the African National Congress (ANC), Trevor Manuel. More eyebrows were raised when Manuel, a lifelong community activist, said in a July 1993 interview with the popular *New Nation* newspaper, "We will certainly need foreign aid, but not from the IMF or the World Bank."

Although such admirable intentions are by no means typical, it is important to keep in mind that many in the ANC do maintain a traditional hostility toward international finance. South Africa's external debt has fallen to $18 billion -- from a peak of $23 billion in 1985 -- and is therefore not an ongoing balance of payments hazard. But a 1991 ANC banking handbook suggested that it be repaid into a local currency development fund (à la Susan George): "Morally, it could be argued that this debt, used to bolster apartheid, should be used to assist economic reconstruction in South Africa." ANC General Secretary Cyril Ramaphosa periodically threatens not to repay any foreign loans taken out by the South African government prior to the installation of a democratic government.

But contrast these with other, more politic statements. On trips to the United States in 1990 and 1991, Nelson Mandela used Preston to back a post-apartheid aid program, and the Bank president made a one-day visit to Johannesburg in 1992 to confirm progress to that end. In September 1992, as the South African finance minister began aggressively soliciting an IMF loan purportedly related to drought relief, Manuel commented, "it would be wrong to refuse the issue."

Queried about the Bank in May 1993, Manuel reported that "positions are drawing closer as we talk to them." And during a business banquet speech, ANC economist Tito Mboweni confirmed the rightward drift by citing "IMF pressure" as a reason for the leadership's decision "to give up nationalization." Cynics say that when the issue of the Bank and the IMF is raised, ANC leaders degenerate into telling audiences what they want to hear.

The mixed signals reflect the ANC's delicate wavering on a tightrope whose endpoint is, very likely, a close working relationship with the Bank. Meanwhile, however, the unsure strides are all the more treacherous because of insistent tugging from competing ideological directions: neoliberals who enthusiastically embrace the Bank and its ideas, and radical democrats and Afrikaner welfarist nationalists who don't. The first category of lobbyists are based in corporate headquarters, various think-tanks and parastatal agencies; the second are in the movements of civil society and affiliated "service organization" NGOs; and the third are mainly in commercial farm and white service lobbies. In at least one venue, the Johannesburg Metropolitan Chamber (a forerunner of democratic municipal government), the latter two camps have allied to hold the Bank at bay, at least temporarily.

More generally, the ANC is increasingly intent on stitching together a winning social democratic electoral coalition. Although the resulting mixture of populism and neoliberalism is ridden with potential conflicts in the medium term, it seems to be working for now.

On the one hand, the neoliberal influence grows, ironically, with the continued success of international financial sanctions. These provide ANC leaders with the power to either open the gates or keep them closed to renewed foreign loans. Even short-term foreign debt rescheduling has involved the ANC's new chairperson and international director, Thabo Mbeki. Until the ANC gives word that "democracy is irreversible," South Africa's credit rating remains suspect. It is thus in the ANC's self-interest to link its role in government to new loans.

Repeated assertions in the business press that international financial aid is South Africa's only savior reinforces this perspective. So does the ruling elite's implicit understanding, as expressed by the head of the Johannesburg Stock Exchange, that the ANC "must talk to people like competent economists at the IMF. If they go to Washington, they'll find all of a sudden that they'll be doing what everybody else is doing, which is privatizing and reducing the state's share of the economy."

In reality, it is not altogether logical that the Bank and the IMF are portrayed as saviors of South African capital, especially in view of the extensive trade protection on which most local businesses depend. Bank and IMF funding for project finance and structural adjustments are probably unnecessary, given the massive untapped liquidity in South Africa's own financial markets, the limited need for foreign exchange-dominated loans to underwrite basic needs development programs and the fast declining currency (which makes even local 15 percent money market interest rates cheaper than Bank loans). As a result, even a few enlightened business leaders are now talking about avoiding a foreign debt trap.

Regardless, the general consensus among South Africa's present rulers remains simple: it is preferred that the economy be run from Washington during the next few years rather than taking a chance on a potentially redistributionist ANC. This is rarely discussed in polite company, of course, and neither is the process of "comprador" formation within the ranks of the democratic forces. Instead, the Bank's technical expertise is acclaimed by most commentators, and there is little or no threat of a boycott.

To be sure, Bank staff have done a splendid job of putting forth a friendly face to critics. Transparency is unprecedented. Mission leaders have become good at mimicking the local lingo -- reports are now peppered with accolades to equity, consultation, participation, nonracialism -- and at schmoozing with the left intelligentsia, bringing many on board as co-authors of background papers. At universities and non-governmental organizations (NGOs), generally white, middle-class progressives with research skills are hungrily eyeing $500-a-day consultancies.

On the other hand, many thousands of ANC cadres spent their lives exiled in Zambia, Tanzania, Uganda and the like, where they witnessed first-hand the social mauling of structural adjustment policies (SAPs). Vibrant South African movements based in union, community, rural, religious, women's health and education sectors are intrinsically suspicious of the Bank, and this will become apparent over the medium term. Citing the "universal outcry and misery" caused by the Bank across the Third World, Rev. Frank Chikane (leader of the South African Council of Churches) argues, "We cannot believe that the salvation of our country lies in an uncritical and undemocratic subjection of our country to IMF and World Bank policies."

Bank opponents are gathering momentum, particularly as a result of a recent Johannesburg conference (funded by the Dutch aid agency NOVIB) on the implications of Bank policies. Institute of African Alternatives director Ben Turok -- who is also an ANC regional leader -- and staff at NGOs such as Group for Environmental Monitoring, International Labor Rights Working Group and various other internationally networked critics, argue that Bank loans will inexorably lead to the introduction of a full-fledged SAP.

Already, in the midst of South Africa's longest depression ever, the IMF has endorsed the present finance ministry's SAP, which is characterized by some of the highest real interest rates in the world, imposition of an enormously unpopular Value Added Tax (designed by the IMF), a sharp rise in unemployment to 47 percent and a GATT proposal that will devastate many more industries and jobs dependent on high levels of tariff protection. One IMF report pronounced, "Real wage growth must be contained," notwithstanding the sub-living wage that apartheid bequeathed today's economy.

But other, more specific attacks on the Bank that focus on its philosophies of development are also emerging. "Market-assisted" (actually market-dominated) land redistribution, shack (not housing) policy, small-scale credit (at above-market interest rates) and cost-recovered health and education could well be imposed on South Africa through project conditionality.

The Bank vision of transforming South Africa's cities is seen as extremely important both in material and political terms -- most money will flow through urban infrastructure credits, and, as the capacities of nation-states deteriorate across Africa, both the World Bank and USAID increasingly prefer the metropolitan scale as the unit of analysis, control and implementation.

Moreover, South Africa's urban social movements have played a profound historical role -- in part by making the broader apartheid society "ungovernable" in the course of struggle over local grievances -- to a degree that strategists of state, capital and international finance have had to take notice. The contest over the hearts and minds of the urban movements represents possibly the greatest hint as to whether the Bank will break the apartheid mold with a neoliberal hammer.

17

Zimbabwe: SAP Means "Suffering for African People"
Michael O'Heaney

Two years after the implementation of structural adjustment in Zimbabwe, it is becoming clearer day by day that the impressive gains made under the government's "growth with equity" program are being reversed. The SAP implemented by the government has acquired another name among the majority of Zimbabweans, "Suffering for African People." One unemployed Zimbabwean claims, "For most of us, SAP has brought all the hardships and none of the benefits expected when it was introduced."

Far from bringing greater democracy and equality in a "second revolution" to wipe out poverty, the SAP in Zimbabwe is driving a wedge between the people and their government, hijacking the goals of liberation and reversing the social advances made following independence in 1980. While the Zimbabwean government, World Bank and IMF blunder ahead in a fog of optimism about the progress of structural adjustment, suspicion is growing about where the SAP is taking Zimbabwe and at what cost.

Structural Adjustment Programs

A cornerstone of the adjustment program is the withdrawal of government from the economy of the country. Zimbabwe has now opened its doors to external investment and external competition in the hope that these two principles of free market ideology will stimulate its industry and boost its share of exports in world trade. But, as one worker recently dismissed from his job complained, "competition is fine, but if you run a race you have to make sure that everyone starts off from the same place. These industries from abroad are decades ahead of us. How on earth are we supposed to match their resources?"

The IMF and World Bank demanded that the Zimbabwean economy be opened up for competition through the SAP. Some claim it is hypocrisy to ask a poor country like Zimbabwe to open itself up to economic competition when this is not repeated at the global level. They protest, "High subsidies and high tariffs have guaranteed the wealth of the industrialized world. Why are we being asked to swallow a different medicine?"

The deregulation of price controls and the abolition of subsidies, another component of the SAP, have had a disastrous impact on many families both in urban and rural areas. Cooking oil, margarine, sugar, bread, maize-meal, meat, electricity, water and transport prices have more than tripled over the last year and a half. This increase compromises the ability of many Zimbabweans to adequately feed, clothe and shelter their families. As a result, begging and crime, indications of intense economic hardship, have risen dramatically in Zimbabwe, particularly in cities like Harare, the capital.

Father Brian MacGarry, an economic researcher, questions why Zimbabwe should choose to follow the SAP path at all in a booklet entitled "Growth Without Equality?" As he sees it, structural adjustment will lead to a situation where all trade will be directed to rich countries. The SAP strategy is "to impoverish primary producer countries," and the only winners will be international bankers, multinational corporations and commercial farmers. The Catholic researcher concludes that to accept the IMF conditions "will only make most of our people poorer." Father MacGarry's claims are materializing today in Zimbabwe, especially in the areas of health and education.

Health and Education

The withdrawal of government as a controlling and monitoring influence has not only taken place in industry. Price controls, subsidies on essential goods and provision of services such as health and education have also been affected by a series of measures that adversely impact the more vulnerable sections of society. Zimbabweans have experienced a drastic slip in incomes since the SAP was introduced. This, coupled with the reduction of government social services in health and education, means people no longer can afford these services.

Zimbabweans are unable to visit their doctors or attend hospitals because of the introduction of fees. Unfortunately, doctors have pointed out that this increasingly common problem has in some cases led to late diagnosis, resulting in the deaths of patients who might have been cured if they had sought attention earlier. For example, UNICEF recently reported that the number of women dying in childbirth has doubled in Harare in the two years since Zimbabwe introduced the SAP. Lack of money has also affected diet, and in rural areas a sharp increase in malnutrition has been recorded. While this cannot be blamed entirely on the reform program, the withdrawal of subsidies on essential goods and services at the time of one of the worst droughts in southern Africa this century has exaggerated the problem. Still, all of this illustrates some of the damaging impacts of the SAP on Zimbabwe's health care, one of the country's greatest successes since independence in 1980. It is predicted that if the cuts continue in line with the budget targets, all of the health gains of the past decade will be reversed within two years.

Education, another area of advancement after independence, is also suffering. Increases in the costs of education have meant the removal of many children from school. Families are now being forced to choose which children should receive education. In addition, the cuts in expenditures on education are increasing divisions within the society between those who can afford to send their children to private schools and those who can barely afford the fees for under-resourced state schools. One headmaster claims, "we are reaching a situation where the children of poor households have no chance of competing in the job market even if their academic potential is high." This reverses the gains made since independence, when the state decided to intervene in education to reverse the former racial bias.

The economic reform program is not responsible for all of Zimbabwe's current woes. A protracted drought, an unfavorable international economic environment, regional conflicts and destabilization have all taken their toll on Zimbabwe's development. But in chastising the country's investment in education, health and social welfare for being "non productive," the SAP has compromised one of the country's main achievements since independence. As one economist concluded, education, health care and protection of the poorer sections of society is as much an investment as pouring money into commerce and industry. "Without healthy, educated people, how can we hope to achieve all the other things that economic reform promises?"

> *"Behind structural adjustment there is a model for the development of our society. It is a model to reorganize society and natural resources that has two fundamental characteristics. One is the reinforcement of an elite that will increase exploitation of producers. And the second is the reinforcement of the patriarchy."*
>
> Diana Lima Handem, Co-founder,
> *Associacao de Estudos é Alternativas*
> Guinea-Bissau

18

Stealing from the State
Natalie Avery

"The 1990s have started with a bang," said William Ryrie, executive vice president of the International Finance Corporation (IFC), an affiliate of the World Bank, as he addressed the Seventh Annual Conference on Privatization sponsored by the British think tank, the Adam Smith Institute. "Privatization will, I am sure, be a continuing theme of the remaining years of the century, and the potential benefits to the countries concerned will, I have no doubt, continue well into the new century."

Ryrie's enthusiasm for privatization of publicly owned enterprises is reflected in World Bank policy during the last decade. Ahmed Galal, a senior economist at the World Bank, says, "Privatization has featured in almost every structural adjustment program in the last 12 years or so." As of 1992, the World Bank and its affiliates had supported privatization in more than 180 Bank operations and had provided investment, support and advice to privatized firms in dozens of IFC operations. The World Bank has pushed privatization in countries ranging from Argentina to Zimbabwe.

The Bank's use of privatization as a condition for the receipt of structural adjustment loans has escalated in the last few years. The proportion of World Bank structural adjustment loans made conditional on specific privatization targets has risen from only 13 percent in 1986 to 59 percent in 1992.

The Bank's emphasis on privatization over the last decade has drawn sharp criticism from a wide array of government officials, academics, community activists and institutions, perhaps most notably the United Nations Development Program (UNDP). They charge that privatization has primarily benefited multinational corporations, which have gained access to previously closed industries in the Third World and Eastern Europe, and local elites in those countries, who have bought up privatized enterprises at discount rates. As the UNDP's 1993 World Development Report asserts, "In many countries the privatization process has been more of a 'garage sale' to favored individuals and groups than a part of a coherent strategy to encourage private investment."

Privatization and related policies have widened the gap between rich and poor and increased human suffering throughout the Third World and Eastern Europe, contend critics. Although the Bank insists that its promotion of privatization is based on "pragmatic" considerations and that privatization will eventually lead to a reduction of poverty, the effect of Bank-inspired privatizations carried out so far has been to intensify poverty. The UNDP concludes that "the long-term objectives of privatization may be to increase economic growth and human development, but the immediate effects [on human development] have been traumatic."

Many of those who most harshly condemn World Bank-directed privatizations are quick to assert that they are not detractors of privatization per se. For example, Brendan Martin, author of *In the Public Interest? Privatization and Public Sector Reform*, says,

> The global privatization drive has been guided by a dogmatic ideological insistence that the market is better than the state at allocating resources and the private sector can run anything better than the public sector. It has been able to happen in part because the opposition to it has all too often fallen into the trap of simply reversing these propositions equally rigidly.

Martin, whose London-based organization Public World monitors and analyzes privatization and public sector reform worldwide, asserts:

> The point is that privatization can and indeed must contribute to establishing a balance of state, market and society. It can help to improve sustainable economic performance, combat poverty and give people more control over their local industrial and agricultural development. In practice, however, it is having the opposite effect because it is serving an opposite agenda -- that of concentrating wealth with the transnational corporations, income with elites and power with remote bodies and individuals far from the reach of political accountability.

Mexico: Privatizing Monopoly

Mexico was one of the early countries to undertake a large-scale privatization scheme under the World Bank's tutelage. In 1986, with the government itself turning to a neoliberal economic agenda, the deeply indebted country assented to demands from the Bank and other financial institutions to undergo a major restructuring of its economic policies, including an extensive privatization program.

The Mexican privatization program, developed with the advice of the World Bank, failed in many ways to meet the objectives the Bank and the government had defined at the outset of the program. Instead of distributing wealth, improving efficiency and breaking up monopolies, says Carlos Heredia, an ex-deputy director of international economics in Mexico's Ministry of Finance and now director of international programs at Equipo PUEBLO, a Mexican non-governmental organization, "Mexican privatization basically transformed public monopolies into private ones." Heredia asserts, "Privatization has worsened the already steep concentration of wealth in the country. Along with structural adjustment policies in general, privatization has benefited the friends of President Carlos Salinas."

Privatization in Mexico was supposed to improve the fiscal situation of the new government, demonstrate the government's commitment to the private sector, improve the efficiency of enterprises, eliminate monopolies and improve the quality of public service. "The government has achieved the first two goals," Heredia says, "but the last three have largely been forgotten." *El Financiero*, a Mexican daily newspaper, reported in December 1992 that a large number of privatized industries have seen efficiency fall, monopolies maintained and serious financial problems exacerbated.

One of the largest privatized enterprises is *Telefonos de Mexico* (Telmex), which the government sold to a Mexican firm headed by Carlos Slim, a close political ally of Salinas. "The privatization of Telmex," Heredia says, "illustrates how Mexican privatization has benefited a few private capitalists at the expense of consumers." Since privatization, consumers' telephone bills have skyrocketed, and, according to Equipo PUEBLO, Telmex has not managed to improve services.

The World Bank recently subjected some results of the privatization of Telmex to an econometrics model, devised by Galal and others, who claim it reveals the overall effects on a country's economic welfare. According to Galal, who managed the project, the researchers concluded, "In the case of Telmex, the bottom line is positive. The Mexican economy was better off with the privatization of Telmex." In response to assertions that the privatization of Telmex has hurt consumers, Galal says, "You have the winners and the losers -- among these actors are government, the consumers, the workers. We do have numerical values as to who won how much. It is true that in the case of

Telmex consumers were worse off and that is probably okay from an economist's point of view."

Martin is critical of this type of research and methodology. He says, "The Bank assigns numerical values to the interests of various categories of people -- workers, service users, shareholders, and so on -- which at best are totally arbitrary and at worst reflect existing inequalities. Then they say if the gains of the rich are greater than the losses of the poor, the welfare of society as a whole has improved."

Hungary: A Multinational Feeding Frenzy

Hungary's privatization program, like that of Mexico, has resulted in a massive transfer and reallocation of power. Yet, unlike the Mexican experience, in which assets were transferred primarily to local conglomerates, the Hungarian experience has been marked by a massive transfer of wealth to foreign multinationals. As is the case in many Third World and East European countries, Hungary's industrial and service sectors need investment and could benefit from more efficient management and production structures. The divestiture of public enterprises is central to the post-communist Hungarian government's policy. The World Bank, however, has played a substantial role in determining the pace and structure of the country's privatization program, loaning Hungary $200 million in April 1992, for example, on the condition that the government meet highly specific privatization targets.

By 1992, significant sectors of the Hungarian economy, including brewing, cement, glass, bread, vegetable oil, sugar confectionery, paper and refrigerators were in the hands of foreign multinational corporations. In 1991, nine of the largest ten privatizations went to Western multinational corporations. Eighty-five percent of privatization proceeds came from foreign investors. Multinationals, including Electrolux, Unilever and General Electric, have plucked attractive state enterprises.

This concentration of ownership in the hands of foreign multinationals has upset many Hungarian citizens. Facing plummeting popularity and public alarm over the level of foreign control over the economy, in early 1993, the government began to institute policies designed to favor Hungarian investors over foreign ones in future privatizations. By May 1993, purchases of state enterprises by Hungarians outnumbered those by foreigners.

Nevertheless, Hungary's privatization program continues to be plagued by controversy. In May 1993, Imre Korosi, a member of parliament for the Hungarian Democratic Forum, the country's largest coalition party, charged that the nation's privatization minister, Tamas Szabo, was in charge of a "destructive privatization process." In June, the country's State Privatization Agency (SPA) launched an investigation into allegations of fraud, blackmail and bribery during previous sales, announcing that it will investigate over 400 separate incidents of possible criminal malpractice.

Disputes over the role of foreign investors, despite the government's recent reforms, are also ongoing. Public outrage erupted following revelations that the Hungarian American Enterprise Fund (HAEF), a U.S. investment fund, was paying part of the salary of the chair of the AVRT, a state holding company. The chair, Paul Teleki, was earning $130,000 per year, an amount that far exceeds the salary that AVRT alone would have provided him. He resigned effective July 1, 1993, in the wake of publicity about HAEF's payments.

The fact that a U.S. fund, with a significant interest in facilitating the purchase of Hungarian assets, subsidized the salary of the person who was in charge of half the nation's business portfolio outraged many Hungarians. But the president of the HAEF, Alexander Tomlinson, says he saw nothing wrong in the arrangement. "We agreed to supplement [Teleki's] salary in order that he be able to take the job," he said. "We were able to do this because we have a certain amount of money allocated to technical assistance." He adds that the HAEF concluded that "we would have no reason to do business with them [AVRT] because we are dealing with small companies, and they are dealing with big companies. If it [a conflict of interest] did arise, we would make sure that we didn't act in such a way that we would take advantage of some kind of a conflict. We've had no business with them so far."

Kenya: Confusion and Corruption

Privatization has been a feature of World Bank structural adjustment loans to Kenya since 1983, when the Bank asked the government to consider the privatization of its maize marketing board. In order to receive desperately needed aid to help repay its mounting debts, Kenya implemented market-friendly economic policies designed to boost exports. It lowered exchange rates and cut social services. It has also slowly begun to privatize state-owned enterprises.

"The Bank's strategy has been extremely short-sighted," asserts Jasper Okelo of the Kenyan Economic Association. "It has failed to acknowledge the important role state-owned enterprises have played in the Kenyan economy." After independence in 1963, indigenous

Kenyans lacked the capital and the experience to take over the enterprises left by the colonists. The new government set up the Industrial and Commercial Development Corporation and the Kenya Industrial Estates to help Kenyans enter business. Okelo contends, "When assessed in terms of efficiency and profitability, many of these firms have not been great successes. However, when they are assessed in terms of their original goals these firms have been relatively successful. They have succeeded in helping Kenyans participate in industrial and agricultural development and increased employment opportunities."

Furthermore, some studies indicate that Kenyan parastatals perform better than private enterprises on a range of economic indicators. A recent study of Kenya's industrial sector by Kenyan researcher Barbara Grosh found that, by sector, Kenyan parastatals were generally less protected and more profitable and efficient than private firms. Citing Grosh's research, Susie Ibutu of the National Council of Churches of Kenya told a conference on the social impact of structural adjustment in November 1991 that the "advantages of privatization have been supposed rather than based on Kenya's experience."

Interested in obtaining information on the impact of privatization on the vulnerable poor and in opening up discussion on alternatives to privatization, Ibutu distributed a questionnaire to representatives of non-governmental organizations and religious institutions. Ibutu reported that most respondents felt that privatization had the potential of releasing state resources so that government could "do what it does best" -- provide social services. The respondents believed that any privatization program should be blended with a commitment to increase employment, improve efficiency, facilitate more involvement by indigenous Kenyans in the economy and transfer skills and technology. According to those who responded to Ibutu's questionnaire along with many others, the Kenyan privatization program and advice from the World Bank have failed to meet or even address these goals.

Some Kenyan members of parliament have also been extremely critical of the country's privatization program. On November 6, 1991, members of parliament charged that the government's Ministry of Privatization was guilty of corruption and that the country's privatization program was a conduit for transferring money out of the country. They also complained that government sales have been made to parties lacking managerial capacity and that state-owned enterprises have been shut down without authority.

A Head-in-the-Sand Policy

Community groups, government officials, trade unions, academics and even the UNDP have criticized the way in which the last decade's wave of privatization has been carried out under the World Bank's direction. Despite widespread evidence that privatization has undermined communities, transferred power to remote bodies, concentrated wealth and income and contributed to growing poverty in many countries throughout the world, the Bank continues to pressure countries to embark on massive privatization programs.

The UNDP's 1993 *World Development Report* asserts that the impact of privatization on human development has been given minimal attention by those intent on promoting it. The Bank's research concentrates on the macro-economic impact of these policies at the expense of providing comprehensive assessment of the impact of these policies on human welfare and communities.

Galal responds, "With every public policy you have a debate going both ways. You have those guys that like it and they are going to support it no matter what, and the guys that oppose it. And they are going to oppose it no matter what."

But Brendan Martin argues that a more nuanced view is called for. "The trouble is that the debate has been polarized between whether or not privatization in general is a good or a bad thing," he says. "That misses the point, because neither public nor private ownership and control is necessarily right for every sector in every time. Like any other policy instrument, much depends on what privatization is designed to achieve and whose interests it is intended to serve."

19

International Institutions Practicing Environmental Double Standards
Vandana Shiva

S tatements and reports from the World Bank indicate that this *Northern-dominated international agency does not view the global environmental crisis in terms of a "common future," but in terms of environmental apartheid in which the North grows richer and cleaner and the South grows poorer and more polluted. The World Bank economist mentioned at the beginning of the article, Lawrence Summers, has since moved on to a job as President Clinton's top international economist at the Treasury Department.*

Lawrence Summers, who was the World Bank's Chief Economist and is responsible for the 1992 *World Development Report* devoted to the economics of the environment, has suggested that it makes economic sense to shift polluting industries to the Third World countries. In a memo to senior World Bank staff dated 12 December 1991, the Chief Economist wrote, "Just between you and me, shouldn't the World Bank be encouraging more migration of the dirty industries to the LDCs [less developed countries]?"

Summers has justified his economic logic of increasing pollution in the Third World on the following grounds. Firstly, since wages are low in the Third World, economic costs of pollution arising from increased illness and death are lowest in the poorest countries. Summers thinks "that the economic logic behind dumping a load of toxic waste in the lowest wage country is impeccable, and we should face up to that."

Secondly, since in large parts of the Third World, pollution is still low, it makes economic sense to Summers to introduce pollution. "I've always thought," he says, that "under-populated countries in Africa are vastly under-polluted; their air quality is probably vastly inefficiently low compared to Los Angeles or Mexico City."

Finally, since the poor are poor, they cannot possibly worry about environmental problems. "The concern over an agent that causes a one-in-a-million change in the odds of prostate cancer is obviously going to be much higher in a country where people survive to get prostate cancer than in a country where under-five mortality is 200 per thousand."

The World Bank apologized for Summers' memo. But that does not alter the fact that the World Bank has, in fact, been financing the relocation of pollution-intensive industry to the Third World. As steel plants close in the North, the Bank helps the expansion of steel manufacturing in India. It has financed the displacement of millions of tribals to build the Challdil and Icha dams of the Suvernarekha project and to support the expansion of the Tata's Steel Plant at Jamshedpur.

It continues to finance super thermal power plants to facilitate the relocation of energy-intensive industry to the Third World. When fertilizer surpluses grew in America, the World Bank gave credit to push chemical fertilizers on India.

The World Bank's practice shows that Summers' memo is not an aberration, but is consistent with the vision of an environmental apartheid, separate development for the North and South. The North benefits in four ways from this arrangement of apartheid.

Firstly, Northern businesses are able to sell, through so-called "transfer of technology" financed by loans and debts, obsolete production systems and products, which they would otherwise have to dump because of stricter environmental regulations at home.

Secondly, Northern banks, including the multilateral development banks like the World Bank, are able to make interest on loans and credits given for the transfer of environmentally unsound technology.

Thirdly, the resultant financial debts give the North more political and economic control over the Third World through International Monetary Fund (IMF) conditionalities and structural adjustment loans, which push the Third World further into debt.

Finally, the increased pollution and environmental degradation in the Third World is also used as a new reason for control through green conditionalities.

The Third World is thus pushed inexorably into deeper debt, deeper poverty, deeper environmental degradation and deeper erosion of its sovereignty and democratic structures. The malaise that allows these processes to grow is not limited to one economist like Summers or one agency like the World Bank.

Apartheid seems to have become the way of thinking of all the dominant powers of the North. Apartheid is, in the final analysis, a racist world view that moralizes injustice on grounds of the false assumption of the superior status of the white race and the inferiority of the rest of us. We can be polluted and poisoned because we are lesser beings in the eyes and minds of those who want to rule the world. A brown or black child does not deserve the same protection from health and environmental hazards because he or she is not white.

This apartheid philosophy is fast emerging as the ruling philosophy in the North. It finds its echo in a paper by Dr. Maurice King's in the *Lancet,* in which he recommends that health care should be removed from children in the Third World and that they should be allowed to die because Third World populations are a burden on the planet. Apartheid is also the underlying philosophy of the report from the General Agreement on Tariffs and Trade (GATT) on Trade and the Environment.

On the face of it, GATT's report opposes environmental imperialism. It refers to the recent GATT ruling against a U.S. decision to ban imports of Mexican Yellowfin tuna because fishing methods led to the deaths of dolphins that swim about the tuna shoals. The GATT ruling says, "A country may not restrict imports of a product solely because it originates in a country whose environmental policies are different." GATT says that "countries are not clones of each other. They have a sovereign right to declare different environmental priorities and policies."

However, when it comes to intellectual property rights (IPRs) and patents, GATT insists on a uniform law globally. IPRs are in effect instruments of control over biological resources and biodiversity that are concentrated in the Third World. When applied to living resources and life forms, they are ultimately laws about the environment.

GATT's report is, in reality, the recipe for an environmental apartheid. The report on Trade and the Environment appears to be against protectionism in the North, but environmental laws are treated uniformly and as being "global" when they relate to controlling the resources of the Third World. All countries are treated as clones of each other in the case of patents on life forms. On the other hand, when environmental laws relate to pollution and hazards, the Third World is treated differently. "National Sovereignty" is used to justify the localization of pollution in the Third World, but "National Sovereignty" is sacrificed to justify the globalization of access to the biological wealth of the Third World.

The environmental "bads" inherited from the North are thus made the South's exclusive legacy. Environmental "goods" like biodiversity, which have been the South's heritage in the past, are transformed into a "global heritage of mankind."

Some Third World elites and governments will be happy with this arrangement of apartheid because it allows them to participate in the robbery of people's resources, and it frees them of social responsibility to protect their fellow citizens from pollution and other environmental hazards. They have taken the resources from local communities. The pollution they invite will not be theirs to suffer. A part of the South will thus be jubilant as this face-saving device of "National Sovereignty" is used for "free" export or resources from South to North and "free" import or pollution from North to South.

The words "freedom" and "protection" have been robbed of their humane meaning and are being absorbed into the double-speak of corporate jargon. With double-speak comes a double standard, one for citizens and one for corporations, one for corporate responsibility and one for corporate profits, one for the North and one for the South.

The U.S. is most sophisticated in the practice of double standards and the destruction of people's rights to health and safety in the Third World. On the one hand, it aims at regulating safeguards within its own geographical boundaries, while on the other hand, through Super 301 [the U.S. law that allows for penalties against foreign goods sold in the U.S. below costs of production], it aims at destroying the Indian Patents Act of 1970 and replacing it with a strong U.S.-style system of patent protection, which is heavily biased in favor of the industrially developed countries.

The World Bank and GATT consider the transnationals' lack of patent protection as unfair trading practice. It does not consider the destruction of regulations for public safety and environmental protection as unethical and unfair for the citizens of the Third World. The Northern agencies want to limit and localize laws for the protection of people and universalize laws for the protection of profits. The people of India want the reverse -- a universalization of the safety regulations protecting people's livelihoods and right to live and a localization of laws relating to intellectual property and private profits.

All life is precious. It is equally precious to the rich and the poor, whites and blacks, men and women. Universalization of the protection of life is an ethical imperative. On the other hand, private property and private profits are culturally and socio-economically legitimized constructs holding only for some groups. They do not hold for all societies and all cultures. Laws for the protection of private property rights, especially as related to life forms, cannot and should not be imposed globally. They need to be restrained.

Double standards also exist in the shift from private gain to social responsibility for environmental costs. When the patenting of life is at issue, arguments stemming from the concept of "novelty" are used. Novelty requires that the subject matter of a patent be new, that it be the result of an inventive step, and not something existing in nature. On the other hand, when it comes to legislative safeguards, the focus of the argument shifts to the concept of "similarity," to establishing that biotechnology products and genetically engineered organisms differ little from parent organisms.

To have one law for environmental responsibility and another for proprietary rights and profits is an expression of double standards. Double standards are ethically unjustified and illegitimate, especially when they deal with life itself. However, double standards are consistent with and necessary for the defense of private property rights. It is these double standards that allow the lives and livelihoods of the people and the planet to be sacrificed for the protection of profits.

And it is these double standards that support the emergence of an environmental apartheid in which the last resources of the poor are taken over by the rich, and the poor are pushed into "pollution reservations" to live with waste. They themselves are treated as waste, to be dispensed with either through poisoning and pollution, as Lawrence Summers has suggested, or through population control and denial of health care to children, as Maurice King has suggested.

An environmental order that is full of contempt for the poor of the Third World and tries to rob them even of their right to life cannot be the basis of our common future.

20

World Bank Takes Control of UNCED's Environment Fund
Patience Idemudia and Kole Shettima

n an effort to promote its environmental profile, the World Bank's 1992 World Development Report was devoted to the theme of Development and the Environment. The following article evaluates the Report's analysis from an African perspective.

"Our lifestyle is not up for negotiation."
George Bush

The 1992 World Development Report, *Development and the Environment*, makes a number of claims about the environmental problems facing developing countries. Like the economic debt, the environmental debt is erroneously placed on the shoulders of the poorest countries.

According to the report, the most important and immediate problems facing developing countries are overpopulation, unsafe water, inadequate sanitation, soil depletion, indoor smoke from cooking fires and outdoor smoke from coal fires. While these issues do figure in the environmental equation, the report virtually ignores the practices of industrialized countries that have contributed to the present crisis: carbon dioxide emission, depletion of the stratosphere and ozone layer, photochemical smog, acid rain and hazardous waste management.

The report also fails to discuss the relationship between current economic development policies and their environmental impact. Rather than address the fundamental disparities between rich and poor countries or the need for a fundamental redistribution of the world's assets, the report simplistically claims that overbreeding by uneducated women and deforestation by ignorant farmers are the major environmental problems plaguing developing countries.

Shifting the Blame

> *"The onus of adjustment is seen to lie on the South and so is the guilt of failure whilst the responsibility of the North in this adjustment is finance and supervision."*

Charles Abugre (Ghana)

It is ironic that population increase is seen as the root cause of environmental degradation. While peoples of the Third World consume only 20 percent of world resources, Western populations (which make up only 16 percent of the world's population and 24 percent of its land) consume approximately 80 percent of the world's resources. In fact, the average North American consumes more energy commuting to work in a week than the average African uses in an entire year. Furthermore, it is estimated that Western countries are responsible for producing over 75 percent of the world's environmental pollution.

The report also attempts to place the blame for the destruction of precious vegetation solely on the peoples of developing countries. It is not the Third World peoples who are destroying their vegetation for the construction of large-scale industries; it is the multinational corporations who are looking for cheaper and greener pastures to exploit for maximum capitalist gains. A recent study conducted by the UN Center on Transnational Corporations concluded that the activities of transnationals "generate more than half of the greenhouse gases emitted by the six industrial sectors with the greatest impact on global warming." For its efforts, the Center was abolished during the recent U.S.-led restructuring of the United Nations.

The peoples of the Third World have traditionally relied on indigenous ways of cultivating crops for feeding their families without damaging the environment. The exploitation of the environment began when colonialism forced the hands of the conquered people of the Third World into the production of export cash-crops that were not indigenous to the soil. Most of the crops and imported production schemes depleted the soil faster than the indigenous food crops.

In view of this evidence there is a need to reexamine the excessive focus on population growth and the so-called ignorance of farmers, and instead, focus on other issues of global environmental and economic justice.

The World Bank Recipe: More SAPs

The World Bank resorts to its standard menu of market-oriented solutions to solve the environmental crisis. Their key policy advice to developing countries: continue to implement Structural Adjustment Programs (SAPs). The key recommendations of the Report are aimed at increasing the role of the market, privatization of land ownership and increased efficiency of labor. By liberalizing their economies, the report argues, poor countries will be able to increase their output dramatically. While greater pollution will occur at first, "rising income will make environmental protection affordable and such protection will enable future income growth."

This vision of economic growth and market-driven environmental protection is offered along with other nuggets of wisdom, such as the importance of improving education for girls. While better education for girls is a laudable goal, the implementation of World Bank supported policies has had the exact opposite effect. Because of the introduction of education user fees -- a standard SAP measure -- most families have had to reduce the number of children they send to school.

There is also a need to carefully examine the high-tech solutions that the World Bank is promoting in its environmental blueprint. The questions that need to be asked are:

• Who stands to benefit from the use of high-tech inputs, farmers or agribusinesses?

• Are the needs of women farmers, who produce over 90 percent of Africa's food, going to benefit from SAP-oriented solutions?

• Are inputs such as herbicides and pesticides contributing to soil depletion and environmental degradation?

Continuing to ignore these questions will mean that the interests of the poor will not be served by the proposed solutions. Instead, the implementation of the World Bank's recommendations may lead to the demise of the majority of the poor and to a form of genocide to achieve the "desired" population control.

SAPs and the African Environment

The current international division of labor casts most African countries as exporters of raw materials: cash crops (cotton, cocoa, coffee), minerals (oil, bauxite, coal, gold) and agro-forestry products (timber, wood). The reimposition of this pattern of development through the policies of SAPs has had serious environmental impacts. Export-led growth based on the exploitation of raw materials has led to creeping "savannization" of the forest, "sahelization" of the savanna and the "desertification" of the Sahel.

For example, Burkina Faso, Mali, Senegal, Niger and Chad increased their harvest cotton fiber from 22.7 million tons in 1961-62 to

154 million tons in 1983-84 during the height of the Sahel famine. In the same year, however, they imported a record of 1.77 million tons of cereal, nine times more than was imported in the 1960s.

The introduction of trade liberalization policies has also had serious environmental implications. Essentially, Africa has become a dumping ground for goods that are contaminated, expired and hazardous.

Trade liberalization involves the removal of most restrictions on imports to facilitate foreign investment. In order to attract foreign business, many African countries have created free trade zones, simplified the process of investment and introduced new industrial policies. Consequently, products that cannot meet Northern environmental guidelines are dumped in the continent, and pollution-intensive production like asbestos and pulp and paper have shifted their base to Africa. The suggestion by former World Bank chief economist Lawrence Summers (lead author of the report) that African countries import toxic wastes and polluting industries is already commonplace in many African countries.

The dumping of toxic waste in the continent can be traced to the struggle to gain foreign exchange to make debt payments and to the liberalization of trade, both of which are conditions of SAPs. In an environment of lax import controls and the virtual collapse of many governments, Africa has become the new site of toxic dumping. Although these products could be dumped more safely in the North, it is more costly to do so. Dumping costs between $160 to $1000 per ton (for the most dangerous waste, between $2000-3000 per ton) but Benin was offered $2.50 per ton!

Diversification of exports, which has become the catch-phrase in the era of SAPs, has also resulted in environmental abuses. In Cameroon, 150 licensed timber operating companies, of which 23 are indigenous, are involved in commercial logging. Africa's SAP "miracle," Ghana, passed a law that provided for numerous investment incentives. Between 1985 and 1989 the number of independent logging companies skyrocketed from 90 to over 800. Some estimate that Ghana will have depleted its forests by the year 2000 if current trends continue. Namibia's department of sea fisheries is involved in the genocide of seals about to be exported to the Far East. According to the Namibia Animal Action Group, the first year mortality rate of seals is as high as 90 percent.

Sadly, the companies and governments involved are preoccupied with the short-term benefits and do not take into consideration the sustainability of their activities. When the environment is abused beyond any profitability, they pack up and leave. Poor farmers, whose lands were taken, have to contend with the menace of erosion, deforestation, drought, famine and communal violence. Pastoralists fight endlessly with peasant farmers over grazing lands.

The gender implications of these activities are quite clear in Africa, where women are the major farmers and providers of fuel wood and water. And yet, the World Bank prefers to blame them for having too many children rather than reexamine their own policies, which have pushed women, the poor and the entire global environment to the very brink of survival.

An Alternative Approach

"The key issue for UNCED is the reform of the World Bank and IMF."

Martin Khor, Third World Network

It is clear that the interests of the global environment and its inhabitants will not be well served by the World Bank. The countries of the South and their allies in the North must lobby hard for the democratization of the World Bank and the Global Environment Facility. In its present form, the World Bank cannot and should not be allowed to control an agenda on which the entire fate of the world depends.

Rather than promote high-tech, market-oriented solutions to the environmental problems facing African countries, approaches are needed that will enhance the role of small-scale farmers. These include the transfer and support of appropriate technology, such as fuel-efficient stoves, waste-to-fuel wood schemes and solar energy. Most importantly, the lack of a just resolution of the debt problem is the single most important cause of environmental destruction and poverty. In resolving the debt burden and addressing the more fundamental issues of global disparity, we recognize the close relationship that exists between our global economic system, the environment, the protection of indigenous peoples and the satisfaction of our basic needs.

21

The World Bank and Tribal Peoples
Survival International

The World Bank embarks on about 250 new projects every year. Having identified which aspects of a country's economy are in need of "development," the Bank looks for projects that will fulfill preselected economic criteria.

Many of the projects that evolve from Bank planning (such as agriculture projects, rural development, water projects, mining and road-building) are in ecologically vulnerable areas. Since it is Bank policy to "develop" previously isolated regions and untapped resources, the Bank's projects have a major impact on tribal peoples whose lands these are.

Big Projects -- Big Mistakes

The manner in which these projects are designed and selected means that they are structurally incapable of being properly adjusted to tribal peoples' needs and demands. Selection is on macro-economic grounds, hence tribal peoples' interests, when considered at all, are from the start subordinated to the wider plan. Concern for local peoples and for environments likely to be affected by projects is typically deferred to the latest phases of the "project cycle."

Also, because it costs as much in staff support services to administer a small project as a large one, the Bank automatically favors large projects. Regional staff are under heavy pressure anyway from the Bank to move large amounts of capital, further encouraging the trend toward more and more ambitious schemes. When the Bank's projects go wrong, they go wrong on a disastrous scale, causing massive social and environmental ruin.

Brazil: A Lesson Unlearned

In December 1981, the World Bank signed an agreement with the government of Brazil to provide a loan of $320 million (later increased to nearly $500 million) as partial funding for the Polonoroeste Program in west-central Brazil. This was to be a large-scale "integrated regional development" program, involving the all-weather paving of highway BR-364, the building of a vast network of secondary and feeder roads, agricultural colonization projects and forestry development. No less than 60 Indian groups with a total population of over 9,000 live in the Polonoroeste region.

Pro-Indian activists and environmentalists mounted a major international campaign opposing those aspects of the Polonoroeste plan that would mean serious environmental degradation and waste of natural resources and a harmful impact on the lives and livelihoods of the Indian populations. Their warnings proved all too well-founded: in the course of 1983 and 1984 there were reports of disastrous deforestation, invasions of Indian areas and outbreaks of violence between settlers and Indians. The situation became so bad that, in the corridors of the World Bank itself, the Polonoroeste was being talked of as "the worst development fiasco of the last ten years." he project became the principal example of failing development in an unprecedented series of hearings held in the U.S. Congress on projects funded by the multilateral development banks.

In early 1985, the Bank finally stopped disbursement of funds to Brazil until the Brazilian Government met a number of loan conditions having to do with protection of the environment and the Indian populations. Unfortunately, in only a few months, the Bank declared itself satisfied that things had improved enough for it to resume disbursement of funds.

This is far from being the case. Survival International has maintained since 1980 that demarcation and registration of Indian lands should be a precondition of any funding, and a Bank official has admitted, "Either these lands are demarcated and defended now, or the Indians will disappear within four or five years."

Medical services to the Indians in the region have deteriorated drastically and, in some areas, have come to a complete standstill; Indians suffering from introduced diseases such as tuberculosis are often without treatment of any kind.

The World Bank has let four years go by, and only now are things even approaching an acceptable level as regards appropriate protection against the life-threatening effects of the ill-designed Polonoroeste Program.

In spite of this experience, the World Bank proceeded to fund another large-scale development project in the Amazon region, the Carajas iron ore project, which threatens at least 5,000 Indians whose lands are being flooded and invaded. The Bank has provided $304.5 million for this scheme to extract iron ore from a massive deposit in the Eastern Amazonian state of Para and transport it by electric railway to the north coast.

Already, the Assurini, Parakana, Xikrin and Gavioes who inhabit the region have suffered compulsory relocation, decimation due to venereal infections introduced by construction crews, water-associated diseases and disorders arising from the use of toxic defoliants. Other communities, such as the Surui and Gavioes of Mae Maria, are losing land and are suffering disruption of their hunting, gathering and farming.

Broken "Support"

The World Bank clearly had in mind the protests and objections made to the Polonoroeste Program when it announced that it was funding an official scheme of "Support for the Indigenous Communities" of the Carajas Project, to be administered by the government Indian agency, FUNAI. However, the Bank has clearly learned nothing from the experience of working with FUNAI on the Polonoroeste program. A mere 1.6 percent of the $13.6 million allowed to the "Indian component" has been allocated for the purpose of demarcating tribal lands. However, FUNAI is neither able nor willing to demarcate tribal territories without external support and pressure. It has spent most of this sum on administration and agricultural projects designed to sustain its own internal bureaucracy and to create an economic infrastructure. As in the case of Polonoroeste, the recommendations of the independent anthropologists appointed to advise the agency have been systematically ignored or overruled.

Among the peoples worst hit by the Polonoroeste project are the Nambiquara Indians, who inhabit the forest and savannah margins in northwestern Mato Grosso and southern Rondonia. They live by gardening and hunting, in small communities generally consisting of groups of brothers and their families, who are linked to other villages in the vicinity by marriage ties and through trading.

The entry of settlers into the region has proved disastrous to the Nambiquara. Decimated by introduced diseases, their lands taken over by ranchers, they have been totally disorientated by the clash of cultures. When they resist the takeover of their lands, they are shot and killed, and when they do not, they fall into dependence on the invaders, the women as prostitutes, the men as cheap labor.

In late 1985, an almost uncontacted group in the Corumbiara valley was attacked by local ranchers. At least ten Indians were killed and their cemeteries, gardens and houses destroyed.

World Bank's Tribal Policy: Rhetoric and Reality

In 1982, after it had sustained heavy criticism for the shattering effects of its projects on the tribal peoples of the Philippines and Amazonia, the World Bank announced its adoption of new policy guidelines for implementing projects in tribal areas, which were set out in its new publication *Tribal Peoples and Economic Development.*

According to this publication, the Bank will not carry out projects affecting tribal peoples, "unless the tribal society is in agreement with the project." Rejecting policies that seek forcibly to integrate tribal peoples with the national society or isolate them from it, the document proposed "an intermediate policy of self-determination" and made special provisions to ensure respect for land rights, ethnic identity and cultural autonomy.

The rhetoric sounds fine, but the reality, since then, has been sadly different. Many, perhaps the majority, of the Bank's projects in tribal areas have been undertaken against the will of the peoples affected. They have led to the rapid takeover of tribal lands and the destruction of identity and autonomy. Some projects have even led to the virtual extinction of whole communities, as among the Surui and Nambiquara in Brazil.

Challenged to explain the gap between its published policies and its practice, the Bank has progressively tried to distance itself from its own publication. Finally, in September 1986, one of the Bank's top lawyers publicly announced to a Committee of the International Labor Organization in Geneva that the published policies are not those it observes.

The Bank's real policy regarding tribal peoples, he revealed, is described in a confidential document that is not publicly available. This document, which became available to Survival International, reveals a somewhat weakened resolve on the Bank's part. According to the document, projects should be designed "to mitigate undesired social effects," and the Bank's commitment to the principle of self determination, with the corresponding right of tribal peoples to veto projects on their lands, has vanished.

Yet, weak as they are, the Bank's "real" policies remain vastly superior to its practice. Only by changing this can the Bank show that it does indeed have at heart the interests of "the poorest of the poor."

Campaigning for Change

Survival International started its campaign against multilateral projects on tribal lands in 1975. The campaign, reinforced by environmentalist groups concerned for the fate of fragile tropical ecosystems, has now begun to bite hard.

In 1985, the international protests received further support when their criticisms were substantially endorsed by members of the U.S. Senate. The resulting furor forced the Bank to briefly suspend loans to the Polonoroeste project in Brazil. Further lobbying by Survival International on behalf of the 60,000 tribal people to be displaced by the Narmada Valley hydropower scheme in India caused the British Prime Minister, Margaret Thatcher, to raise our concerns with the World Bank. The Bank delayed disbursements while a team was sent out to improve the project's resettlement program.

Meanwhile, the Washington-based lobby groups, with the assistance of members of the U.S. Senate, forced legislation through Congress that tied U.S. contributions to the Banks to a package of reforms designed to improve the social and environmental performance of Bank projects.

Recommended Reforms

Survival International, besides calling for a halt to certain particularly bad projects, has urged reforms in the basic project cycle.

We demand:

Openness in the formulation of projects and the provision of free access to information about them.

That tribal and other local peoples be given control over the design and implementation of the projects that affect them.

That tribal and other local peoples be the prime beneficiaries of projects that affect them, as far as possible.

That the emphasis in projects be on self-sustainable development as far as possible.

That the Bank provide funds where appropriate for the demarcation of tribal lands.

That the Bank's Office of Environment and Scientific Affairs (which is responsible for ecological and indigenous questions) be assigned more staff.

That observation of human rights be made a precondition of Bank projects.

22

Fury Over a River
Pradeep S. Mehta

On paper, it promised to be India's Tennessee Valley: the Sardar-Sarovar Project (SSP) for the benefit of one of the dryest areas of the Indian subcontinent -- the Kutch, Saurashtra and north Gujarat -- brought to mind images of water for drinking and for irrigating parched lands through a network of dams and canals. But while they talked of obliterating the images of pain in India's dry regions, the planners of what was called the biggest ever "temple of modern India" took for granted the 800,000 indigenous people who have for centuries inhabited the lands to be submerged.

India's first prime minister, Jawaharlal Nehru, wanted the indigenous people, the inevitable refugees of development, to put national interest before their own. But after scores of dams built during the past five decades displaced an estimated 30 million people all over the country, the anti-dam movement, scattered in numerous peripheral groups across India, has come together to resist.

The dam holding back conflict over models and parameters of "development" burst when the Indian government and its partner in the project, the World Bank, parted ways. Under intense international pressure, sources within the Bank were increasingly calling for a reassessment of the project. A peeved Indian government decided in March 1993 to forego the undisbursed $170 million portion of the $450 million in assistance committed by the Bank.

"It is actually a case of sour grapes," says Medha Patkar, the frail woman heading the Narmada Bachao Andolan (NBA, the Save Narmada Movement). "The World Bank-appointed independent review mission [headed by former UNDP administrator Bradford Morse] vindicated our position that [dam planners allowed] considerations of engineering [to] supersede the implications to life and livelihood of *Adivasis.*"

Adivasis, or "ancient people," are the oldest inhabitants of India. They have long been marginalized by the "new people" and forced to live difficult lives in forests. Patkar, winner of the Right Livelihood Award (also known as the Alternative Nobel Prize) and the Goldman environmental award, points out that "the mission attacked the Bank and the Indian government for not coming up with detailed data on the population to be displaced." Pathar explains,

> The Bank, who was eager to go ahead even at a high human cost, was cornered. The Indian government, which still basically considers environmental issues to be non-sense when weighed against prospects of running water and electricity, now prefers to bury its head in jargons like "self-reliance." Ironically, this was farthest from their minds when the decision was taken to implement this highly unscientific and unsuitable project.

The Narmada movement is bringing the development dilemma to every household across the length and breadth of the subcontinent, asking who are to be the beneficiaries of "progress." Unlike the immediate post-independence generation that was seduced by the Nehruvian model of big factories, bigger irrigation projects and state control of key industries, today's intelligentsia are increasingly questioning the premise that the human and environmental costs of development can be ignored.

Significantly, Nehru's grandson, Rajiv Gandhi, India's prime minister from 1985 to 1989, first introduced the idea of evaluating development projects in ecological terms. But even he was bulldozed by the juggernaut of "progress." It was during his tenure, in April 1989, that the green light was given to the Narmada Valley Project (NVP), the consolidated project integrating three distinct ventures -- the Narmada Valley Development Project, the Narmada Sagar Project (NSP) and the SSP.

Since 1947, the year of India's independence, the largest river project in the world had been caught in various deadlocks, mostly for reasons of financial paucity. Until 1979, it was also bogged down in interstate disputes between Gujarat, Maharashtra and Madhya Pradesh, all three large and populous central and western states of India, through which the Narmada flows.

The project finally began to move forward after the World Bank assured credit assistance representing 15 percent of the project cost. The entire project was to be spread over 30 large, 135 medium-sized and 3,000 small dams. Gujarat's (or SSP's) share of the cake was to be the greatest -- apart from dams and reservoirs, two giant hydroelectric power plants and a 75,000-kilometer canal network were to be built.

But the World Bank came under enormous international pressure to withdraw its support for the massive dam project. According to Lori

Udall, a staff attorney with the Environmental Defense Fund, the Narmada project had become known worldwide as the "test case" of the Bank's willingness and capability to adhere to its own environmental and social guidelines. "Narmada was only one example of the World Bank's negligence on environment and forcible resettlement of people."

Ultimately, the Bank came to rethink its support for Narmada, for reasons of political expedience or otherwise. After India decided to forego Bank assistance, World Bank president Lewis Preston said, "I think it was, alas, in everybody's interest. I think we would have had an awkward time if it had come to forcing a date because of the civil strain and stress that goes with the implementation of the time table. It was a sensible thing to do."

However, Bimal Jalan, India's executive director on the World Bank board, is confident the project will go forward without Bank support. "The Indian government will be able to go it alone." Patkar retorts that the federal and Gujarat governments are now fighting a "prestige battle." Muchkund Desai, an executive with the state corporation executing the project, says:

> The government had always claimed that it was committed to full implementation of the action plan on resettlement and rehabilitation of the population to be displaced by the project. The government contends that it still hopes to complete the SSP by the end of the decade at a cost of about $3 billion. Some financial assistance may be coming from expatriates. Rich Gujaratis settled in Europe, Africa and the United States have come together to establish funding consortiums for Narmada in the absence of World Bank aid.

Perhaps to indicate that it is serious, in August 1993, the government decided to go ahead with the flooding of the little cluster of villages called Manibeli, bordering Maharashtra. Patkar and her activists vowed to perform Jal Samadhi, sacrificial drowning in the water, as their ultimate protest.

The government's first response was to arrest opposition activists. But faced with mounting public outcry at the instances of police atrocities, the government was forced to announce a review of the project. Basically, it saw the impossibility of policing a 30 kilometer-wide front. Patkar herself proved elusive, and the government realized that if she was successful in making her suicide statement, the SSP was as good as lost.

The Indian federal government's pacific overture in offering to review the project gave rise to another dimension of the debate, however. The chief minister of Gujarat state, Chimanbhai Patel, notorious for his sympathies with the contractor interests behind the project, spoke out bitterly against the central government's mollification of the activists. "There can be no compromise, the SSP will be the lifeline of Gujarat," he asserted. The federal government views Patel as an important ally, and so, to soothe his nerves, it amended its statement.

The federal Water Resources Minister, V.C. Shukla, assured parliamentarians from the state in early August that any change in the basic design of the SSP can only be implemented with the consent of the state government. He also said that the so-called review will not significantly change the character of the SSP.

While wide cracks are appearing in the government's front, the opposition is experiencing major problems of its own. Together for years, the NBA has been a loose assortment of groups unified by a variety of concerns over the SSP. Some decried the project in ecological terms, while others concentrated on the combined seismic impact of all the reservoirs. The uncertainty shrouding the fate of the indigenous people offered an emotive chord to tie them together into a somewhat cohesive movement.

But now the government, which has gone through similar, albeit smaller-scale motions over the past five decades, is exploiting the vulnerability of the impoverished people to be affected by the project. The lure of "jobs" in the new project, cash compensation and dreams of proper homes right out of movies, have proven too much for many of them to resist. These promises often result in a sudden, though short-lived upward mobility in their lifestyles. Bandi Umrao, an *adivasi* villager to be affected eventually, is looking forward to an urban lifestyle complete with a motor scooter. "The government has also assured me a job in the project. A fixed salary is sometimes preferable to an uncertain life as a shepherd," he says.

Within their community, the displaced often become subjects of envy. With goodies like transistor radios, jewelry and simple household consumables becoming a reality, many look at leaders like Patkar as characters intent on keeping these objects out of their reach through alien concerns. The juxtaposition of this simple reasoning with allegations of "unholy pacts between giant global financial magnates and so-called environmentalists to keep India ever dependent," as raised by the leading pro-Narmada campaigner, Krishnaprasad Patel, give the government's stand a certain legitimacy.

23

The World Bank and the Feminization of Poverty
Inge Khoury

Among the trendy chapter headings, book titles and special new projects that came into vogue among the development set in the 1980s was "Women in Development." Once relegated to footnotes, women surged to the top of the topics-to-be-addressed lists of the aid industry. But beyond the colorful posters, special departments and patronizing literature, are women faring any better?

Halfway through the UN Decade for Women (1975-85), the World Bank published a report, *The World Bank and the World's Poorest*. Though its illustrations portrayed women, the text did not, referring instead to "small farmers," the "rural poor" and the "landless." One rare sentence alluded to the significant role women "may" play in food production (particularly in Africa), and the water supply chapter identified women as the principal drawers of water.

The poverty described in this report was scrupulously gender-neutral, despite the fact that women comprise over half the world's population, yet receive only 1 percent of world income and own less than 1 percent of world property. In 1980, these apparently were not sufficient grounds for women to merit special attention in the "world's poorest" category.

Times have changed, in the corridors of the World Bank and in development circles generally. If measured by the proliferation of Bank publications on the topic, the importance of women in development is increasingly recognized. There are other signs, too.

In 1975, there was one solitary advisor on Women in Development (WID) at the Bank. In 1987, a WID division was established, and women became a "special operations emphasis." The division was charged with integrating women's needs into the Bank's analytical work and lending. Last year, that division placed a coordinator in each of the Bank's four regional complexes.

And what are the results? Certainly there is a greater awareness of women's concerns as measured by an increase (from 11 percent in fiscal year 1988 to 40 percent in fiscal year 1991) in the number of Bank operations that include some specific actions to help women. Most of these actions, however, center on areas associated with women's traditional roles, such as population, health, nutrition and, to a lesser extent, on promoting female education.

In contrast to these lending practices, the WID rhetoric coming out of the Bank is that women should not be viewed as passive recipients of services, but rather as important economic actors who should be helped to increase their productivity. Women are even viewed as a good investment. In a recent address, the Bank's vice-president and chief economist, Lawrence Summers, commented on the subject. "Investment in the education of girls," he declared, "may well be the highest return investment in the developing world."

The World Bank has found that for every year of secondary schooling, women's wages are boosted by 10 to 20 percent, and their mortality and fertility decline by five to ten percent. The value of these benefits far exceed the cost of girls' education. A study in Kenya shows that female farmers with the same access as men to productive inputs, extension, credit and education produce about 2.8 percent more per hectare. Such facts provide an economic rationale for allocating funds to women for even the most profit-oriented of World Bankers.

The reality, however, is that the World Bank has a dismal record in investing in the productive capacity of the poor in general, especially poor women. Bank WID publications are full of sound statements on the importance of low-cost, consumption-oriented agriculture and of giving credit and other types of production assistance to women's groups, yet lending is increasingly concentrated in capital-intensive, export-oriented agriculture typically controlled by men.

Though Summers proclaimed the merit of investing in women's education, Bank-promoted structural adjustment lending systematically slashes government social spending and then merely tacks on something like an improved cook stoves project as an "action to assist women."

By stressing the need to increase women's productivity without providing women with better access to productive resources, does the Bank mean to imply that women should simply work more? Whether this is the intent or not, that seems to be the effect of most World Bank policies and projects. The reason for this lies in the all-encompassing nature of women's work.

A large part of women's work, even in the North, is not measured in the official economic statistics upon which the Bank relies for its information on productivity. As New Zealand economist Marilyn Waring has pointed out in her book *If Women Counted,* activities such as child rearing, cooking, fetching water and fuel, tending the sick and other services often performed by women are not traded in formal markets, so officially they produce nothing.

Making women more productive, officially, means enabling (or compelling) them to sell their goods and/or labor in the formal market. Structural adjustment policies that aim to shift resources into the "tradeables" sector are a prime example of the Bank's notion of increased efficiency and productivity.

But what does this mean for women? Often it means a lot more work. All the "unofficial" work -- fetching fuel and water, raising the children, cooking the meals, cleaning, tending to the sick, producing and processing food for household consumption -- does not go away when women switch to producing goods that the bean counters can count. As women enter formal labor markets and produce cash crops, GNP may increase, and the Bank may pat itself on the back for its so-called successes. Women, on the other hand, simply find themselves working harder for less return.

For all its research papers, WID, coordinators and fine rhetoric about the value of women's work, the Bank projects have failed to transfer the resources to women that would improve their lives and ability to sustain their families.

Worse still, macroeconomic policies promoting growth as measured by increases in the GNP exacerbate women's heavy workload and perpetuate the feminization of poverty. Under these circumstances, the question is not whether women are better off as a result of World Bank programs, but whether they can survive them at all.

24

Women, Structural Adjustment and Empowerment
Merle Hodge, Interviewed by Eloise Magenheim

Merle Hodge is a professor in the Department of Language and Linguistics at the Univerity of the West Indies, St. Augustine Campus, in Trinidad and Tobago. A long time activist, scholar and feminist, she is active in movements for popular education, economic justice and grassroots empowerment.

Eloise Magenheim: **What are the impacts of structural adjustment programs on women?**

Merle Hodge: Under the structural adjustment programs designed by the IMF and World Bank, the burdens of women increase because State spending in the social sector is cut back. For example, when, as a result of these cut-backs, the health services deteriorate, women have to become both doctor and nurse to their families.

In the Caribbean, women have always been breadwinners, and today they are taking on two or three jobs to feed their families. The informal sector grows in countries under structural adjustment, and here women are predominant in this sector.

Another feature of structural adjustment is the assumption that you can get women to work as cheap labor in the Third World countries. One of those models is the Export Processing Zone (EPZ). Foreign companies pick themselves up, abandon their workers and come here to pay women workers starvation wages.

The rise in vagrancy, the rise in crime, the rise in the prison population, all of those are results of imposed structural adjustment programs. Who picks up the mess? It is women.

Violence against women increases. Men are being fired in the thousands, and their frustration contributes to this. It is a very unfortunate, natural human response to take out your frustration on somebody who is perceived as weaker. Women and children are bearing the brunt of the frustration of men caused by structural adjustment imposed by agencies external to our society. Women are under a lot of stress.

EM: **Have women been empowered by international alliances during structural adjustment programs?**

MH: That is the case in the Caribbean here. We, for example, are in touch with women's organizations in Guyana, Jamaica, Barbados. Specifically, it was because we were in contact with women's organizations in Jamaica that we knew so much about EPZs. We were able to mount a campaign of public education on what EPZs were, what the effects were, what the implications were for the economy. We used a video-tape called "The Global Assembly Line." We asked groups to host us, and we went along with the film, had a discussion, handed out information. We wrote articles in the papers, statements to the press.

The government had already done a lot of the infrastructural work on the proposed EPZ. They had laid down concrete and pipelines, but the places are overgrown with vegetation now. The government has never officially gone back on the decision, but we suspect that businesses were frightened off as resistance had been put up here before they had even come.

EM: **What is the historical perspective preceding women's organizing around structural adjustment today?**

MH: Historically, the first women's organizations were welfare organizations basically set up around charity and social welfare issues. The fact that women's organizations now are taking on the business of trying to affect the economic environment rather than just dealing with the fall-out from it is a new development. This might be due to the increased education of women. The earlier organizations were mainly upper-class women providing welfare for poor people. Now that women from all strata of the society have access to education, the consciousness is a little different. It's not a charity, it's a question of empowering all of ourselves.

EM: **How do you define action and empowerment and how they relate to each other?**

MH: Gathering information and devising strategies is an important part of action. Even the period of talk — as long as it is directed talk and informed talk and sharing with a lot of people who are affected by whatever it is you are talking about — already is a part of the action. Action can only come out of awareness. Action can only have an effect if it is directed, if it is properly planned. Very often we are told, "oh, you're only talking," but I think that the talk stage is important. A lot of the work of our organization [Working Women] is simply spreading the information about what this thing [structural adjustment] is —

what is this thing that is happening to us?

You must start with the awareness that you have power, the awareness that you have within you the power to change things, that you don't just have to suffer things that are done to you, and then it is the confidence to act on that. The worst kind of disempowerment is not knowing that you are able to do something about your environment. That is the worst form of slavery.

EM: **What actions has Working Women taken around structural adjustment programs?**

MH: Stopping the introduction of EPZs is one. Our action has been to interest women in the issue of structural adjustment and also to spread the word that it is affecting women. That was not accepted widely before. We started to spread the analysis.

One of our most important roles is the way that we impact thinking at the government level. When I hear government ministers talk, I know that the women's movement is having an impact. A lot of the information they are using about women's issues and a lot of the awareness that is evident in their speeches comes from the women's movement.

EM: **Why do you think the IMF and World Bank continue to implement structural adjustment programs?**

MH: Because our governments have no backbone — all of the governments of the Third World. They don't stand up to the Bank and the Fund. There is a real problem — and I don't think it's only in the Third World — of alienation of people at the top from the rest of the population. It's almost as though they forget how it was or how it is. It's almost as though the impact on people is an abstraction to them. They approach the thing with far too much politeness and not enough creativity and not enough gumption.

EM: **How has women's organizing been most successful?**

MH: In Trinidad and Tobago, and that's really the only place I can speak for, even though the women's movement isn't that vast numerically, the impact has begun to embolden women. This is why we are aware of the domestic violence that is taking place and increasing with structural adjustment. Women are standing up for their rights in the home and in the workplace. Women are coming out and complaining of exploitation in the workplace. Because of pressure from the women's movement, we have also had certain pieces of legislation passed. Recently [in 1991], we had the very controversial Domestic Violence Bill passed, which allows family members to have the offending family member expelled from the home temporarily. The fact that women are using the bill, that they are emboldened to use it, is one of the successes of the women's movement.

EM: **Have structural adjustment programs provided a new opportunity for organizing?**

MH: Yes, it does tend to squeeze us together in one boat. More and more people of all kinds are recognizing that the only way to fight something as big as that is through collaboration. In the same way that the Caribbean governments are being squeezed together by impending developments in Europe [through economic integration] — we won't have preferred status for our products any more. It's time to start pressuring Caribbean governments to make Caribbean unity a reality. Caribbean unity has been on the agenda forever, but there haven't been any real, concrete steps toward it. What is happening now, in the world economic environment, is that they are actually being forced to start to take concrete steps toward Caribbean unity — otherwise we'll all sink. All the groups in the society which are affected by structural adjustment are liable to take the same decision.

EM: **Is unity spreading?**

MH: Yes. There is greater awareness in people's organizations, greater focus given to economic issues and to the urgency of banding together.

EM: **How have grassroots groups been fighting back?**

MH: The important thing to understand is that we are not powerless. Each of us won't fight the IMF, but as a united people in Third World countries getting together to talk back to the IMF, it will be a success. The only way it will happen however, is if we put pressure on our governments.

"The Rio conference on environment and development constantly referred to 'sustainable development.' But we in the South would rephrase that in light of policies such as structural adjustment, because what they actually promote is unsustainable underdevelopment. The adjustments that really need to be made are adjustments in global production, consumption, and distribution patterns. These patterns need to promote social and ecological justice."

Maria Onestini, Co-director,
Center for Environmental Studies,
Argentina

25

Battling the World Bank
Nilufar Ahmad, Interviewed by
Multinational Monitor

Trained as a statistician and an economist, Nilufar Ahmad is a
university professor in Bangladesh and works with grassroots
organizations of rural women. She first came face-to-face with
hunger as a university student working with rural women during
Bangladesh's 1974 famine. "At that time," she says, "I made up my
mind to work with rural people, especially rural women, because they
are at the bottom of the pit."

Multinational Monitor: **Could you describe your work in
Bangladesh?**

Nilufar Ahmad: My associates and I mobilize rural women, help
them form their own organizations. The first step is awareness-rais-
ing. These people are illiterate. They have no information. They do
not know their rights as citizens. They have basic human needs, and
they have the right to the resources that are available in our country.

After a little while, if we see that the women are becoming more
powerful, we make credit available to them, so they can set up small
businesses to make -- I would not call it a sustainable living -- but a
living at their own subsistence level.

MM: **Do you work independently or with a group when you're
working with the rural women?**

NA: We work in groups because, in Bangladesh, we found that net-
working is most important. In times of stress, we need each other's
help, so if there is a problem in some village, we can immediately call
on our friends to come to our support or legal aid.

MM: **How are the International Monetary Fund (IMF) and the
World Bank involved in Bangladesh?**

NA: It is a sad situation. We fought a nine-month war with Pakistan
in 1971. The United States supplied arms to Pakistan, so after
Bangladesh was liberated, the Americans had no great footing in
Bangladesh. In fact, they were very much hated. And the World Bank
did not have much footing in Bangladesh at that time, either.

But, during 1974, there was a big flood and a great famine in Bangladesh. At that time, Bangladesh was politically more connected to the Soviet Union, which helped us during the war with Pakistan. We also sold the Soviets and the Cubans jute, a fiber mainly used to make grain sacks -- that was our main export. Because of its trade embargo on Cuba, the United States stopped all the grain supply to Bangladesh. Thousands of people died during the few months when the grain supply was cut off. So though we tried to maintain an independent international policy, Bangladesh had to go begging on bended knees to the United States. The World Bank started to gain a footing in Bangladesh at the same time.

During that period, Sheikh Mujibur Rahman, the leader of our country, was attempting to get rid of the military. He said that we only needed the police and militia, not a big military. In 1975, the military came out one night with tanks and killed Sheikh Mujibur Rahman and his family. Under military rule, Bangladesh shifted its policies toward the United States and World Bank.

At the time of the military takeover, Bangladesh was suffering; a lot of people were dying of famine. Everybody wanted to help out. The World Bank somehow convinced all donor countries that Bangladesh would not be able to manage all this money coming into the country; that it would not be able to fashion programs and strategies. So the World Bank took the coordination of relief and aid out of our hands.

The World Bank became the coordinator of a consortium of donor groups. Now the World Bank decides what our policy and our budget will be, and it allocates all the money to different sectors. We are totally beholden to the World Bank.

Whatever the World Bank says, we have to say yes. For example, the World Bank and Western states all say that population is Bangladesh's biggest problem. Bangladesh is a highly populated, very small country -- we have about 2,000 people per square kilometer. So the first priority of foreign lenders is population control. Of all the money that goes into Bangladesh, 55 percent goes into population control. They give us Depo-Provera, Norplant, all kinds of IUDs. And they actually set targets for the number of each type of contraceptive that has to be distributed. If we do not satisfy the target, they can keep the money in the pipeline and not give it to other sectors. They give only 2 percent to education and only 0.4 percent to women's health. We have no control over our population policy; it is totally controlled by the World Bank.

In the last 20 years, however, Bangladesh's population has not decreased. This is because population is not the problem; the problem is poverty. We have a high infant mortality rate in Bangladesh. If a woman does not know if her child is going to survive or not, she's not going to use contraceptives. So our first priority is to put money into basic human needs: education, health, shelter, food. But the World Bank decides that population control is the first priority.

MM: **How are World Bank-imposed structural adjustment policies affecting the country?**

NA: The World Bank is trying to liberalize Bangladesh's trade laws and promote export-oriented policies. It has cut off all of the money for the social sector, so there is more and more poverty in Bangladesh.

In Bangladesh, the industries were nationalized. But the World Bank has forced us -- and all the weak countries in the world -- to privatize state-owned enterprises. In selling off the enterprises, government officials took many bribes. The public industries that earned millions of dollars each year were sold to the private sector for just a couple of million dollars. Those were public goods. And the people got nothing for them.

Because we are a land-poor country, our economic policy should promote industrialization. Sixty percent of our population is landless, and there is simply not enough land for everybody. But the people who bought the privatized factories just sold the machinery, took the money and sent it abroad. They just ran away. Now there is almost 50 percent unemployment in Bangladesh and a lot of additional shadow underemployment.

MM: **One of the export products the World Bank is urging for Bangladesh is shrimp. Could you talk about the origin of the shrimp industry and its impact on life in the coastal areas of Bangladesh?**

NA: The shrimp industry right now is a very touchy subject. The World Bank has planned a big project for the shrimp industry, designed to bring in a lot of foreign exchange for Bangladesh. The shrimp we grow is not for our own consumption; it is for rich countries to buy.

In the 1960s, the government built embankments around the coastal area to stop the tail-line waters from coming in, to gain more land from the ocean. The coastal areas were the surplus food areas where a lot of grains grew. One fourth of the population of Bangladesh lives in the coastal areas.

In the late 1970s and 1980s, the World Bank said, "Go for shrimp." And some rich people who lived in the area -- with the compliance of the government -- cut through the embankments and let the tail-line water come in. They leased a lot of land from the local people and said they were going to cultivate shrimp. The local people didn't know what was going to happen: their fields were flooded with salt water and used by the shrimp cultivators to grow the shrimp. They catch the shrimp right from the ocean and put it in these flooded areas, inside the land. When the shrimp reach a certain size, the cultivators sell them to outside markets.

People are living on bamboo huts on top of the saltwater because they have no place to go. They are sort of like hostages to the shrimp cultivators; the shrimp cultivators hire goons to intimidate the local people.

The women working those shrimp areas must go in the ocean to catch shrimp, and they are in the cold water from eight to ten hours each day -- many of them die of heart attacks or catch fever. When the shrimp are bigger, the women catch them from the cultivating areas where salt water is mixed with lime, which does a lot of internal damage to the shrimp workers' bodies. They wear no gloves, and their hands and feet are totally decayed, totally rotten.

The foreign exchange that shrimp exports earn is just going to the pockets of a few rich people. The poor people are not able to eat the shrimp, they're not getting agricultural production, they're not gaining anything in any way. The World Bank says development is growth, but the point is, development for whom? Not for a few rich people, when 25 million people are dying of hunger.

So we do a lot of mobilization in the coastal areas. The women form groups, and they guard embankments so that shrimp cultivations do not invade land and cut new embankments. There was a big demonstration in November 1990 involving thousands of people. The goons working for one of the very rich cultivators attacked the women. One woman was killed, another was abducted -- she was never found. But the women there are not afraid. They are still in groups, they make protests. They say that they are going to win this battle, that they are not going to go away, that they are going to stay on their land and continue whatever agricultural production they have. They just will not give up.

MM: **What are some of the other impacts of the shrimp industry?**

NA: The shrimp cultivation causes serious environmental problems. The land that has been flooded by salt water is already damaged, and agricultural cultivation there has decreased by 30 percent. There is simply no vegetation -- no trees, no plants. Scientists say that it will take three decades to relieve the land of this salinity. It also contributes to deforestation. In the coastal areas, we have the great mangrove forest. They cut the mangrove forest to make room for more shrimp cultivation, and this has depleted the forest by about 40 percent.

We are going to have an ecological disaster in Bangladesh. Only 4 percent of the land is forested, and we need at least 25 percent. We have big cyclones in the bay -- last year there was a big cyclone and about one million people were killed. The bay is tunnel-shaped, and when the cyclone comes it creates a big tidal wave about 20 or 30 feet high. Because the people live in huts, they're all washed away into the ocean. They just cannot survive. But where the coastal area is forested, the water cannot come in, and people are protected.

The government simply has no policy on forest protection. Forestation in the coastal areas should protect the people, protect their land, protect their livestock, protect their resources. But the government is going to deforest the whole coastal area. That is the sad truth.

MM: **So it is almost guaranteed that there will be future disasters on the scale of the recent flood?**

NA: Yes. Let me tell you a story. In 1988, we had a big flood in Bangladesh. Fifty percent of the land was flooded. Even Dhaka, the capital city, was totally underwater. I have never seen such water in my whole life. And the whole world was really concerned when the flood was shown on international television. The donor countries really wanted to help Bangladesh; they wanted to find policies and strategies to help the people.

The World Bank again got into the act and became the coordinator of the relief effort. It came up with a strategy called the flood action plan. The proposal was to build embankments beside the main rivers. We have the three biggest rivers in the world in Bangladesh -- the Ganges, the Brahmaputra and the Meghna. Can you imagine building embankments on those rivers? Those are totally unstable rivers. We already have 7,000 kilometers of embankments, and still every year we are flooded. But the World Bank is going ahead with the plan.

At the time, we had a corrupt, autocratic ruler, and he was very happy to implement this plan. Ten billion dollars will be spent just to make the embankments, and $600 million will be needed every year to maintain them. We are going to borrow $10 billion from the whole world. How is it going to be repaid? It's all loans, not aid.

When we heard about this, we started to protest, but the government went ahead anyway. In 1989, the government built an embankment around Dhaka without conducting any feasibility studies. Now in Dhaka we are drowning in our own drain water because the government didn't put in any sewage -- the water inside Dhaka cannot go out.

Meanwhile, the World Bank has already spent $150 million just on the 26 studies it has done for the flood action plan. The Bank has put in all sorts of wasteful conditions we have to follow. For example, for each study we have to include something like six foreign consulting firms. Each consultant that comes to Bangladesh gets paid something like $800 per day -- while the average per capita income in Bangladesh is $160 per year. Do you think these people are really helping Bangladesh? We have calculated that for each dollar that comes into Bangladesh, we have to repay $1.50 back. Where is this money going to come from?

What I am saying is that the donor countries are not actually helping the developing countries, the poor countries. They're just doing good business for themselves. It is their own self-interest they are satisfying.

But I also want to say another thing: that it actually takes two parties to do it. Our government is complicit. The World Bank could not force all these policies on us if our government didn't agree to them. The government consents because government officials do not have enough political will and because they want to line their own pockets. Only the people can stop this process. Our main work should be to help the people understand that the government is selling them to the donors. Then we can make the government accountable and devise our own policies without being beholden to the World Bank, the International Monetary Fund, U.S. Agency for International Development or anybody else.

MM: **How optimistic are you that the people of Bangladesh will be able to successfully resist World Bank and government policies?**

NA: A great story of hope just happened two months ago. This is delta country. In Ramgati, on the coast, 50 landless families went to a piece of land that rose up in the ocean. They just stayed there and cultivated a bit of that land. After the harvest, the landlord who lived nearby came with the police, claiming that it was his land and that he was going to collect all the grain that had been harvested.

The women asked their men to leave. They knew there was going to be violence because the police always protect the interests of the landlords. The women gathered the grain in a field and stood around that grain with their babies in their arms. They told the police, "You have to kill all of us to get this grain." And the police backed away.

I was in a nearby area when I heard this story, so I went to meet these women who were so brave. I asked one of them where they got the courage. And this woman, who is only in her twenties, told me that she is an orphan, that she does not have any parents or brothers or sisters, that she has lived in the streets all her life, that she has been raped many times because she sleeps on the streets and that she does not know the names of the fathers of her children. She told me that she has no money, that she has no shame, that she has nothing left. She has only her life to lose. And if she loses it to help other women who are in the same condition, she said, then it is no loss at all.

I think it's a great sign of hope that these people will really fight and that they are going to get what they want.

"In 1991 the government of Kenya and the World Bank signed an agreement for $100 million for an 'Education Sector Adjustment Credit.' The credit required the government to reduce its current expenditure in the education sector. Now the personal allowance for students (known as 'boom') has been halved. Reports are rife that women students from poor families have resorted to prostitution to raise money, and they're trading and taking toifo (illicit brew) and drugs, or becoming matatu (minibus) conductors instead of studying. The 'pay as you eat' scheme has left students without meals. Cases of students fainting during examination sessions are very common due to malnutrition. Demonstrations held at two of the major universities resulted in the government reversing its announcement that student allowances would be cut completely."

Susie Ibutu,
National Council of Churches of Kenya

26

Internal Report Card Looks Bad for Structural Adjustments
Cameron Duncan

A confidential World Bank report on structural adjustment suggests that the short-term impacts could endanger the long-term success of adjustment efforts. According to the report, expected increases in the efficiency and growth rates of economies currently undergoing adjustment have failed to materialize, with two thirds of the countries experiencing declines in both public and private sector investment.

The report, entitled *World Bank Structural and Sectoral Adjustment Operations*, was prepared in June 1992 by the Bank's Operations Evaluation Department. It reviews project completion reports through 1991 for 99 structural adjustment loans in 42 countries. Economic recovery under adjustment programs is particularly sluggish in Africa. In the 18 sub-Saharan African countries reviewed, no less than 14 had experienced a fall in investment rates during adjustment.

For the Bank's adjustment-related technical assistance loans, 60 percent of which were implemented in African countries, the news is also bad. According to the report, "less than 20 percent of these operations were substantially effective, and 15 percent had only negligible impact."

While the Bank report emphasizes that "the social impact of adjustment has not been uniform," with differences between countries, it does acknowledge that "income inequality in rural areas appears to have gone up in some countries, as landless farm workers bear the greater burden of higher food prices."

Case studies of the social impact of adjustment are presented for Cote d'Ivoire, Ghana, Indonesia, Jamaica and the Philippines. Adjustment in Cote d'Ivoire had the most severe impact on the poor. The report says that

> poverty increased by 4.8 percent a year during 1980-85,
> and hard-core poverty by 7.9 percent a year. The urban
> poor were the hardest hit because of both unemployment

and wage reductions. In the rural areas, the prices of trad-
able food crops fell relative to those of export crops. This
had an adverse impact on income distribution in rural areas as food-crop farmers, who were hardest hit by the
price movements, were the poorest social groups in Cote
d'Ivoire. The incidence of hard-core poverty among this
group increased from 13 to 20 percent.

The report finds that in half of the 20 countries undergoing structural adjustment programs where data were available, the adverse effects of the overall reductions in government spending were intensified by a cut in the share of social spending. The Bank concludes that
"the trends in social sector expenditures were thus not very satisfactory in the adjustment period in many countries."

The case of Indonesia receives special praise as "a good example
of the successful combination of adjustment, growth, and favorable
social impact." Though few figures are presented for employment,
health and poverty, the report concludes that the Indonesian adjustment policies "were the best, in terms of their social impact, compared
with the alternatives." Alternative policies are not specified.

Even more ambiguous are the report's conclusions on the impact
of adjustment on the environment. In the one page devoted to the topic,
the paper notes that "increased export crops in response to currency
depreciation can occur at the expense of forests that are cut down to
provide land for the crops. This has happened in Cote d'Ivoire and
Ghana." The report goes on to suggest that some adjustment policies
may have a positive environmental impact, as "trade liberalization may
facilitate the transfer of low-polluting technologies."

Despite its mixed findings, the report largely ignores environmental degradation, social breakdown and economic failure associated with
structural adjustment loans. Its conclusions call for more of the same
orthodox medicine and for closer collaboration between World Bank
and the International Monetary Fund.

The environmental destruction caused by World Bank and IMF
structural adjustment loans has led some groups, such as Friends of
the Earth and Greenpeace, to demand that the institutions conduct full
environmental and social impact assessments of the programs.

27

World Bank Failures Soar to 37.5% of Completed Projects in 1991
Pratap Chatterjee

Over a third of World Bank projects completed in 1991 were judged failures by its own staff, resulting in a dramatic 150 pecent rise in failures over the last ten years, according to a leaked internal Bank report. The report lends considerable weight to charges by activist groups like Greenpeace and Friends of the Earth that Bank loans have paid for environmental and social destruction in poor countries.

The World Bank lent a total of $16.4 billion last year to developing countries and the former Soviet bloc. The Bank is one of the largest sources of money for development projects like dams, roads and timber management. Among other criticisms, activists have long said that projects like the Bank's forestry management plans have paid for the razing of the Amazonian rain forest in Brazilian states like Rondonia, that projects for irrigating the Nile have destroyed the same lands because faulty designs allowed the intrusion of sea water and that its present plans for dam projects in India and China will displace hundreds of thousands of people.

Now it appears that a high-level Bank internal team has come to exactly the same conclusions. This summer a report entitled "Effective Implementation: Key to Development Impact" prepared by Willi Wapenhans was sent to the Bank's president Lewis Preston. Wapenhans reviewed about 1,800 current Bank projects in 113 countries for which the Bank had lent $138 billion, and met with a number of policymakers from borrowing countries.

Specifically, Wapenhans noted that 37.5 percent of the projects completed in 1991 were deemed failures, up from 15 percent in 1981 and 30.5 percent in 1989. Bank staff also said that 30 percent of projects in their fourth or fifth year of implementation in 1991 had major problems. The worst affected sectors were water supply and sanitation, where 43 percent of the projects had major problems, and the agricultural sector, where 42 percent of the projects were failing.

The report says that far from being isolated sector phenomena, the problems are spreading. "New areas of lending were also encountering major problems: poverty (28 percent), environment (30 percent) and private and public sector reform (23 percent)."

The meeting with policymaker representatives from half of the borrowing countries in May 1993 provided some startling comments on the Bank. Wapenhans recorded over 400 pages of anonymous testimony that slammed the Bank for ignoring local input in favor of policy mandated from Bank headquarters, which was not consistent.

One borrower said the Bank staff "take a negotiating position not a consulting position -- they know what they want from the outset and aren't open to hearing what the country has to say," while another said that governments feel "psychologically pressured" to take the loan or leave it, and countries then end up with conditions that they have no way of honoring and contracts that cannot be implemented.

Others said that the Bank "changes its wisdom with the passage of time. We saw the Bank talking about import substitution in the sixties, then export substitution, then social problems and then the environment." Bank staff were accused of being high-handed and insensitive, insisting on designing projects according to Bank policies at the time instead of consulting with the borrowers and local people.

The borrowers agreed that the Bank staff appeared more driven by pressure to lend than a desire for successful project implementation. The Bank staff often insisted on international consultants to prepare projects resulting in poor quality suggestions because the consultants "from New York or London" had no experience in the country. In an analysis of the success rate for major country portfolios, a number of countries had a success rate of less than two thirds for completed projects -- Bangladesh (66%), Philippines (65.8%), Algeria (58.3%), Mexico (56%), Brazil (55.9%), Kenya (48.2%),Tanzania (34.8%), Nigeria (26.3%) and Uganda (17.2%).

28

The World Bank After the Wapenhans Report-- What Now?
Richard Gerster

The World Bank Group is by far the most significant institution in development financing. In 1992, 140 billion dollars were committed in 1,800 projects and programs. Each year, new loans totalling 18 to 20 billion dollars are granted to finance about 225 new operations.

In February 1992, the president of the World Bank established an internal task force under the chairmanship of Willi Wapenhans to analyze problems with the quality of projects financed by the World Bank. The extremely critical Wapenhans Report, "Effective Implementation: Key to Development Impact," released on September 22, 1992, deserves serious recognition. With this report, the already self-critical tradition of the World Bank reaches a new depth. Moreover, the fact that the World Bank, following the recommendation of Switzerland, released the report for publication in December 1992 is encouraging.

A few months earlier, on June 18, 1992, the independent commission appointed by the president of the World Bank to investigate the Sardar-Sarovar Dam in the Narmada Valley of India had completed and released its findings. What this report, under the direction of Bradford Morse, demonstrated for the particular case of the Narmada Project was largely confirmed in the analysis and conclusions of the Wapenhans Task Force.

The criticisms in the Wapenhans and the Morse Reports confirm the many standpoints and evaluations that have been put forward by nongovernmental development and environmental organizations for years. Presently, the World Bank is under pressure to reform as never before.

Major Conclusions of the Wapenhans Diagnosis

"The methodology for project performance rating is deficient; it lacks objective criteria and transparency," states the report. The World Bank employs the standard of profitability it has set for itself: projects that do not bring at least a 10 percent rate of return or its qualitative equivalent in cases in which quantification of benefits is not feasible are considered "unsatisfactory." This in itself demanding hurdle, however, says little about the contribution of World Bank projects to sustainable development.

It is true that historically, three quarters of all completed projects are considered satisfactory and one quarter are deemed failures. However, the proportion of problematic projects among current projects as well as the proportion of projects judged to be unsatisfactory upon completion is continuously increasing. The Operations Evaluation Department (OED) has designated 37.5 percent of the projects completed in fiscal 1991 as unsatisfactory, a proportion that ten years ago was still at 15 percent. Forty-two percent of the agricultural and 43 percent of the water supply and sanitation projects in their fourth and fifth years of implementation are classified as projects with "major problems."

Problem projects remain problem projects: "The Bank and its borrowers usually struggle unsuccessfully to resolve difficulties." Initially, the project managers attempt to solve problems, but after three years of difficulties, the level of effort falls off "dramatically," and the project is, for all practical purposes, given up. And yet, suspension of funding proves to be practically impossible, probably because no one has an interest in outright failure.

Project appraisals are perceived by many Bank staff "as marketing deuces for securing loan approval (and achieving personal recognition)." The Wapenhans Report especially criticizes "the frequent absence of explicit consideration of alternative technical solutions and options." In the aura of the "approval culture" of the Bank, the appraisals are not sober evaluations, but instead serve to support positions and are correspondingly skewered. According to Wapenhans, "the credibility of the Bank's appraisal process is under pressure."

Although only partial data was available, the Wapenhans Report found that "the evidence of gross noncompliance is overwhelming." An internal survey showed that in only 15 percent to 25 percent of the cases were the borrowers in compliance with the covenants; noncompliance did not have any consequences. Specifically, "financial covenants are often complex, frequently unrealistic and usually ignored."

Beyond the aspects already mentioned, the reasons for project difficulties are manifold:

• The projects are too complex and often do not make allowances for the weak institutional structures in the developing country.

• The developing countries as borrowers are often overwhelmed and do not identify with the project: "The negotiations stage . . . is seen by many borrowers as a largely coercive exercise designed to 'impose' the Bank's philosophy and to validate the findings of its promotional approach to appraisal."

• The economic risks that result from the macro-economic environment (i.e., terms of trade) and the limited implementation capacity in the developing country are not taken into account when quantifying the rate of return.

The corporate culture of the World Bank orients itself along false values and offers the wrong incentives. Loan agreements, nice appraisal reports and disbursements rather than development impact are at the forefront. On October 2, 1992, World Bank President Lewis T. Preston wrote a commentary on the Wapenhans Report: "We should recognize that the emphasis on lending is rooted as deeply in past as in current objectives; in the views of managers and staff as in the views of Executive Directors; in the views of our borrowers as in the expectations of the international community."

Recommendations

The objective of the necessary measures is to strengthen the contribution of the World Bank Group to sustainable development in a qualitative, need-oriented sense.

The measures enumerated below are regarded by the Swiss Coalition -- Swissaid/ Catholic Lenten Fund/ Bread for All Helvetas/ Caritas -- as being of central importance. In part, they are recommendations already mentioned in the Wapenhans Report in one form or another and whose importance from the viewpoint of the Swiss Coalition needs to be emphasized. However, in addition to that, further proposals are put forward.

Wapenhans Proposals

The Wapenhans Report contains many proposals the thrust of which deserve endorsement, even though the details often cannot be thoroughly grasped by outsiders. As important as accuracy and formal clarity are in themselves, there is also the danger of over quantification and technical formalism -- i.e., the proposed project poverty-reduction index. Sustainable development as a societal, economic and ecological process can be but insufficiently comprehended by means of quantitative indicators. Neverth. 'ess, it is encouraging that quality as defined by sustai ble developm t have moved into the limelight.

Country performa c as a whole must gain importance in relation to the present projec by-project approach to portfolio performance management. Identification, preparation, implementation and evaluation of projects must ensue from the specific priorities and capacity of each country. The primacy of the country as the unit of analysis meets the widespread demand for true policy dialogue, which is not to be equated with the one-sided imposition of conditions.

Borrower identification with the project must be one of the prerequisites for loan approval. "The most satisfactory projects tend to be those in which there has been the most borrower participation during preparation and, as a result, the greatest likelihood of high borrower commitment." A survey of a representative sample of borrowers revealed that they tend to view the projects as "a World Bank project" rather than as their own undertaking.

The capacity of the World Bank to properly track project implementation must be strengthened. Until now, only 12 work-weeks were available per project per year. Additional resources for project management, enhancement of the role of the resident missions in developing countries and new criteria for career advancement are a few of the measures proposed. If, in spite of all efforts, no satisfactory project results can be obtained, the World Bank should suspend the loan.

The mandate of the Operations Evaluation Department (OED), which answers directly to the president and has complete access to information, must be enhanced so that *evaluation of development impact* becomes the nucleus of its future work. "OED should help ensure that the prevailing focus upon capital flows is matched by an equally intense interest in the benefits that flow from them."

Recommendations from the Viewpoint of the Swiss Coalition

From the viewpoint of the Swiss Coalition (Swissaid/ Catholic Lenten Fund/ Bread for All Helvetas/ Caritas), the recommendations in the Wapenhans Report are not sufficient to lead to the reform breakthrough at the World Bank that the Wapenhans analysis indicates is urgently necessary. The Wapenhans Report only marginally touches upon the issue of people's participation and the participation of nongovernmental organizations, and neglects questions of transparency and accountability vis-a-vis the public.

The Wapenhans Report points out in several places that its analysis "reflects views that are widely held." Former World Bank staff members also report that many of these issues were already being raised five to ten years ago. Thus, the question arises why these problems, recognized as such long ago, still haven't been solved. That internal and external criticisms have obviously brought about few results until now is probably not due to a lack of good will on the part of the staff, but rather to institutional constraints that have defined the present corporate culture in such a way and not another.

Under the present corporate culture of the World Bank, quantitative commitment of resources has priority before qualitative considerations. This corporate culture could only develop because the World Bank is not held financially accountable for its mistakes; in the last analysis, frank self-criticism does not cost anything, either. The loans of the international development banks are also not included in debt rescheduling, but receive privileged treatment. It is, therefore, urgent that mechanisms be sought to ensure that the World Bank assumes its share of the financial consequences of failures. It is only when a development fiasco, for which the World Bank is jointly responsible because of its misguided advice, has a negative effect on the balance sheets that entrepreneurial interest will be expressly directed toward project quality and implementation. For example, it will then be in the interest of the World Bank to think of project appraisal as factual analysis rather than as project promotion. Without banking obligations making it imperative to take into account qualitative factors, there is great danger that the reforms will only go half way.

Transparency and accountability of the World Bank vis-à-vis the public must be improved for participation to be at all possible. The principles of good governance and unequivocal administration of the law demand people's participation in all phases of the project cycle, as well as fair and adequate compensation for encroachment of legally obtained rights. The following measures are steps in this direction:

• Accredited nongovernmental development and environmental organizations should be granted observer status at the meetings of the Executive Directors, as is already the case in the Montreal Protocol.

• The people affected by a project must be able to turn to an independent ombudsman or to an independent commission with corresponding jurisdiction.

• Public access to information must be expanded in the direction of the U.S. Freedom of Information Act, as in the saying, "Sunlight is the best disinfectant."

• The newly convened UN Commission for Sustainable Development is to be granted total access to information under agreed upon conditions. Possibly, a committee of the Commission could take on the role of independent commission or ombudsman for the persons affected.

Progress in the realization of reforms must be reviewed yearly. To this end, the Executive Directors together with management should give the already well-functioning Wapenhans Task Force Working Group a new mandate. This mandate should at least cover the period necessary for implementing the reforms, that is, beyond the retirement of the present chair. The findings are to be accessible to the public.

Consequences for Nongovernmental Development and Environmental Organizations

Pressure for reform vis-à-vis the World Bank must be maintained in such a way that the Wapenhans and the Morse Reports really do become a turning point in the Bank's operations. To this end, the nongovernmental development and environmental organizations need to lobby their respective governments, put forward their reform proposals and insist that the Wapenhans Report become a major topic to be actively taken up by the individual Governors.

The primacy of the country as the unit of analysis at the World Bank must find expression in the lobbying efforts of the nongovernmental development and environmental organizations:

• Internationally concerted lobbying must be concentrated on priority countries whose structural adjustment programs and projects are monitored over the long term.

• The consultative country groups under the direction of the World Bank deserve more attention; in the case of Cambodia, nongovernmental organizations have been granted observer status for the first time.

• INGI (International NGO Forum on Indonesian Development) gains significance as a model for intensive, country-specific cooperation by nongovernmental organizations from the South and the North.

World Bank reforms aimed at improving project quality reduce at least temporarily monetary flows to the South. When there is sand in the money machine of the World Bank, macro-economic difficulties may develop in individual countries. This is desirable and increases the pressure for reform in those countries. Beneficiaries should be those countries willing to institute reforms and in which projects with good prospects for success can be realized. With the reductions in the lending volume of the World Bank, nongovernmental development and environmental organizations must work toward ensuring that developing countries willing to undergo reform have higher bilateral budgets at their disposal.

With regard to many politically sensitive issues such as resettlement, the major stumbling block is that official guidelines exist on paper only. The reform proposals in the Wapenhans Report aimed at problems of implementation ought to bring improvements in this respect. Besides institutional questions, the nongovernmental development and environmental organizations should not neglect other unsatisfactory, politically charged issues such as energy, forestry and structural adjustment and should above all also contribute their project experience.

50 Years of Bretton Woods

It is very important that the reform proposals be taken up and implemented by the World Bank. Nineteen-ninety-four is the 50th anniversary of the Bretton Woods Conference. Having had a significant hand in shaping half a century of global economic history is reason enough for a critical review by the World Bank of its own role in a world which has changed so much. This ought to include the political willingness to rethink and, if need be, revise the Articles of Agreement. Several of the reform proposals put forward here point toward a revision of the statutes.

> *"During the 1980s under structural adjustments, instead of flowing North to South through loans and aid investment, more money flowed from South to North in debt servicing, capital flight, and profits from transnational corporations and the privatization of state-owned companies. In truth and fact, the countries of the South are subsidizing the countries of the North. We are helping to subsidize the United States deficit."*
> David Abdullah,
> Oilfield Workers' Trade Union,
> Trinidad and Tobago

29

The World Bank's New Rules (Same as the Old Rules)
Patricia Adams

The World Bank, which for the past 50 years has developed scores of guidelines, directives and other rules to combat criticism from internal and external sources -- and then blithely ignored them -- has established a new set of measures in the wake of a high-level report critical of the Bank's loan portfolio.

The Wapenhans Report, released in December 1992 after being ordered by incoming Bank President Lewis Preston, found that over one third of the Bank's projects were failing and that the deterioration of the Bank's $140 billion portfolio was "steady" and "pervasive."

So damning were the details and so widely was the draft document leaked that an official version of the Wapenhans Report was soon released to the public. This led to member governments demanding that Bank staff reverse the downward trend in project performance.

The Bank's first attempt, prepared by former Vice President Visvanathan Rajgopalan, was rejected by the Executive Directors in May 1993 for being too casual, too anemic and too unmonitorable.

Bank management then appointed its Central Operations Director, James Adams, whose new draft was accepted by the Board on July 8 and promptly repackaged into a booklet for public consumption.

But *Getting Results: The World Bank's Agenda for Improving Development Effectiveness*, as the final plan is called, is a pathetic, unconvincing and ultimately futile attempt to reform an unreformable institution.

As the core of its action plan, the Bank pledges to "look at its whole portfolio of operations" in each country in order to identify systemic obstacles in the country's economy that are handicapping all Bank projects. Most troubling, however, is the Bank's intention to then seek "remedial actions," designing economic policies with country authorities to make Bank projects work. But history shows that what is good for World Bank projects -- monopoly structures, subsidies and market distortions -- is often bad for the rest of the economy.

To ensure that individual Bank projects succeed, the Bank insists that borrowing nations and their implementing agencies take more "ownership" without considering that borrowers don't stand behind the Bank's projects because the projects are ill-conceived and because the borrowers are often more interested in the projects' pork-barrel opportunities than in their success.

To foster "a genuine partnership" with its borrowers, the Bank will hold workshops and trumpet "broad, meaningful participation" in its projects. But this attempt to counter accusations of unaccountability is belied by the Bank's actions; just weeks after the release of *Getting Results*, the Bank approved a new information disclosure policy that is more like a muzzle to keep the public at bay about Bank activities.

Projects that maintain a "problem" status for more than 12 months, claims the Bank, will be dealt with summarily. Action plans "will specify the basis on which support for the project can be sustained. If the actions are not implemented, the project will be cancelled or restructured." Only a fool would believe this, after the first ever Independent Review Team to investigate a World Bank project documented how, in the case of the Sardar Sarovar Dam in India, systematic "violations of legal covenants are flagged and then forgotten . . . conditions are relaxed or their deadlines postponed."

In another attempt to rewrite history and confound its critics, the Bank claims in its detailed action plan that "in administering its loan portfolio, the Bank has always emphasized the importance of compliance with loan covenants" even though Wapenhans found that "the evidence of gross noncompliance [with legal covenants] is overwhelming" and the remedies available to the Bank are "rarely exercised."

Bank critics have Lewis Preston to thank for the official confirmation of their suspicions: the former chairman of J.P. Morgan and Co. did what any commercial banker would do in taking the helm; he asked for a no-nonsense reading of the state of his new bank's portfolio.

Now that the genie is out of the bottle, Preston must despair at the prospects of putting it back. Because the bank is legally and constitutionally unaccountable to the taxpayers that keep it in business and the people who must pay for its activities, no one can force the Bank to abide by *Getting Results* or any other policy. Borrowing and lending member nations of the Bank prefer it this way: the absence of private-sector discipline and public-sector accountability give them broad scope for directing funds to favored projects and governments, and for awarding contracts to favored firms. In the end, only the propagandists and the perennially gullible will find comfort in *Getting Results*.

30

World Bunk
John B. Judis

From the end of World War II through the 1980s, Japan's diplomats dutifully maintained that their kind of capitalism and that of the United States were alike. But in recent years, Japanese officials have begun to assert in public what they previously would have only said in private: that Japan's capitalism is fundamentally different from -- and in some ways superior to -- American-style economics.

More is at stake than bragging rights. At the World Bank, where Japan is now the second-largest contributor, Japanese officials have begun to challenge the economic advice that American academics and Bank officials are giving to Eastern Europe, Africa and Latin America.

The Japanese are arguing that these developing countries should look to East Asia rather than to the United States and Great Britain for their model of capitalist development. So far, World Bank officials have held off Japan's challenge. But as Eastern European economies crumble under the burden of U.S.- and World Bank-sponsored "shock therapy," Japan's argument has become increasingly difficult to dismiss.

Japan's dissent was sparked by a recent change in the way the World Bank loans money. From its founding in 1945 until 1980, the bank primarily provided loans for dams, schools and other infrastructure projects in the Third World. But in 1980, it began to provide "structural adjustment" loans that were not tied to specific projects.

These loans, however, required the recipient country to meet certain conditions. These conditions -- dictated by neo-classical economics -- consisted of eliminating tariffs and restrictions on foreign investment, privatizing public banks and industries, eliminating subsidies for domestic industries and removing any controls on credit and currency. Developing countries, in other words, were supposed to adapt their economies to the theoretical ideals of the most conservative U.S. economists.

Most World Bank aid to Eastern Europe and the countries of the former Soviet Union has taken this form; these countries -- on the rebound from the failure of communist economics -- willingly accepted the Bank's conditions. Advised by Harvard University's Jeffrey Sachs and by World Bank economists, they undertook programs of "shock therapy" designed to convert them overnight into burgeoning capitalist economies. But these policies have produced very high unemployment and declining output and are now leading to a widespread political revolt, one manifestation of which was the abortive October 1993 counterrevolution in Russia.

The Japanese began complaining about the Bank's aid policies in the early '90s. They pointed out that Japan, Korea, Taiwan and other East Asian nations developed economically according to a far different model than that recommended by the Bank and by Sachs. In East Asia, the Japanese noted, governments work closely with business to develop strategies for economic growth. Nationalized banks selectively grant low-interest-rate loans to targeted industries. Governments restrict foreign investment to maintain control over the direction of economic development. Subsidies are granted to business -- but only in exchange for meeting specific performance requirements. And planners place a high priority on becoming competitive through higher productivity rather than through lower wages.

Since 1960, the East Asian countries have prospered, while countries that followed a western model of development have floundered. Japan, South Korea, Singapore, Taiwan, Indonesia, Malaysia, Hong Kong and Thailand have grown three times as fast as Latin American and South Asian countries and five times as fast as economies in sub-Saharan Africa. Real income per capita has increased more than four times in Japan, Hong Kong, Korea, Singapore and Taiwan.

Japan's displeasure with the Bank first surfaced publicly at the organization's annual meeting in October 1991. In a speech, Bank of Japan Governor Yasushi Mieno declared, "Experience in Asia has shown that although development strategies require a healthy respect for market mechanisms, the role of government cannot be forgotten." Mieno argued that government could "create the kind of environment in which free markets can function effectively."

That fall, at Japan's urging, the Bank's economists completed an internal study of the East Asian model. The study urged the Bank to consider the East Asian model as an alternative. Japan's executive director at the World Bank, Masaki Shiratori, vigorously campaigned for its publication, but the Bank's other managing directors opposed making the study public. Finally, the Bank's new president, Lewis Preston -- formerly CEO of Morgan Guaranty Bank -- agreed to publish the study's summary and to commission a public study that would incorporate the data of the internal study, but that would be under the control of the Bank's managing directors. Japan's Finance Ministry agreed to fund it.

World Bank economists spent the next two years putting the internal documents into publishable form and writing an overall analysis and conclusion. The result, recently published as *The East Asian Miracle*, is a masterpiece in obfuscation. While the factual accounts of the different countries are useful and accurate, the Bank's economists superimposed upon them conclusions that bear out the institution's own theoretical and ideological preconceptions. The conclusion consists of a plethora of debating devices used to evade the facts of East Asian success.

Early in the text, the authors try to undermine the very idea of an East Asian model. By comparing Hong Kong with South Korea, the bank officials come to the conclusion that "there is no single East Asian model." That's fine, except that no one would ever suggest Hong Kong -- a long-time British colony and an outpost of London's financial district -- as a model for Ukraine or Nigeria.

Then they concede that there might be an Asian model, but that the success of the South Asian nations, Thailand, Malaysia and Indonesia, is more relevant to other developing nations than the success of the more dirigiste Northeast Asian countries -- an assertion for which they offer no argument. Finally, they concede that the Northeast Asian nations -- Japan, South Korea and Taiwan -- might provide a model, but they insist that these nations' success has had nothing to do with "industrial policy" and government intervention. "Industrial policy," the study concludes, "was generally not successful. In Japan, Korea, Singapore, Taiwan and China, promotion of specific industries had little apparent impact."

The study asserts that the East Asian countries have succeeded because they pay attention to the "fundamentals" of fiscal and market discipline championed by the World Bank. "Attempts to guide resource allocations in international trade, financial markets and labor markets have reduced competitive discipline, guided resources into low productivity and internationally uncompetitive sectors and resulted in widespread rent-seeking."

In an appendix, the Bank's officials attempt to ground these conclusions in arcane equations, but their findings have already been discredited by South Korean economist Jene Kwon. In a paper that appeared recently in the journal *World Development*, Kwon shows that in South Korea, the industries that enjoyed the highest increase in output, productivity and sales were those subsidized and overseen by the government. The same kind of results could be demonstrated for Japan and Taiwan.

Japanese officials, who kept their distance from the project, have already expressed their disappointment with the study's results. At an October breakfast meeting at the Economic Strategy Institute, Finance Ministry official Eisuke Sakakibara reaffirmed Japan's conviction that the United States' and the Bank's shock therapy strategy was ill-suited for developing nations. Sakakibara, the author of an impressive new study, *Beyond Capitalism: The Japanese Model of Market Economics*, also attributed part of the upheaval in Russia to the Yeltsin regime's acceptance of the dictums of Sachs and the Bank.

Sakakibara and the Japanese are continuing their challenge to the World Bank and its economic orthodoxy. That's a good thing, because the Japanese are basically right about the Bank's policies -- and about the poverty of the U.S. neo-classical model in Eastern Europe.

"What has structural adjustment meant for our people? Greater poverty, greater inflation, and greater unemployment. According to data from the Honduran College of Economists, poverty grew from 68 to 73 percent, over 54 percent of the economically active population is unemployed, and inflation has increased 63.4 percent since 1990. Misery is reflected in the faces of men, children, women, and old people, who must wander through the city in search of food, housing, and work. The World Bank officials who have visited the country must have seen this misery from the moment they disembarked from the plane, since at the airport, as much as in the streets of the city, it is evident that many people subsist only thanks to the few pennies they manage to collect by begging."

Narda Melendez, Coordinator,
Asociación Andar,
Honduras

31

Banking on Poverty:
An Insider's Look at the World Bank
Michael H. K. Irwin

ichael H. K. Irwin joined the World Bank in April 1989 as director of the Health Services Department, following a 32-year career with the United Nations. During August and September 1989 he also served as the World Bank's acting vice president for personnel. On March 30, 1990, after completion of one year at the Bank, he resigned out of frustration with "the Bank's bloated, over-paid bureaucracy, its wasteful practices, and its generally poor management."

In 1987, facing complaints from its major donor nations that it was "inefficient and drifting," the World Bank undertook an extensive, corporate-style reorganization. The Bank publicized the reorganization heavily in an attempt to convince donor nations that it could trim bureaucratic fat and thereby merit a $75 billion increase in its capital to finance an enlarged annual lending program. The funding boost was received in 1988 (the U.S. share is $14.3 billion), and the Bank has expanded its lending activities in Latin America, Africa, Asia and, more recently, Eastern Europe.

In 1990, however, three years after the reorganization, the administrative budget continues to grow. The staff will soon top pre-reorganization levels. Extravagant benefit packages characterize the institution more than ever. As discussions at meetings of senior World Bank officials regularly disclose, the institution is plagued by massive overstaffing, bureaucratic gridlock and staff preoccupation with further salary and benefit hikes. Public proclamations to the contrary, poverty reduction is the last thing on most World Bank bureaucrats' minds.

$150 Million Reorganization a Wash

In 1987, the World Bank's regular staff numbered about 6,150, and its administrative budget was $81 million. (New loans approved that year totaled $17.7 billion.) As a result of the reorganization, 498 staff left -- 80 elected voluntary separation and received golden handshakes averaging $134,000, and another 418 who were let go when no appropriate positions were found for them received average packages of $291,000. The total cost of the reorganization -- for separation payments, retraining, and office moves -- came to $148.3 million. The World Bank's president at the time, Barber Conable, estimated that "the Bank's operating costs will be cut about $50 million a year due to greater operating efficiency."[1]

The regular staff of the World Bank number about 6,100, and the present administrative budget is $900 million. In addition to the regular staff, there are approximately 500 long-term consultants (average length of service is 1.3 years), another 500 temporary staff (some of whom have been in the same job for three years or more) and 375 contractual staff. At least 50 of those who left during the 1987 reorganization have returned on short-term consultancies.

In short, although the reorganization removed a few hierarchical layers, it did not measurably reduce staff numbers, and it did not save any money. On May 4, 1989, William Cosgrove, then the vice president for personnel, admitted to his senior staff that the Bank "could do twice as much with its present staff or only needs half the staff for the present workload."[2] Indeed, while some areas are adequately staffed, and even a few are understaffed, most departments have a surplus of personnel looking for work to do. Yet, as Cosgrove admitted, it is still "difficult to remove dead wood."

Bureaucratic Gridlock

The World Bank today remains highly bureaucratic. For example, some staff never meet their director, several offices still have vague or overlapping functions, there are uncertain staffing predictions and gridlock in the senior grades, and budgeting procedures are complex. The organization, as Francisco Aguirre-Sacasa, then the director of external affairs, noted at a meeting on August 23, 1989, "is choking on reports." The bank suffers from many poor managers who, as noted by personnel consultant Michael Macoby at a senior personnel managers' meeting on January 27, 1989, act as "dukes, running their departments or offices like fiefdoms."

There is a serious staff morale problem at the Bank. A Staff Association survey in 1988 revealed that "there is little trust between staff and senior management." Sixty-five percent of the staff describe morale among their immediate co-workers as "low." At a senior managers' meeting on December 21, 1989, Willi Wapenhans, then the senior vice president for external affairs and administration, remarked that there is "a declining level of job satisfaction and a preoccupation with salaries and promotions."

The Bank's problem of generally poor management is compounded by the excessively legalistic manner in which much of the work is done and by complicated staff rules that, as former Bank staffer James Jones noted at a personnel meeting on July 7, 1989, "have layers of exceptions and modifications."

The executive directors, who represent member governments at the Bank and are charged with making policy, are, in fact, little involved in the management of the organization. Indeed, the Executive Board is regarded contemptuously by many senior staff. At a budget seminar on May 22, 1989, Robert Picciotto, vice president for corporate planning and budgeting, stated that often the "mushroom approach" is taken with the board: "Keep it in the dark, and feed it garbage." And Aguirre-Sacasa, at a senior managers' meeting on September 13, 1989, noted that "many would be concerned" if the board received certain documents several weeks before they were to be discussed because there "might be too many comments" from its member governments.

Inflated Salaries

The World Bank pays high, tax-free salaries. The World Bank president earns $154,000 a year; the 15 vice presidents earn, on average, $123,000 and the 58 directors earn, on average, $105,000. The World Bank's top 74 officials thus enjoy salaries averaging $120,000. Just below the top levels are hundreds of "technical advisers" who earn between $80,000 and $105,000. Again, all salaries are tax-free.

In recent years, World Bank salaries have been rising faster than the U.S. inflation rate. In 1988, professional staff received an average 6 percent increase, compared with a 4.2 percent U.S. inflation rate. In 1989, they received an average 11.1 percent increase (ranging from 7.7 percent for 174 staff at the low end to 17.5 percent for 31 staff at the high end), compared with a 5.2 percent U.S. inflation rate. In 1990, according to a January 8, 1990, report from the Department for Corporate Planning and Budget to the President's Council, there was projected "a salary budget increment of 6 percent . . . compared to a general U.S. inflation rate projected at about 4.5 percent."

Bank salaries are annually reviewed and set by the Executive Board. One reason for salaries that surpass the general inflation rate is that, in the salary reviews prepared for the board by the Bank's Personnel Department, great weight is given to comparators in the private sector. In 1989, for example, data on 95 private U.S. companies were used, whereas data on only eight public-sector agencies were included. Moreover, the Bank's Staff Association has been actively campaigning to get the U.S. Civil Service removed as a comparator for the Bank's salary system.

Another reason for the growth of Bank salaries is that the salaries and benefits of the Bank's 22-member Executive Board regularly reflect increases in Bank staff salaries. (The U.S. executive director is the only exception. He is paid by the U.S. Treasury Department, which he represents at the World Bank.) There is thus little incentive for the board to control salary growth. That seriously contravenes the executive directors' role as the representatives of the Bank's member governments who compose the Bank's policy-making body.

In addition to salaries, the number of the Bank's regular (core) staff also continues to grow. It is projected at 6,211 for 1991, up from about 6,150 before the reorganization. With the 1990 salary increase and continued staff growth, the Bank's administrative budget reached $1 billion in 1991. That growth in overhead comes despite the fact that the same January 8, 1990, report to the President's Council mentioned above notes that, in some areas of development, the "Bank Group response tends to be constrained less by inadequate numbers of staff than by difficulties in coordination . . . and by the training, orientation and attitudes of Bank staff."

Perquisites Galore

In addition to salaries, Bank staff enjoy many further benefits, such as a salary supplement of up to $3,000 a year to make up for a spouse's "inadequate" income. A Bank professional need only submit a simple form stating that his or her spouse received less than $10,000 from employment in a given year in order to receive such a salary supplement. Certification through presentation of tax forms is almost never requested. My own rough estimate is that one half of the Bank's professionals avail themselves of that benefit.

Bank professionals also receive $420 annually for each dependent child, subsidized meals at work, a good medical and dental insurance plan (staff pay only one third of the premiums) and excellent life insurance coverage. Internationally recruited staff can receive up to $5,480 in education grants for each child between the ages of 5 to 24. Expatriate staff are also entitled to home-leave travel for themselves and their families, flying first class if they go every three years and business class if they return to their home countries every two years. In addition, a staff member receives a grant (pocket money) of $1,070 -- and a spouse and dependent children each get $534 -- for every home-leave trip.

Until 1985, staff joining the Bank from abroad who had acquired "green cards" (that is, had become permanent U.S. residents but were still using their national passports) received expatriate benefits. Such benefits are no longer officially available for new staff; however, about 900 Washington-based staff who had green cards before 1985 and had joined the Bank before that year continue to take home-leave to their countries of birth and receive education grants for their children.

Washington-based professional staff who are reassigned to overseas posts in developing countries (only about 240 at present) do very well in terms of benefits. In addition to their Washington-based salaries and benefits, they get free furnished air-conditioned housing, with all utilities paid, and free security guard service when local conditions warrant. A regular assignment allowance of $5,000 annually is provided and, in most locations, a "special overseas allowance" is also paid (that allowance can vary from a 10 percent bonus of one's salary in Ankara or Brasilia to a 25 percent bonus in Addis Ababa or Brazzaville). Then, in places where the cost of living is higher than in Washington, a post adjustment allowance is additional. Also, there are handsome installation and "settling-in" grants and a further "grant on return" when staff come back to Washington, as well as allowances for shipping personal effects. Because of all those benefits, many staff can save most of their Washington-based salaries when they are reassigned overseas and living like "Lords of Poverty," to borrow from the apropos title of British writer Graham Hancock's 1989 book about the global foreign aid elite.[3]

World Bank staff away from Washington also work in comfortable surroundings. A December 1989 report in a Pakistani newspaper, describing the new Bank building in Islamabad, mentioned that "those who visit the office will think they are in the lobby of a luxury hotel rather than a fuddy-duddy Bank."[4]

All Bank staff members based in Washington can eventually benefit from a generous pension plan. If I had completed my two-year assignment, beginning at age 62 (the present retirement age), I could have received a pension, starting at $5,872 annually, for the rest of my life. (That is a typical pension, adjusted for years of service, for the lowest level of director at the World Bank.) Staff members contribute 7 percent of their salaries, and the Bank provides an amount equal to twice the total contributions of all participants as well as any additional amount that may be required to cover the costs of the plan. The present assets of the Bank's plan total about $2.7 billion. Retired staff are guaranteed a lifetime pension, with cost-of-living increases, and financial security for their survivors.

Because of the excellent salaries and benefits, it is no wonder, as Macoby, who himself once received $3,000 a day from the Bank, said at a senior personnel managers' meeting on January 27, 1989: "Nobody leaves; many staff are too comfortable." (About 5 percent of the staff do leave every year, but approximately half that number are at the normal retirement age.)

Since salaries (about 5 percent higher) and benefits (including an even better pension plan) are greater at the International Monetary Fund, it is easy to understand why the Bank's management and Staff Association frequently refer to the need for "parallelism" between the two organizations so that the World Bank's emoluments can rise to the IMF's levels.

Flying First Class

Given that about 90 percent of the World Bank's total staff live in the Washington area, one major expense of operating the Bank is travel to the developing world. In the present budget, $5 million is provided for such travel. When the most distant destination of a trip is more than nine flying hours from Washington, staff fly first class; otherwise, they fly business class, never economy. If all of the Bank's overseas travel was business class, at least $12.5 million would be saved.

In February 1990, on a trip to East Africa, I gave up my first-class entitlement and, by flying business class, saved $1,900. That resulted in considerable internal criticism from the Staff Association,[5] Senior Vice President Ernest Stern[6] and many individuals. One wrote to my vice president that first-class travel is necessary to protect the "health of frequent flyers." He concluded: "My family and I will not feel safe again until Mr. Irwin has been replaced by someone who really cares."[7] Another, a physician, maintained that there might be "a modest increase in the numbers of post mission travel induced strokes among our more elderly frequent travellers."[8] And the editor of *Bank's World*, the staff journal, who printed a letter from me saying that I believed there were no important advantages to flying first class,[9] told me that, in his nine years as editor, he did "not recall ever running a story prompting so many angry responses."[10]

Of course, flying first class allows staff to accumulate "frequent flyer mileage" very quickly, which the Bank allows them to use for personal travel. In addition, the first-class entitlement made it possible for the Bank to reach an agreement with British Airways that provides staff with a free upgrade to Concorde for first-class travel to from Washington, subject to availability within 96 hours of departure.

When traveling officially, staff can stay in first-class hotels (such as the Grosvenor House in London and the Nairobi Safari Club) with all expenses paid. Staff are reimbursed for food or hotel expenditures without presenting receipts, and many such claims go undocumented. The Staff Association has successfully resisted attempts to institute a simple money-saving per diem arrangement, such as that followed by the State Department for U.S. government employees. On official trips staff use U.N. "laissez-passers," which give them a preferred status when passing through immigration and customs inspections.

Borrowers May Now Be More Skilled Than Bank Staff

The World Bank also wastes considerable funds on training programs and "retreats." In a September 12, 1989, report to then President Conable, it was noted that, between July 1988 and June 1989, 5,763 participants were involved in 188 retreats at a total cost of $5.8 million. Although the Bank has several good training and conference rooms, 90 percent of the retreats were held outside the Bank. One third were held in Washington hotels, including such expensive establishments as the Watergate and the Willard.

Training, especially for maintaining professional skills, is very important in any organization, and there is $6.9 million for training in the fiscal year 1990 Bank budget. However, there is little overall coordination of training activities. As Conable wrote in a June 16, 1989, memorandum: "The training budget, training objectives and training results are increasingly controversial." In a discussion on training in the President's Council on June 30, 1989, Wapenhans noted that "there had been a deterioration in the skills of Bank staff" and that "the bulk of training resources went to basic skills areas: technology, language, writing and communications and orientation."

Timothy Thahane, vice president and secretary to the Executive Board, said that "increasingly the skills of the Executive Directors' advisors were superior to some of the Bank staff they have to deal with." The question was raised whether staff should not be more responsible and take courses on their own time, but the minutes recorded that "Bank staff have become used to having training courses provided during working hours." Afterwards, in a July 7, 1989, report to his senior staff, then vice-president Cosgrove reported that "borrowers may now be more skilled than Bank staff."

Burn Bags and Shredders

A January 1987 World Bank directive states: "It is the Bank's policy to be open about its activities and to welcome and to seek out opportunities to explain its work to the widest audience possible." Yet discussions within the organization and in the Executive Board are often conducted with the greatest secrecy. Notes attached to the transcripts of the proceedings of the board's meetings state that they "should not be copied without the permission of the Vice President and Secretary" (Thahane) and that his office must be notified "if the transcript is to be passed on to another staff member."

Circulation of countless other records, reports and documents is also restricted. Most documents are classified "strictly confidential" (defined as "information of a highly sensitive nature," for example, many papers on fine-tuning the reorganization); "confidential" (defined as "information to be confined to recipients who have a need to know," for example, the annual budget); and "for official use only" (defined as "information available to all staff of the institution but to which external access is limited," for example, a staff appraisal report on a project).

According to a March 1989 instruction, staff "should use 'burn bags' to dispose of all classified records, including drafts, one-time-use carbon paper, notes, etc. Burn bags containing classified records should be stored in locked file cabinets until they have been collected" by the security division. And "certain classified records of Controller's and Personnel . . . require shredding before disposal." As an example of shredder mania, the World Bank's Health Services Department maintains three shredders for a staff of 30.

The Bank also requires "regular and frequent password changes to assist in managing access to computerized information." Passwords "should be memorized and not written down where unauthorized persons could easily retrieve them," according to Bank guidelines. Passwords have to be changed at least once every six months, and sometimes even monthly. For access to the personal computer in my office, I worked my way through my three daughters' names in a single year.

Early in 1989, World Bank officials tried to prevent the publication of a June 1989 *Reader's Digest* article entitled, "The Alarming Truth about the World Bank." *Reader's Digest* editor-in-chief Kenneth Gilmore confirms that William Stanton, counselor to Conable, telephoned him with a request that the magazine not publish the article. Later, at a May 17 World Bank senior managers' meeting within the administration complex, Aguirre-Sacasa noted that the Bank had been unable to "suppress" the article's publication, but had achieved a few pre-publication "corrections."

Conclusion

The Bank staff, living and working comfortably in the Washington area and venturing forth in luxury, with first-class flights and hotels, are out of touch with both the realities and the causes of poverty in the Third World. World Bank staff, who deal almost exclusively with ministers and senior civil servants on their "missions," are simply bureaucrats talking confidentially with autocrats, getting only information that the borrower governments want the Bank to have. In fact, the well-paid World Bank staff strikingly parallel the Third World's own senior bureaucrats, whose padded salaries have contributed to the economic ruin of most of their nations.

The World Bank is hypocritical in prescribing financial discipline and savings for developing countries while it lavishes handsome salaries and other benefits on its own bureaucrats. Moreover, the Bank's continued internal malaise and financial extravagance three years after reorganization, along with the lack of any "graduates" from its lending program, raise serious questions about whether the United States or any other Western nation should give the institution another dime.

Notes

1. Hobart Rowan, "World Bank Retrenchment May Cut Up to 600 Jobs," *Washington Post*, May 5, 1987, p. C1.

2. The author was present at this meeting, and the quote is taken from his meeting notes. Other quotes in this paper attributed to World Bank officials at meetings, with dates given, are taken from the author's notes.

3. Graham Hancock, *Lords of Poverty: The Power, Prestige and Corruption of the International Aid Business* (New York: Atlantic Monthly Press, 1989).

4. Ishrat Hyatt, "World Bank Building Inaugurated," *The Muslim*, December 1, 1989.

5. World Bank office memorandum to Michael Irwin from Paul Cadario of the Staff Association, February 16, 1990.

6. Note from Ernest Stern to Bilsel Alisbah, vice president of Michael Irwin's department, February 16, 1990.

7. World Bank office memorandum to Bilsel Alisbah from Gottfried Ablasser, February 9, 1990.

8. World Bank office memorandum to Michael Irwin from Grant Sinclair, February 9, 1990.

9. *Bank's World*, letters to the editor, February 1990, p. 19.

10. World Bank office memorandum to Michael Irwin from Thierry Sagnier, editor of *Bank's World*, March 14, 1990.

32

Fighting Poverty at the World Bank
Margie Snider

A few years ago, Maria Elena Flores made up her mind to flee the two big adversities that marked her life in eastern El Salvador: war and poverty. So, like millions of other immigrants with similar motivations, she came to the United States. As luck would have it, she wound up working at an anti-poverty agency, of sorts--and a very richly endowed one, at that.

But things haven't turned out quite the way Flores had hoped. She escaped the war, but the poverty is still with her. Working as a janitor in downtown Washington, D.C., Flores earns the D.C. minimum wage ($4.75 an hour) and has no health insurance. To make ends meet, she shares a small apartment with three other adults.

"The pay is not much," she said, standing outside the large office building she helps clean at night, "and if you are one minute late, they take away money."

Her words came quickly as she spoke of her previous life in El Salvador and why she'd come to this country. It was almost time for her to clock in, and it was clear from the anxiety in her voice that she didn't want to be late, that even a minute's pay was precious.

The building Flores works to clean five nights a week is one of several housing the Washington headquarters of the International Bank for Reconstruction and Development -- better known as the World Bank.

Like Flores, the World Bank knows plenty about poverty in El Salvador -- and in dozens of other countries throughout the developing world. In fact, the World Bank's professed purpose is to fight poverty by promoting economic development in poor countries. It prefers to characterize itself as "a central force for development . . . in the struggle against poverty," as former Bank President Barber Conable declared in 1988.

"Poverty on today's scale prevents a billion people from having even minimally acceptable standards of living," Conable said. "To allow every fifth human being on our planet to suffer such an existence is a moral outrage."

Apparently, however, that "outrage" doesn't apply to the impoverishment the Bank allows to persist among people who work right in its own headquarters -- people like Flores, who clean the offices.

The Bank's major shareholders are Western-bloc industrialized countries -- the U.S., Britain, France, West Germany and Japan. Established in 1944 to aid postwar recovery, the Bank more recently has focused on promoting economic activities in Third World countries. Its "main business," as one of its publications puts it, is to make loans for specific projects such as schools, dams, roads, crop production and fertilizer plants. Such loans have totaled billions of dollars to scores of countries -- including millions to Flores' El Salvador.

The people whose offices Flores cleans have good jobs. They are engineers, economists and technical experts in such areas as agriculture and telecommunications. They come from all over the world. Their pay is generous, and so are their benefits and health coverage. Eighty percent of the Bank's 5,500-member staff are from countries other than the United States; they and their families get free round-trip airfare to their home countries every three years.

There are about 250 janitors who clean the Bank's office buildings. They, too, come from all over the world -- from Ghana, Egypt, Brazil, Jamaica, Sierra Leone, Nigeria, as well as from El Salvador and the United States. Most are women. And, like Flores, many are from countries to which the Bank has made development loans.

Employed by a private cleaning contractor, these janitors are offered only part-time work. Their pay averages about $115 a week, or less than $6,000 a year. This forces some of them to rely on public assistance. An example is Denise Speed, 24. While working as a janitor at the World Bank, Speed had to live in a homeless shelter for several months. Now she lives in an apartment subsidized by the D.C. government and qualifies for food stamps.

The World Bank janitors are overwhelmingly in favor of a campaign for union representation begun in 1988 by SEIU (Service Employees International Union) Local 525 in Washington. (The Bank used to have a unionized cleaning contractor, but changed to a nonunion contractor several years ago.) But Conable and other Bank officials refused to support the demand for union recognition. They even indicated that, should the cleaning firm sign a union contract with the janitors, the Bank might switch to another cleaning company. In addition to union recognition, the janitors have sought a pay increase to $6.50 an hour, health insurance, paid sick days and holidays.

In the Bank's 1988 annual report, there is a photograph from Bangladesh. It shows a group of women and children huddled outside a public health clinic. The report says providing "essential and affordable health care" for the rural poor is one goal of Bank-supported projects in Asia.

Back in Washington, Delmar Simpkins, a World Bank janitor, is expecting her first baby. She has had to borrow money from friends to pay for some of the medical care she needs, since she has no health insurance. She now lives in a rooming house, but she doesn't want to have to raise a child there.

Said Speed: "I have nothing against the World Bank sending money to undeveloped countries. But I think justice should start at home."

Nevertheless, the janitors' demands initially fell on deaf ears. Bank officials continued to focus their customary attention on poverty in the Third World while overlooking, or ignoring, the working poor in their own backyard. So the janitors decided to recast their message in terms the Bank would be more likely to understand.

Early one morning, a delegation of janitors rang the bell at Conable's residence. No one answered, so they slipped their specially printed invitation under the door and left. It read:

"We have set up 'Janitorville,' our own country. Maybe we can get better treatment from the World Bank as a Third World country than as janitors who clean here daily.

"Like many Third World countries, tourism is our major industry. This special tourist visa is your invitation to visit us in Janitorville."

Conable never visited Janitorville, a mock shantytown of colorful tents, exhibits, banners and lively lunch time rallies in a public park across from the Bank's main building. But a lot of other people took tours during the five days it was in operation. They ranged from World Bank staffers and federal office workers to unionists, bemused tourists, and a famous former janitor who dropped by one afternoon, saw a leaflet asking "What does the World Bank do?" and added his written reply to the others: "Keeps black people broke -- Harry Belafonte."

In fact, the World Bank has its share of critics who contend that its policies and projects harm as well as help poor people in Third World countries. Cheryl Payer, author of several books about the Bank and a former consultant to the U.N. Center on Transnational Corporations, asserts that the Bank's lending does more to help multinational corporations than the poor. She writes "the bank equates good economic management with policies favorable to foreign investors and is quite willing to overlook the fact that such policies may be incompatible with a genuine commitment to abolish poverty."

Patrick Bond, a political economist who specializes in international finance, says that "infrastructure" projects like roads and dams funded by the Bank primarily benefit multinational corporations drawing raw materials from the Third World. Asked whether the Bank's policies truly help the world's poor, Bond replied: "By and large, no. The Bank makes things worse."

Asked to comment on the low wages paid to janitors at the Washington offices, Payer said: "It's absolutely consistent with their policies, because their aim in the Third World is to reduce the real wages of workers."

At Janitorville, passersby were occasionally startled by the sight of janitors wearing black and white "prison stripe" uniforms to dramatize that their low wages make them "economic prisoners."

"They're taking in billions, yet we're still working for pennies, and can't afford a decent house or apartment," said Louis Sharp, a janitor who was "mayor" of Janitorville for one day. He was wearing handcuffs and standing near a large banner that read, "End Poverty at the World Bank."

That goal eluded Janitorville, as Bank officials refused during the week even to discuss the issue of unionization -- not to mention the janitors' demands for decent pay and benefits. At one point, eight protesters were arrested in a peaceful sit-in demonstration at the Bank building's main entrance.

But the janitors and their union haven't given up. SEIU has been enlisting international support from service unions in other countries where the World Bank operates. And some members of Congress -- who have something to say about the U.S. government's annual appropriation for the Bank -- are expressing concern about the gap between the Bank's words and deeds.

Meanwhile, Maria Elena Flores and the other janitors continue to clean the Bank's offices and to live on the edge of poverty. And the Bank continues to send massive antipoverty loans to the same countries, in many cases, where these janitors came from. Apparently, poverty is not easily eradicated when the World Bank has a hand in it.

[Although the Service Employees International Union has continued its fight for union rights at the World Bank, as of April 1994 the janitors at the World Bank were still not working under a union contract.]

International Tribunal Judges the G-7
Peoples' Tribunal

T*he following document is excerpted from the Final Declaration of an International Peoples' Tribunal held in Tokyo, July 3-4, 1993. The G-7 is the Group of Seven industrial countries that dominate the world economy and have controlling influence over the policies of the IMF and the World Bank: USA, Britain, Germany, France, Italy, Canada and Japan. In attendance and supporting the following statement were representatives from development organizations, academia, trade unions and research centers from around the world. For a complete text of the tribunal's final report contact AMPO (Japan/Asia Quarterly Review, P.O. Box 5250, Tokyo, JAPAN).*

Response and Redress

Redressing the policies and practices that form the basis of our indictment is indeed a formidable challenge. This will involve changing the basic structure and organization of multilateral agencies (such as the World Bank, the IMF and GATT) that the G-7 uses as instruments for the advancement of its economic objectives, for the preservation of present power relationships and for the perpetuation of its domination of the peoples of the South. This, in turn, will involve the drastic reorganization of the G-7.

It would be simplistic to underestimate the difficulties ahead. But equally, it would be tantamount to despair and surrender to be fatalistic in the face of such difficulties. Indeed, the Tribunal was presented with several cases in which the mobilization of people in both South and North effectively blocked, and in some instances reversed, destructive G-7 policies.

It is important, therefore, that both short- and long-term responses be mobilized within the sphere of transnational participatory democracy, which must be the main arena for such struggles. But selective use (recognizing their limitations) of the institutions of the international, intergovernmental system and of the national state systems in the South and North alike need not be totally abandoned. A creative mix of responses in both of these arenas may well prove necessary.

In the domain of peoples' movements and civil society, more effective South-South and South-North linkages need to be forged at the micro-level to strengthen the political and economic base. At the macro-level, the forging of effective peoples' alliances to advocate and lobby for policy changes and multilateral institutional-redesign are essential, if visionary. Thus, for example, to press for recognition by the G-7 (and its multilateral institutional agents) of human and social indicators and of ecological indicators to address human and social deficits and ecological deficits is crucial. But it is important that these alternative indicators, as well as the norms and standards they will help to implement and enforce, be articulated and elaborated at grassroots levels through an exercise of transnational popular sovereignty and as an expression of transborder participatory democracy.

Of special concern is the enormous concentration of unaccountable power in the hands of transnational corporations that are the driving force behind the G-7 governments and the international financial institutions. Our response must be at different levels, ranging from grassroots resistance when whole communities are threatened by the intrusion of TNCs to a concentrated effort at the global level to monitor their performance and make them truly accountable to international human rights law. Responses must also include continuing resistance to attempts to consolidate TNC dominance of the global economy through the GATT.

More immediately, however, the struggle for a better tomorrow needs to take place within the context of addressing today's disablement, disempowerment and victimization. So far as this legacy of the G-7 is concerned, there are important and immediate tasks of:

• Effecting relief, rehabilitation and de-victimization of the ever-growing legion of victims of the G-7.

• Ensuring the protection against revictimization of those whose very humanity has been victimized by the G-7, its multilateral agents and its transnational corporate principals.

• Securing the accountability at the institutional level (be it multilateral, bilateral or national) of those responsible for the creation of such victims and of treating people as "disposable and expendable."

• Establishing responsibility at the personal level in terms of both criminal and civil liability as well as popular censure and social ostracism. "Iron-clad guarantees" of immunity from liability and institutional opacity and anonymity breed covertness and clandestine corruption. The more that personal responsibility can substitute for institutional accountability, the further along we will be in identifying those truly responsible rather than holding out the sacrificial lambs that the North will give to the South.

• Compensating, not in a narrow legalistic sense, but rather in terms of a human impacts equivalent of the "polluter pays" principle in the environmental sphere. The question here is, who pays compensation to the human victims of structural adjustment policies and other development policies and programs? On what basis: how and why? Once again, the matter of compensation must not be a matter only of legal liability -- tortuous, criminal or other -- alone. It must be based upon principles of justice, fairness and non-discrimination. Compensation must be delivered both through legal and extra-legal community-based processes as well.

• Voicing public censure and imposing penal and other sanctions through both state and popular processes. Delegitimization and disempowerment are powerful mechanisms that the processes of transnational participatory democracy must rely upon. The institutions of state law may, at times, be able to play a supportive role. But the challenge lies in finding ways for the people to devise mechanisms for dealing with crimes against humanity rather than relying on state structures alone for that purpose.

• Enacting preventive and injunctive remedies and relief. The Chipko movement, which courageously protects endangered forests in India, clearly underscores the merit of preventive rather than remedial relief. It also highlights the capacity of people to act collectively even while their governments remain paralyzed or unwilling to act or even react.

While each of the above seven responses may be initiated in civil society or the state sector or the intergovernmental sector, it is crucial that existing international normative frameworks (in respect of human rights, environment and development) serve as the foundation for such actions. Only then can principle prevail over subjectivity. Only then can denials and grievances become the basis for popular mobilizations and the exercise of popular sovereignty.

Conclusion

The Tokyo Peoples' Tribunal has drawn up this indictment to clarify the realities surrounding the role being played by the G-7 framework in the "new world order." It is a role destructive of human well-being, with cruel and adverse effects on the poor everywhere and on the habitat of the planet. In preparing this indictment we have no illusion that the struggle can be won quickly or easily.

Yet there are reasons to be hopeful. The cooperation of peoples across borders in a common endeavor to promote justice and nonviolence, to reduce human suffering and deprivation and to protect the environment is building something new -- a real network of social activists with local roots and a global outlook. We identify these developments as the beginnings of a transnational democratic order that might be called globalization-from-below, a movement of peoples being formed to resist and transform the kind of structures being maintained by the G-7 states, what we have labeled here globalization-from-above. There is also encouraging evidence that the critique of the World Bank/IMF approach to development is gaining credibility, and is beginning to put even officials of these institutions on the defensive in public discussion and debate.

In the end, our confidence about the future arises from the conviction that transnational democracy best represents the changing tide of history. No one a decade ago anticipated the collapse of the oppressive Soviet internal and external empire, but it happened quickly and decisively. We should not rule out the possibility that deep flaws in the G-7 approach to global domination will create a variety of opportunities for drastic reform and reconstruction. Sharpening the critical perspective is essential preparation. The Tokyo Peoples' Tribunal seeks to contribute to this readiness on the part of the peoples of the world and their representatives.

We therefore invite all those around the world who share both our concern about the destructive role of the G-7 in maintaining and intensifying its global domination and our hope that, through transnational democratic processes, this trend can be thwarted and a more just and sustainable social order be created, to:

1) Signify affirmation of this indictment by joining us in signing it.

2) Organize peoples' tribunals at the local, national or regional level to refine, revise or extend this indictment, to render judgment based on their own experience and to formulate remedies appropriate to that experience.

3) Join together a year from now at the next G-7 Summit and 50th Anniversary of the IMF and the World Bank in a worldwide demand that widespread violations of human rights by the G-7 governments, the international financial institutions and the transnational corporations and banks be stopped and those responsible be held accountable for their actions.

34

African Alternative Framework to Structural Adjustment
UN Economic Commission for Africa

The African Alternative Framework to Structural Adjustment Programs for Socio-Economic Recovery and Transformation (AAF-SAP) originated from studies by Adebayo Adedeji and other economists at the United Nations Economic Commission for Africa in Addis Ababa, and was originally presented as a proposed framework in July 1989. Intended as an alternative to orthodox prescriptions presented by international agencies such as the World Bank and the International Monetary Fund, the draft was welcomed as "a basis for constructive dialogue" by the United Nations General Assembly in November that year. Only one country, the United States, voted against the resolution. The document published here is an abridgment of a popular version of the AAF-SAP that was published by the Economic Commission for Africa in Addis Ababa in April 1991.*

An Alternative Framework to SAPs

The failure of African countries to bring about a process of sustainable development in spite of SAPs as well as the suffering of the people led to an outcry for an alternative. It was generally agreed that any alternative to SAPs must at least have the following basic features:

• It must be a broad framework and not a standard program to be applied uniformly in all countries;

• The concepts of the framework must be viable and relevant to the present African situation;

• The framework must be practicable, meaning that it should be easy to implement and should not impose unbearable hardships and suffering on the people;

• The alternative should seek, hand in hand, adjustment with long-term development objectives and strategies;

• For the framework to be effectively operational, it must, right at its conception and formulation, involve all people at all levels.

Any alternative to SAPs should attempt to find convincing answers to at least the following four fundamental questions:

First, to what should African countries be adjusting? While most, if not all, SAPs in African countries have taken the short-term view that Africa should be adjusting to the financial crisis, what the African economies require is to bring about structural transformation, diversification and increased productivity.

Balancing budgets on its own can never make the African people richer and can also never bring about real development. The alternative framework was, therefore, anchored on the premise that any adjustment program must not compromise long-term development.

Second, what should African countries adjust? This was one of the most difficult questions. It touches on almost all aspects of socio-economic life: political, social, cultural, environmental and economic. The answer that was found was that African countries should adjust three basic elements:

• The different forces in the African society such as the domestic systems of government, the nature of the public sector, the learning systems, the cultural motivations and value systems, etc.;

• The different ways and means African countries produce what their people need: the human resources in terms of know-how and imagination; natural wealth in terms of minerals, land, forests, livestock, wildlife, energy, etc.; the financial wealth in terms of what people can keep or have kept aside for the future;

• The goods and services that are vital for the welfare of the people and for keeping the process of production running smoothly and continuously. These include vital goods and services like food, water, basic clothing, soap, energy for cooking, medicines, educational facilities and school supplies, cheap transport in rural and urban areas, sports and recreation as well as raw materials for small- and medium-scale industries.

The third question that the alternative set out to answer is that of how to adjust? Any adjustment that a country engages in should be done in such a way that human welfare is improved rather than worsened and that economic transformation will occur along with the adjustment.

The last, but not the least, important aspects of the alternative framework relate to the question of adjustment for whom and by whom? adjustment must be for the benefit of the majority of the people, and, as such, adjustment programs must derive *with* rather than *without* the people. Hence the alternative framework insists that adjustment with transformation must involve:

• Access of the poor to basic factors of production;

• Creation of employment opportunities;
• Improving the way national wealth is shared throughout the population.

Regarding the issue of who is to implement the alternative framework, it is necessary to emphasize the role of popular participation. Programs of adjustment with transformation should not be the property of only the government or the Ministry of Finance They should be the property of the people and the people's own grassroots organizations. It is the people who should decide on the main thrust of such programs and also devise the means and actions to be taken to implement these programs.

Policies for the Alternative

[The African Alternative] maintains that meeting the needs of local populations and investment in basic development goals are not luxuries to be easily dismissed or pushed aside while austerity programs stretch on into an indefinite and unknown future. Indeed, the framework further maintains that solving the people's basic problems and establishing a momentum for transformation are the real solutions.

This chapter takes a close look at the broad range of policy options to be applied flexibly to the specific cases of individual countries. It is a sort of menu from which each government can select a set of policy measures that suits its purpose, the condition of the country and the problems to be tackled.

[There are] four main categories or blocs. It is imperative in order to pursue the path of adjustment with transformation -- to have a wholesome and balanced meal, as it were -- to select from each and every one of the four blocs:

• Strengthening and diversifying Africa's production capacity;
• Improving the level of people's incomes and the pattern of its distribution;
• Adjusting the pattern of public expenditure to satisfy people's essential needs;
• Providing institutional support for adjustment with transformation.

Strengthening and Diversifying Production

The narrow range of goods and services that Africa presently produces either for export or to meet local needs has to be greatly widened. To do this, a number of policies become very important. For example, credit should be extended on favorable terms to food production and to enterprises that manufacture essential goods. Investment from overseas in these sectors should also receive favorable treatment. A larger share of foreign exchange has to be accumulated and channeled for the import of spare parts, fertilizers, chemicals, machinery and other vital production inputs in selected priority sectors.

For Africa to develop, it has to use its strengths in natural resources to build up its weak industrial sector. A strategic starting point is to carry out processing of raw materials, agricultural and mineral, within African countries. Processed exports will always earn more money overseas, and local industrial capacity will be increased and diversified. Employment will increase substantially. Links between agriculture and industry will fortify both sectors and make both sectors dynamic. Certain agricultural products, for instance, may be employed as raw materials in new industries, and some by-products can be used as fertilizers or as sources of energy. Manufacturing for its part would supply agriculture with what the sector needs in order to produce more, and more efficiently: agricultural tools and machinery, irrigation equipment, pesticides, etc. Manufacturing will also produce essential goods such as sugar, salt, soap, clothes, books, etc., to satisfy the needs of the rural farmers.

It is the development of human resources that will, in the final analysis, determine the course and content of the transformation process. The creativity and imagination of the African people will be the real factor in what Africa will be able to achieve. Hard work, understanding of the issues, dedication to African causes and a clear vision of the people will also be essential. [Therefore] it is necessary to focus on the development, mobilization and efficient utilization of one of Africa's most abundant resources: its people. Another requirement to build a broader base for production is to get scientific researchers involved directly with productive enterprises.

An additional area of strategic opportunity is to be found in the informal sector of Africa's economy. Cottage and small-scale businesses like car repair services, sewing, brick-making as well as light manufacture and assembly operations can effectively occupy a large proportion of overall economic activity in Africa. Already, these small enterprises in the informal sector are filling a large vacuum. Instead of harassing this sector, it should be supported and encouraged through access to credit and flexible regulatory procedures.

Food self-sufficiency is a very special category in the area of strengthening and diversifying Africa's production capacity. If it can feed its people, Africa will strengthen its human resources, reduce political instability and stem the loss of foreign exchange that has to be spent on imports of food. Therefore, AAF-SAP accordingly proposes that national governments should allocate a minimum of 20-25 percent of total public investment to agriculture and particularly to food production.

Government spending in agriculture should not only be on direct inputs such as seeds, fertilizers, or on extension services and technical assistance to farmers and farmers' cooperatives, but also on improvement of rural infrastructures like roads and storage facilities. Creating more jobs in the countryside and making the rural area attractive to live in will reduce the exodus of rural people to cities and provide a larger domestic market for national industries.

Land reform -- more equitable distribution of land on which to grow crops or to raise cattle and more open rules for legal ownership of land -- is high on AAF-SAP's agenda for Africa. Special emphasis is placed on granting legal recognition to the rights of African women to land. This is very basic because more than 85 percent of the African women of working age are estimated to be involved in agricultural production.

The common tendency to favor production of crops for export (the so-called cash-crops) over production of food for local consumption needs to be corrected. AAF-SAP strongly advocates price support policies for food production.

Trade and currency exchange rates are also very important in the process of strengthening and diversifying Africa's production base. Thus, a central feature of AAF-SAP is the use of multiple exchange rates. Under this policy, the rate at which the currency of an African country is exchanged for foreign currency will vary in the cases of different imports and exports and other financial transactions. African governments can promote industries of strategic national importance by assigning favorable terms of exchange to designated products. Conversely, vital imports can be encouraged.

Unfavorable rates of exchange on non-essential imports and luxury items and on capital flight (wealth amassed in African countries but taken outside of Africa) will help the balance of payments. Specially assigned currency exchange rates can also be applied to earnings of Africans working abroad, if they wish to send some of the earnings to their families or to transfer their savings to the home countries.

Careful use of multiple exchange rates is an alternative to the problems associated with highly over-valued currencies. It also avoids some of the drawbacks that have emerged from across-the-board and massive currency devaluations, which result in very high price increases, falling purchasing power and blockage of necessary imports such as medicines, spare parts, industrial inputs and petrol.

Improving Income and Its Pattern of Distribution

In undertaking adjustment with transformation, AAF-SAP calls for aiming at increasing levels of income. It is very costly and perhaps even counter-productive to undertake programs of adjustment that deflate the economy like one deflates a balloon. When an economy does not grow or goes into a recession, more people become unemployed, real wages decline and poverty increases. AAF-SAP strongly advises against such policies.

What it recommends are those policies that will increase the dynamism of the economy and increase incomes of the people. In this respect, resource mobilization and its efficient utilization are necessary first steps.

Decisive government action is needed to plug financial leakages, such as payments for unnecessary imports or overpriced imports or underpriced exports, flight of capital to foreign banks by foreigners and Africans alike, government inefficiency and untaxable profits made through criminal activity.

Also, an unacceptably high share of Africa's scarce foreign exchange is tied up in payments on foreign debt. To free financial resources for productive investment, debt relief on the part of international creditors is called for, as is improved debt management by African governments. Only a small proportion of the massive amount of debt that exists worldwide is owed by African countries. Relinquishing a portion of the African debt will not threaten the international credit system, but will make a tremendous difference to national economies that are presently making debt payments that are nearly as large as their export earnings.

Privatization of government enterprises is not neglected by AAF-SAP. The framework recognizes that governments must give up ownership of certain unprofitable operations, by selling them off preferably to national private businessmen and businesswomen. But under current African conditions, governments cannot completely abandon their role in ensuring development. Essential social services must be provided. Protecting the environment, building ports and roads, modernizing communication networks, establishing a system of primary, secondary and technical schools and colleges that will promote mastery of modern technology, to mention but a few, are all functions that must be carried out even if they rarely will produce high visible financial profits. In other cases, it is better to concentrate efforts on improving the quality of management of important state-run enterprises than to sell off valuable public property at a loss.

Therefore, AAF-SAP suggests that African countries should strike a pragmatic balance between the public and private sectors by eliminating subsidies to enterprises that do not provide social services or promote strategic development needs, adopting investment codes to encourage new businesses, making loans available at low interest rates and maintaining government involvement as and when necessary, especially in the crucial sectors of the economy.

Concerned about the need to improve the way national wealth is shared among the population, AAF-SAP proposes a strong policy of guaranteed minimum prices for food crops managed through strategic food reserves. This policy is seen as being crucial in assuring income to farmers. It should always be stressed that the majority of the African people live in rural areas mainly as farmers. According to AAF-SAP, policies must favor and protect this majority rather than the urban elites, as most plans and programs have tended to do up to now.

Adjusting Expenditure Patterns to Satisfy Vital Needs

Old-style SAPs put a lot of emphasis on the adoption of policies that reduce expenditures of governments and peoples: cuts in wages, elimination of subsidies on consumer goods and essential services, shrinking of government enterprises, reductions in the number of public employees and other budgetary reductions. Normally, governments found it easier to slash expenditures of the "soft" sectors like education and health. Governments would also quite readily postpone expenditures on development projects.

AAF-SAP flatly refuses to accept this very narrow view of adjustment. It is possible and better to deal with well-studied government expenditure switching. Such switching can bring about significant changes in the delivery of services and effectiveness of government without increasing spending. For example, resources can be switched from the military to social services and development projects. In this way, social services and development itself need not suffer.

AAF-SAP sees nothing wrong at all with the use of selective trade policies. Unlike traditional SAPs, AAF-SAP sees clear advantages in using import controls, including even the banning of non-essential goods. In this way, the essential goods for the people and the machines and equipment for development projects can be imported. The banning of certain imports can also help the growth of domestic substitutes and protect infant industries that would otherwise be swallowed up by cheap imports.

Rail and highway links that run in a straight line from the interior to the ports -- a legacy of colonial times -- need to be extended into a spider-web network connecting the African countries. Improved transportation and communication links will encourage intra-African trade and ease dependence on overseas markets. Trade within the continent will also be facilitated by taking down barriers between African countries, coordinating exchange rates between countries to make it easier to exchange goods and, when appropriate, bartering commodities of equivalent values without the medium of national currencies.

Marketing is another area of cooperation that needs to be investigated. AAF-SAP calls for agreements between African countries and overseas purchasers to stabilize the prices of primary export commodities. It also envisions the possibility of assigning export specializations, so that competition between African countries for export markets is reduced and downward pressure on prices of basic commodities is eased. It is clearly self-defeating for all countries to struggle to produce more of the same primary commodity (e.g., coffee or cocoa) as this will, in the long run, lower the price of the commodity in question.

Implementing the Alternative

It is certainly not enough to have an African Alternative on paper. It must be put into action. [This] requires the active support and participation of the entire population and their grassroots organizations, the full dedication and commitment of the government as well as the support of the international community.

At the national level, the activities of government will have to be closely coordinated within it and between it and people's organizations like trade unions, employer's associations as well as non-government organizations. Governments must find ways to yield a measure of authority to localities and community self-management.

At the subregional level, [there must be] close cooperation between the countries of the region: specialization of industries and specialized production of commodities for foreign markets, pooling of resources for research and industrial development, environmental protection and channels for increased intra-African trade. Coordination of consumption as well as production should be high on the agenda. It should be stressed that lack of regional cooperation was one factor that bedeviled conventional SAPs. More often than not, exchange rates, interest rates and pricing policies were adjusted at different times and to differing degrees among countries in the same region or subregion, with contradictory impact and, in many cases, with policies in one country nullifying the effect of other policies in a neighboring country.

At the international level, multilateral development and financial institutions, as well as bilateral donor agencies will have a useful role in implementing the policies of AAF-SAP. First, the international financial institutions such as the World Bank and the IMF should encourage and support programs designed by African governments to solve specific national problems of economic recovery and transformation. Second, donors should do all they can to respect the development priorities that African countries set themselves. Third, donors should give their assistance on the most favorable terms.

To adjust the ongoing selection of policy mechanisms and get early warning signals of deviations from objectives, programs need to be closely monitored. National, subregional and regional data systems will have to be in place to assess the success or failure of new policies.

Statistical indicators of economic growth and financial flows need to be studied, but so do qualitative factors, such as the extent to which basic needs are satisfied, political and social vitality and progress in transforming production structures and consumption patterns. National agencies need to become more sensitive to the plight of ordinary citizens, whether this plight is of hunger, disease, ignorance or the inability to educate children.

Gaining the support of the population, however, will require more than an extensive public relations campaign. There needs to be genuine participation of the people in rebuilding African political economies. This will require that decision-making is democratized at the national, local and grass-roots levels.

People will have to be convinced that their leaders are accountable to them and that genuine consultations take place at every stage of policy formulation, planning and implementation with local authorities, non-governmental organizations and village and neighborhood associations. AAF-SAP offers an opportunity for the leadership of African countries to regain the initiative in getting national development going ahead with the people. Its implementation will require perseverance, responsible decision-making, alertness to changing economic conditions and full commitment to genuine democratization.

"The facts of adjustment speak for themselves. Fifteen years after the World Bank and IMF emerged as the dominant force in economic policy making in sub-Saharan Africa, sub-Saharan Africa is now the only developing region in which poverty is deepening, human welfare indicators are worsening and prospects for accelerated recovery are receding.

"Oxfam challenges the claim that adjustment policies have created a framework for poverty reduction. According to the World Bank's argument, market liberalization in agriculture has increased prices and increased rural household incomes. But Oxfam's experience across Africa is that an undue emphasis on market deregulation has exposed vulnerable peasant producers to private sector monopolies that have proved every bit as exploitative as their parastatal predecessors.

"What is needed is an open acknowledgment of the scale of Africa's development failure -- including the failure of adjustment policies to generate sustainable growth and poverty reduction. Instead, we have got an exercise in institutional self-congratulation and public deception that will further erode the already dwindling credibility of both the World Bank and IMF."

Oxfam America

35

Reforming the Global Environment Facility
Cameron Duncan

T*he Global Environment Facility (GEF) was launched in 1990 as a project operated by the World Bank in cooperation with the United Nations Environment Program (UNEP) and the United Nations Development Program (UNDP). The GEF provides grants and technical assistance to Southern countries to help them implement environmental protection measures that the industrial countries failed to implement during their own development. The following recommendations are from a much longer Greenpeace International booklet,* **The World Bank's Greenwash: Touting Environmentalism While Trashing the Planet***.*

The GEF, under World Bank control, has the same critically flawed approach as the Bank. It is run undemocratically, its project information is secret and its decisions are taken without consultation with locally affected people or non-governmental organizations (NGOs). Many of its proposed projects have the potential to be environmentally destructive. Sixty percent of GEF projects are tacked onto existing or proposed Bank loans, which may be used to mitigate the environmental damage of the original project rather than contribute significantly to solving environmental problems.

Public Accountability and Access to Information
Local communities and NGOs must play an active role in ensuring ecologically sound and socially just development, and have meaningful participation in decisionmaking. A critical component to such participation and decisionmaking is access to information.

The Bank, however, severely restricts public access to information about its policies and operations, while paying lip service to the importance of involving local NGOs and community groups. Adequate oversight of Bank operations is not possible unless citizen organizations can review project documents and participate in project design before lending decisions are made. The Bank refuses to make public environmental impact assessments, project identification reports, appraisal reports and evaluations.

Principles for Accountability and Participation

1. UNCED must call for direct public accountability in any financing mechanism for the global environment. Global environmental breakdown cannot be avoided unless citizens and their organizations are given a decisive voice in the use of natural resources. New funding mechanisms must be directly responsive to the needs of local people and NGOs. Such mechanisms must be open to public scrutiny and accountable to locally determined priorities for meeting global targets. Thus, administration of environment and development funds must:

- be based on transparency and provide the public in donor and recipient countries access to complete documentation on projects at every stage of the project cycle;
- allow for consultation and broad participation in policy meetings and an active role for NGOs and affected communities in project development and implementation;
- include mechanisms to monitor funding activities, oversee consultation with local NGOs and communities and hear public complaints and
- acknowledge the right of communities to refuse projects that will damage their livelihoods or culture, and to demand ecologically sound, socially equitable alternatives.

2. Institutions should prioritize financial support to governments that actually adopt policies that uphold the rights to land and livelihood of indigenous people and other traditional communities, curb commercial exploitation of their natural resources and plan for ecological development.

3. Rational resource management and environmental regeneration can only be accomplished with the conscious, empowered involvement of people who live with and depend upon that environment. The involvement of people in the decisions that affect their lives is the essence of democracy.

4. Institutions should cease supporting projects that cause the destruction of forests and non-renewable resources, destroy the livelihoods of people or disregard the rights to land of indigenous peoples.

5. Governments should dissociate their aid programs from structural adjustment schemes. Institutions should recognize the harmful effects of existing forms of structural adjustment and conditional pro-

gram lending on poverty and the environment, and reorient their programs in accordance with such recognition.

Governance Principles: Control of the GEF

1. World Bank control of the GEF should be halted.

2. Donor countries must not have full control over new funds, as they do presently over the GEF. The governing body should include a balanced representation of participating governments, including recipient governments. Local and international NGOs and people's organizations must have the right to observe meetings related to the negotiation and operation of financing mechanisms.

3. Where NGO institutional capacity exists, a substantial portion of new funds should be granted to NGO and local indigenous organizations, which are best placed to develop and employ appropriate technology and to use biological diversity in a sustainable manner.

Sources of Funds

UNCED should consider how new financial resources for the environment could be mobilized through measures that would begin to address the roots of the problem.

1. **Debt relief.** Official debt forgiveness should be granted to all heavily indebted countries, with no conditions that impose orthodox structural adjustment policies on debtor countries.

2. **Reduced military spending.** Oversized military budgets should be converted to environmental, economic and human security budgets under civilian control. Governments should commit themselves to cutting military budgets by 50 percent or more over the next three years and to using the dividend to pursue sound development strategies at home and abroad.

3. **Private sector contributions.** A tax on the use of fossil fuels and electricity in industrialized countries could generate a fund of approximately $30 billion a year raised by a levy, in OECD countries, of $1.20 a barrel of oil or oil equivalent. Detailed studies on alternative forms of such an "ecological tax" should be initiated by UNCED.

Conclusion

Global environmental issues cannot be addressed by the transfer from North to South of the relatively small amount of funds committed in the GEF at a time when debt servicing requires a net flow of $45 billion a year from Southern debtors to Northern creditors. The GEF cannot be a substitute for fundamental changes in the international system of finance and aid. Nor does the GEF address the destructive lending practices of the World Bank and other Multilateral Development Banks.

A truly democratic global environment fund would be directly accountable to both its member governments and the local communities most affected by proposed development projects. As long as the World Bank continues to fund environmentally destructive projects and fails to support a transparent and participatory process, its management of the GEF will amount to nothing more than an expensive and elaborate greenwash.

Unless the world community addresses the problems of increasing international inequity and poverty, global economic and environmental decline are certain to accelerate. The key tasks are to reduce the debt burden, to rechannel development aid and military spending toward protection of the environment and participatory development and to transform and democratize the World Bank and other multilateral financial institutions. Until these realities become the keystone of national and international policies real environmentally sound and socially just development will continue to elude us.

"That social and environmental injustice is currently a condition of the South is simple to see. Take for example the import in the South of wastes and pesticides banned in the North. The pesticides help to produce food for export, reinforcing consumption patterns that we know need to be changed. Twenty percent of the world consumes 80 percent of the natural resources; this . . . was often said [at the Earth Summit] in Rio. In the South, the defense of our economic base isn't merely for ethical or theoretical reasons. We are defending our ability to live off of our own commodities. To do so necessitates commodity markets that truly reflect environmental degradation."

Maria Onestini, Co-Director,
Center for Environmental Studies,
Argentina

36

Little World Banks
Jessica Matthews

One of the most successful development organizations in the world is the Grameen Bank of Bangladesh. Started by professor Muhammad Yunus, the Grameen Bank is noteworthy for the stark contrast between its operating principles and those of the big, international lending institutions, such as the World Bank and the IMF. The Grameen Bank's success in empowering the poor has made it a model that is being emulated around the world.

Muhammad Yunus is an academic turned banker in Bangladesh who has turned the most sacred rules of the profession up-side down and made himself a frequently mentioned Nobel Prize candidate in the process.

He didn't plan it that way. Twenty years ago, Yunus was simply moved to try to help the abject poor who lived near the university where he taught economics. He approached local banks, convinced that what these people most needed was simply a tiny amount of money, as little as one dollar per person. The reception was not warm. Where was the collateral? the bankers asked. These people can't even read.

Finally, Yunus took out the loans himself, despite repeated warnings that the recipients were so poor and the amounts so small that "they'll just eat it up." Nevertheless, the scheme worked. The tiny loans were repaid. Soon, Yunus expanded to several villages, then to the whole district and finally, to five districts. The bankers still could not be convinced that Yunus' vision was sound and would not lend to his borrowers directly. Nothing, he finally concluded, would ever convince them. He would have to set up his own bank. It took another three years to secure government support. The Grameen ("rural" in Bengali) Bank was formally created in 1983, and the rest, as they say, is history.

Today, the Grameen Bank has a record that many a traditional bank would envy. It has more than a thousand branches and 1.6 million borrowers in 34,000 villages in Bangladesh. It lends $30 million per month and enjoys a loan recovery rate of 97 percent. It charges 20 percent interest with a one-year repayment requirement, yet the bad debt on its books is less than one half of one percent. What is its secret?

Yunus saw the banking system as anti-poor, anti-illiterate and anti-women. He set out to reverse all three.

He changed normal practice from "the more you have the more you can borrow" to "the less you have, the higher your priority." His bank would lend only to the poorest of the rural poor, and half of them must be women. Anyone who asks for a loan, he told his staff, is "a fake poor person. The person you are looking for will never come to you. When you find her she will say, 'Oh I don't need money.' When you hear that, you've found your person." The loan officer's job is not to be convinced of the borrower's creditworthiness, but to convince the borrower that she can use money to improve her life.

Banking with Grameen is no picnic. To build commitment and provide community support, the prospective client must find five friends to borrow with. Initial loans are $10 to $20. Average loans are $100. The interest rate is high, the repayment time short and there is a mandatory savings requirement. Yet 48 percent of those who have borrowed from the bank for ten years have crossed the poverty line. Another 27 percent have come close. The remainder have not been helped, usually because chronic ill health erodes any progress.

Experience showed that the payoff from loans to men often did not find its way back to their wives and children. The benefit to whole families was much more reliable when the borrower was a woman. In spite of enormous tensions in borrowers' marriages in a culture where women have few economic rights, today, nearly all borrowers are women.

Scattered around the world are thousands, perhaps tens of thousands, of small success stories like Yunus's program was ten years ago. The particular significance of the Grameen Bank is that it is one of a handful that has been able to grow. It uses a franchise-like system. New staff serve a lengthy apprenticeship. Branches borrow from the headquarters at 12 percent and lend at 20 percent. With that 8 percent spread they have to become profitable, which takes on average seven years. With these requirements and the capital accumulated through borrowers' required savings, the main bank's only need for concessional funds is to fuel expansion.

Now Yunus wants to see his program spread around the world. There are special conditions in Bangladesh, he thinks, that make the idea applicable there and not elsewhere. If anything, Bangladesh should be the acid test. Income is very low. Fertility, malnutrition, illiteracy and gender inequality are high. The communications infrastructure is poor to nonexistent. Yunus' dream is a Grameen Trust of $100 million to capitalize replicas in dozens of other countries: a little World Bank for people. Within the past few weeks, the U.S. Agency for International Development and the World Bank have each pledged $2 million: a small but hopeful beginning.

Many of those who work to ameliorate poverty in developing countries and in our central cities believe that the people they are trying to help have a better idea of what they need than experts in faraway capitals. The perennial stumbling block has been how to tap into this intimate knowledge of local needs on a large enough scale to make a difference. The Grameen Bank is one of few proofs that it can be done.

In Yunus' view, bankers' notions of "bankability" and "creditworthiness" unwittingly create a caste system that locks poor people into poverty. If he is correct, and if his bank can be replicated, he may have found a spark to revolutionary change.

"The World Bank and IMF are public institutions created 50 years ago to solve monetary disequilibrium between countries and to promote development. Unfortunately, the interests represented by them are farther and farther from these objectives. One of the remarkable features of these institutions is their immunity to popular influence and their hostility to democracy. The evolution of a democratic process in Latin America is being threatened by the structural adjustment programs imposed by the World Bank and the IMF. Citizens must press these institutions, which are public institutions, to change their policies and democratize their management. To force them to direct the billions of dollars of public resources that they hold to promote democratic, socially just and environmentally sustainable development."

Maria Clara Couto Soares,
IBASE (Brazilian Institute for
Social and Economic Analysis)

CONCLUSION: What To Do?

The reader who has waded through all the atrocities documented in this book may be tempted to be pessimistic. Yet the good news is that the top-down model of development is being resisted by grassroots community groups throughout the world.

• Trade unions and progressive political organizations are struggling to establish international health and safety standards that will require transnational corporations to treat workers and the environment with the respect they deserve.

• Environmental groups are uniting their efforts to raise global environmental standards to as high a level as possible. This is in contrast to the efforts of international elites to push environmental protection standards down to the lowest common denominator.

• Grassroots organizations in nearly every country are pushing their governments for more accountability and democratic process.

Our most important priority in the North must be to teach our own people that this is not just a "Third World issue." The top-down model of development is not in the best interest of most North Americans.

• Keeping wages suppressed in Third World countries causes companies to move jobs from high-wage countries like the U.S. and relocate to the Third World. This creates unemployment here while exploiting Third World workers at starvation wages. We would gain from increased exports if Third World workers earned decent pay.

• Fresh loans from the World Bank and IMF prop up undemocratic leaders in Third World countries without requiring them to democratize. These repressive regimes foment a spiral of violence and are more likely to create refugees than if they were democratic and shared the wealth more equitably.

• Impoverishment in Third World countries forces people to migrate in search of jobs and a better standard of living for their families. This mass migration in search of work in rich countries is often met with racist attacks against illegal immigrants. This racism is a general pollutant that debases the entire spectrum of social discourse.

• There is a built-in contradiction between poverty and sustaining the environment. Countries desperate to pay off their debts pillage their natural resources to gain new income. This promotes things like global warming and water pollution, which endanger us all.

An alternative vision for the future of the planet is being constructed from the bottom up by a diverse group of people. A simple and direct way for you to get involved in this exciting project is to join in some of the many activities of the "50 Years Is Enough" campaign, which is pushing for fundamental restructuring of the IMF and the World Bank. These banking institutions determine whether millions of people will live or die, and yet they operate in a thoroughly undemocratic manner. The 50 Years Is Enough campaign is demanding the following reforms:

• To limit further damage to subject populations and the environment, structural adjustment programs as implemented by the World Bank and the IMF must be halted.

• The World Bank and IMF must reorient their lending for economic reform to strengthen a wide variety of productive activity by the rural and urban poor, increase local self-reliance and broad-based local demand, promote equity for women and other marginalized groups, enhance workers' rights, ensure environmental sustainability and facilitate increased investment in physical and social infrastructure, especially investments in women's and girls' health, education and economic opportunities.

• The Bank and the Fund must embrace full public openness and citizen involvement in the negotiation and design of economic-reform loans so that reforms are based on local perspectives and local needs.

• The multilateral banks and commercial banks must implement debt relief immediately. Any conditionality associated with this relief should be mass democratic conditionality, as outlined above.

To find out more about the campaign, contact Global Exchange at (415) 255-7296. Better yet, use the coupon at the back of this book to become a member of Global Exchange. You'll receive our quarterly newsletter and Action Alerts, a 10 percent discount on our books and items in our crafts stores, priority on our Reality Tours, and you'll be connected with thousands of other internationalists who understand the importance of democratizing economic *and* political institutions.

The Suggested Readings that follow can help you understand the workings of the global economy, how its managers have abused their power and how we can organize alternative structures.

Finally, please contact the organizations listed in the Resource Groups section to get involved in some of the many campaigns to reform the world economy in the interests of the majority.

SUGGESTED READING

Periodicals

BankCheck Quarterly, 1847 Berkeley Way, Berkeley, CA 94703. $25/year.

Left Business Observer, 250 West 85th St., New York, NY 10024. $20/year.

Multinational Monitor, P.O. Box 19405, Washington, DC 20036. $25/year.

Third World Resurgence, c/o Michelle Syverson & Associates, P.O. Box 680, Manzanita, OR 97130. $20/year.

Books

Africa's Development Challenges and the World Bank, edited by Stephen Commins (Boulder, CO: Westview Press, 1988).

Aid and Power: The World Bank and Policy-Based Lending (two volumes) (London & New York: Routledge, 1991).

Aid for Just Development by Stephen Hellinger, Douglas Hellinger and Fred O'Regan (Boulder: Lynne Rienner Publishers, 1988).

Banking on the Poor by Robert Ayres (Cambridge, MA: MIT Press, 1983).

Bankrolling Disasters: International Development Banks and the Global Environment (San Francisco: Sierra Club, 1986).

A Blighted Harvest: The World Bank and African Agriculture edited by Peter Gibbon, et al. (Trenton: Africa World Press, 1993).

Creating a New World Economy edited by G. Epstein, J. Graham and J. Nembhard (Philadelphia: Temple University Press, 1993).

Dark Victory: The U.S., Structural Adjustment and Global Poverty by Walden Bello, Shea Cunningham and Bill Rau (Food First, 1993).

The Debt Boomerang: How Third World Debt Harms Us All by Susan George (London: Pluto Press, 1992).

Development Debacle: The World Bank in the Philippines by Walden Bello, David Kinley and Elaine Elinson (Oakland, CA: Institute for Food and Development Policy, 1982).

Enough Is Enough (Letter of Resignation to the International Monetary Fund) by Davison Budhoo (New York: Apex Press, 1990).

Faith and Credit: The World Bank's Secular Empire by Susan George and Fabrizio Sabelli (Washington: Institute for Policy Studies, 1994).

Global Visions edited by Jeremy Brecher, et al. (Boston: South End Press, 1993).

Hot Money and the Politics of Debt by R.T. Naylor (New York: Simon and Shuster, 1987).

The IMF, World Bank and the African Debt edited by Bade Onimode, [vol. 1 *The Economic Impact*, vol. 2 *The Political and Social Impact*] (London: Zed Press, 1989).

In the Name of Progress: The Underside of Foreign Aid by Patricia Adams and Lawrence Solomon. (Toronto: Energy Probe, 1985).

In the Public Interest?: Privatisation and Public Sector Reform by Brendan Martin (London & New Jersey: Zed Books1993).

Lent and Lost: Foreign Credit and Third World Development by Cheryl Payer (London and New Jersey: Zed Books, 1991).

Lords of Poverty: The Power, Prestige and Corruption of the International Aid Business by Graham Hancock (New York: Atlantic Monthly Press, 1989).

Mortgaging the Earth: The World Bank, Environmental Impoverishment and the Crisis of Development by Bruce Rich (Boston: Beacon Press, 1994).

Perpetuating Poverty: The World Bank, the IMF and the Developing World by Doug Bandow and Ian Vasquez (Washington, DC: Cato Institute, 1993).

The Silent Revolution in Africa: Debt, Development and Democracy by Fantu Cheru (London and New Jersey: Zed Books, 1989).

Storm Signals: Structural Adjustment and Development Alternatives in the Caribbean by Kathy McAfee (Boston: South End Press, 1991)

The World Bank: Global Financing of Impoverishment and Famine, special issue of *The Ecologist*, vol. 15 (1/2); and *Banking on Disaster: Indonesia's Transmigration Program,* special issue of *The Ecologist*, vol. 16 (3/4) available from Ecosystems Ltd., Worthyvale Manor Farm, Camelford, Cornwall PL32 9TT, UK.

RESOURCE GROUPS

Bank Information Center
Contact: Martha Hall
2025 I Street, NW, Suite 522
Washington, DC 20006
tel. (202) 466-8191
fax (202) 466-8189

The Bretton Woods Committee
Contact: Abbie Sutherland
1990 M Street, NW, Suite 450
Washington, DC 20036
tel. (202) 331-1616
fax (202) 785-9423

Center of Concern
Contact: Jo Marie Griesgraber
3700 13th Street, NE
Washington, DC 20017
tel. (202) 635-2757
fax (202) 832-9494

**Development Group for
Alternative Policies**
Contact: Ross Hammond
927 15th Street, NW, 4th Floor
Washington, DC 20005
tel. (202) 898-1566
fax (202) 898-1612

**Environmental and Energy
Study Intitute**
Contact: Inji Islam
122 C Street, NW, Suite 700
Washington, DC 20001
tel. (202) 628-1400
fax (202) 628-1825

**Environmental Defense
Fund (EDF)**
Contact: Mimi Kleiner
1875 Connecticut Avenue, NW
Suite 1016
Washington, DC 20009
tel. (202) 387-3500
fax (202) 234-6049

**EURODAD -- European Network
on Debt and Development**
Contact: Ted van Hees
Square Ambiorix 10
B-1040 Brussels, Belgium
tel. 32-2-732-7007
fax 32-2-723-1934

Friends of the Earth
Contact: Marijke Torfs/Jim Barnes
1025 Vermont Avenue, NW
Suite 300
Washington, DC 20005
tel. (202) 783-7400
fax (202) 783-0444

Global Exchange
Contact: Kevin Danaher
2017 Mission Street, Suite 303
San Francisco, CA 94110
tel. (415) 255-7296
fax (415) 255-7698

**Global Legislators'
Organization for a Balanced
Environment (GLOBE)**
Contact: Patrick Ramage
409 Third Street, SW, Suite 204
Washington, DC 20024
tel. (202) 863-4153
fax (202) 479-9447

Greenpeace International
Contact: Cameron Duncan
1436 U Street, NW
Washington, DC 20009
tel. (202) 462-1177
fax (202) 462-4507

**Institute for Agriculture and
Trade Policy**
Contact: Kristin Dawkins
1313 Fifth Street, SE, Suite 303
Minneapolis, MN 55414-1546
tel. (612) 379-5980
fax (612) 379-5982

Institute for Food and Development Policy
Contact: John Gershman
398 60th Street
Oakland, CA 94618
tel. (510) 654-4400
fax (510) 654-4551

Institute for Policy Studies
Contact: John Cavanagh
1601 Connecticut Avenue, NW
Washington, DC 20009
tel. (202) 234-9382
fax (202) 387-7915

International Rivers Network
Contact: Juliette Majot or Owen Lammars
1847 Berkeley Way
Berkeley, CA 94703
tel. (510) 848-1155
fax (510) 848-1008

Organizing for Development: An International Institute
Contact: Turid Sato
2134 Leroy Place, NW
Washington, DC 20008
tel. (202) 483-6344
fax (202) 234-1392

Oxfam America
Contact: James Arena-DeRosa
26 West Street
Boston, MA 02111
tel. (617) 728-2475
fax (617) 728-2596

PROBE International
Contact: Patricia Adams
225 Brunswick Avenue
Toronto, Ontario, Canada M5S 2M6
tel. (416) 964-9223
fax (416) 904-9230

Student Environmental Action Coalition (SEAC)
815 16th Street, NW
Washington, DC 20006
tel. (202) 783-3993
fax (202) 783-3591

Third Global Structures Convocation
Contact: William R. Pace
420 7th Street, SE
Washington, DC 20003
tel. (202) 546-1095
fax (202) 546-1156

The Transnational Institute
Contact: Susan George
10, rue Jean Michelez
91510 Lardy, France
tel. 331-6456-4715
fax 331-6082-6668

Witness for Peace
Contact: Carol Richardson
2201 P Street, NW, Room 109
Washington, DC 20036
tel. (202) 797-1160
fax (202) 797-1164

For a more complete list of groups involved in the "50 Years Is Enough" campaign and a calendar of events, contact The Bank Information Center in Washington at (202) 466-8191.

For a comprehensive list of groups around the world working on development issues from a grassroots perspective, consult the *International Directory of Non-Governmental Organizations* by WorldWise, 401 San Miguel Way, Sacramento, CA 95819, (916) 456-9205.

CONTRIBUTORS

Patricia Adams is Director of PROBE International in Toronto, Canada.

Nilufar Ahmad is an economist working with rural women in Bangladesh.

Marcos Arruda is coordinator of the Institute of Alternative Policies for the Southern Cone of Latin America (PACS-PRIES), based in Brazil, Chile, Uruguay and Argentina. He is a professor of philosophy at the Institute of Advanced Studies in Education/Getulia Vargas Foundation in Rio de Janeiro.

Natalie Avery is a researcher and writer at Essential Information.

Walden Bello is a senior analyst with the Oakland, California-based Institute for Food & Development Policy (Food First).

Patrick Bond is an analyst specializing in the South African economy.

Davison Budhoo is an economist from Grenada. He resigned in protest from the International Monetary Fund in 1988 due to what he called the Fund's "increasingly genocidal policies." He is now Executive Director of the Bretton Woods Reform Movement.

Pratap Chatterjee is an Indian journalist specializing in environmental and development issues.

Kevin Danaher is the director of the Public Education Department at Global Exchange, a non-profit education and action center in San Francisco.

Cameron Duncan is the Multilateral Development Bank campaigner for Greenpeace International, based in Washington, DC.

Susan George is a prolific writer, thinker and campaigner on the subject of third world debt. Her books include *A Fate Worse Than Debt*, *The Debt Boomerang*, and *Faith and Credit: The World Bank's Secular Empire* (with Fabrizio Sabelli, forthcoming in September 1994).

John Gershman is a policy analyst for the Oakland, California-based Institute for Food and Development Policy (Food First).

Contributors

Richard Gerster is Director of the Swiss Coalition of Development Organizations (Swiss Aid/Catholic Lenten Fund/Bread for All/Helvetas/Caritas).

Ross Hammond is an analyst with the Development Group for Alternative Policies in Washington, DC.

Karen Hansen-Kuhn is a Program Associate at the Development Group for Alternative Policies in Washington, DC. Karen and the Hellinger brothers listed below were major contributors to the articles written by the International NGO Forum.

Doug Hellinger is a co-founder and Co-Director of the Development Group for Alternative Policies in Washington, DC.

Steve Hellinger is a co-founder and Co-Director of the Development Group for Alternative Policies in Washington, DC.

Doug Henwood is Editor and Publisher of *Left Business Observer* in New York.

Merle Hodge is a professor in the Department of Language and Linguistics at the University of the West Indies, Trinidad and Tobago.

Patience Idemudia is a doctoral candidate in Sociology at the Ontario Institute for Studies in Education.

International NGO Forum was organized in 1992 by the Development GAP and other progressive non-governmental organizations. It brought together development activists from around the world to share information and devise strategies for combatting the World Bank and the IMF.

Michael H. K. Irwin is a former Director of the World Bank's Health Department and former Acting Vice-President of Personnel.

John B. Judis is Washington correspondent for the alternative newspaper *In These Times*.

Inge Khoury is a London-based writer specializing in issues concerning women and development.

Alicia Korten was a Fulbright scholar in Costa Rica. She is writing a book on structural adjustment and Costa Rican agriculture.
Eloise Magenheim is a San Francisco-based writer focusing on women, environmental issues and human rights.

Juliette Majot is a policy analyst for International Rivers Network (IRN) in Berkeley, California. She is also the editor of *BankCheck Quarterly* and *World Rivers Review*.

Jessica Matthews is a senior fellow at the Council on Foreign Relations.

Kathy McAfee is the author of *Storm Signals: Structural Adjustment and Development Alternatives in the Caribbean* (Boston: South End Press, 1991)

Lisa McGowan is a policy analyst for the Development Group for Alternative Policies in Washington, DC.

Pradeep S. Mehta is the general secretary of the Consumer Unity and Trust Society in Calcutta, India.

Abdoulaye Ndiaye is a Senegalese engineer and private development consultant in Senegal.

Michael O'Heaney is a researcher with the Maryknoll Justice and Peace Office in Washington, DC.

Bruce Rich is a senior attorney with the Environmental Defense Fund, Washington, DC. He is the author of *Mortgaging the Earth: The World Bank, Environmental Impoverishment, and the Crisis of Development* (Boston: Beacon Press, 1994).

Kole Shettima is a doctoral candidate in Political Science at the University of Toronto and a member of the Economic Justice Working Group of the Inter- Church Coalition on Africa.

Vandana Shiva is a leading environmental scientist in India. She is the author of *Staying Alive* and many other books and articles on women and the environment.

Margie Snider is an editor and writer for *UNION*, the bimonthly magazine of the Service Employees International Union (SEIU).

Survival International is a London-based group working for the rights of tribal peoples.

Muhammad Yunus is the founder and Managing Director of the Grameen Bank in Bangladesh.

INDEX

Index

Index

Index

Index

Index

Index

Reality Tours

ENJOY adventure travel in some of the world's most controversial and beautiful places. On Global Exchange reality tours participants meet local people, appreciate other cultures, learn about the most pressing issues confronting the world today, while having a great time! Our experienced trip leaders will introduce you to some of the most exciting people and issues of the day.

Global Exchange organizes regular reality tours to the following destinations:

Cuba, Mexico, Honduras, Haiti, Senegal, Vietnam, Cambodia, South Africa, Puerto Rico, El Salvador, Brazil, Guatemala, Chile, Bolivia, Panama, Nicaragua, India, Washington, DC, *and more...*

What is included in a Reality Tour?

Most of our seminar packages include round-trip airfare from Miami, Los Angeles, San Francisco or New York, double room accommodations, all transportation inside the country (including ground and air travel), two meals per day, translation of all programs, a qualified trip leader, seminar fees and reading materials. Global Exchange will also arrange personal meetings to suit your particular interests (as available).

Contact:
Global Exchange,
2017 Mission St. Rm. 303,
San Francisco, CA 94110
(415) 255-7296

JOIN US!

GLOBAL [⚉] EXCHANGE

YES! I want to help Global Exchange build a strong internationalist movement. As a member I will receive:

- ☆ A free copy of *Bridging the Global Gap: A Handbook to Linking Citizens of the First and Third Worlds*
- ☆ Our quarterly newsletter *Global Exchanges* informing me of Global Exchange activities and trends in the internationalist movement
- ☆ Regular updates on the Global Exchange tour program
- ☆ Priority consideration on tours, often limited to 12-15 people
- ☆ 10% discount on Global Exchange crafts and educational materials

❏ Enclosed is my tax-deductible membership donation of:

___$35 ___$50 ___$100 ___ other ___$25 (low-income)

Total enclosed for membership $_____

❏ Please send me more information about your Reality Tours

❏ Please send me the following:

___ copies of *Bridging the Global Gap* at $11.95 each	$_____
___ copies of *The Peace Corps and More* at $6.95 each	$_____
___ copies of *Beyond Safaris: A Guide to Building People-to-People Ties with Africa* at $6.50 each	$_____
___ copies of *Don't Be Afraid Gringo: A Honduran Woman Speaks from the Heart* at $9.95 each	$_____
SUB-TOTAL	$_____
Calif. residents add 8.5% state sales tax	$_____
Add 15% of book total for shipping/handling costs	$_____
TOTAL ENCLOSED payable to Global Exchange	$_____

Name_____

Address_____

City_____State_____ Zip_____

Phone_____

Send to:
Global Exchange, 2017 Mission St.
Rm. 303, San Francisco, CA 94110
(415) 255-7296

Please charge to my

❏ VISA
❏ MASTERCARD

Card #_____ - _____
       _____ - _____

Expiration Date_____

Name on card_____

About South End Press

South End Press is a non-profit, collectively run book publisher with over 180 titles in print. Since our founding in 1977, we have tried to meet the needs of readers who are exploring, or are already committed to, the politics of radical social change.

Our goal is to publish books that encourage critical thinking and constructive action on the key political, cultural, social, economic and ecological issues shaping life in the United States and in the world. In this way, we hope to give expression to a wide diversity of democratic social movements and to provide an alternative to the products of corporate publishing.

Through the Institute for Social and Cultural Change, South End Press works with other political media projects—*Z Magazine;* Speak Out!, a speakers bureau; the New Liberation News Service and the Publishers Support Project—to expand access to information and critical analysis. If you would like a free catalog of South End Press books or information about our membership program, which offers two free books and a 40 percent discount on all titles, please write to us at: South End Press, 116 Saint Botolph Street, Boston, MA 02115.

Other South End Press Titles of Interest

Global Visions: Beyond the New World Order
Edited by Jeremy Brecher, John Brown Childs and Jill Cutler

Trilateralism: The Trilateral Commission and Elite Planning for World Management
Edited by Holly Sklar

Hear My Testimony: María Teresa Tula, Human Rights Activist of El Salvador
Translated and edited by Lynn Stephen

Confronting Environmental Racism: Voices from the Grassroots
Edited by Robert D. Bullard, Foreword by Benjamin Chavis, Jr.